Suicidal behaviour in South Africa

Aussage über Zunahme S. 46

About the author

LOURENS SCHLEBUSCH IS an academic, clinician and author. He is Professor and Head of the Department of Behavioural Medicine at the Nelson R. Mandela School of Medicine at the University of KwaZulu-Natal, and the Chief Consultant in Behavioural Medicine for the Hospital Services of the KwaZulu-Natal Provincial Administration in Durban, South Africa. He is an internationally recognised authority in his area of expertise in suicidology, a stress management consultant and a medico-legal consultant, a member of many national and international scientific editorial boards, organisations and societies. In addition, he is a regular reviewer of scientific publications both nationally and internationally. He has many professional listings, honours and awards, has made significant research contributions and has published widely (including several video- and audiotapes on stress management). His bestselling book *Mind Shift: Stress Management and Your Health* (University of Natal Press, 2000) has been used extensively as a practical aid in stress management workshops and seminars. His current research interests include various aspects of suicide prevention, HIV/Aids and suicidal behaviour, traumatic stress, psycho-oncology and bridging the mind-body dichotomy in contemporary health-care delivery. He is currently one of the Vice-presidents of the International Association for Suicide Prevention (IASP) and the Congress President for the XXIII World IASP Congress to be held from 12 to 16 September 2005 at the International Convention Centre in Durban, South Africa. He is also a member of the WHO Multisite Intervention Study on Suicidal Behaviours (SUPRE-MISS).

Suicidal behaviour in South Africa

Lourens Schlebusch

UNIVERSITY OF KwaZulu-NATAL PRESS

Published in 2005 by University of KwaZulu-Natal Press
Private Bag X01, Scottsville, 3209
South Africa
E-mail: books@ukzn.ac.za
Website: www.uknpress.co.za

© 2005 Lourens Schlebusch

All rights reserved. No part of this publication may be reproduced or transmitted in any form or by any means, electronic or mechanical, including photocopying, recording, or any information storage and retrieval system, without prior permission in writing from University of KwaZulu-Natal Press.

ISBN 1-86914-077-X

Editor: Andrea Nattrass
Cover designer: Sebastien Quevauvilliers, Flying Ant Designs
Typesetter: RockBottom Design
Indexer: Cynthia Harvey-Williams

Printed and bound by Interpak Books, Pietermaritzburg

Contents

Figures and tables ix
Acknowledgements xi
Foreword xiii
Abbreviations xv

INTRODUCTION 1
Types and variants of suicidal behaviour 4
A major public health responsibility 9

CHAPTER ONE: THE AGONY OF A SURVIVOR 11

CHAPTER TWO: SUICIDE IN HISTORY, THE ARTS AND
RELIGION 27
History and the arts 27
The copycat effect 30
Suicide and religion 30
Key points 34

CHAPTER THREE: TRENDS WITHIN AN INTERNATIONAL
AND AFRICAN CONTEXT 35
The global situation 35
The African situation 37
Key points 40

CHAPTER FOUR: TRENDS WITHIN THE SOUTH AFRICAN
CONTEXT 41
Fatal suicidal behaviour 42
Gender distribution 46
Age distribution 47
Ethnic distribution 48
Non-fatal suicidal behaviour 50

Suicidal behaviour in hospital	52
Conclusions	53
Key points	54

CHAPTER FIVE: CHILDREN AND ADOLESCENTS 55
Fatal suicidal behaviour	55
Non-fatal suicidal behaviour	56
Conclusions	58
Key points	58

CHAPTER SIX: REPORTS IN THE SOUTH AFRICAN PRESS 59
Suicide pacts	60
Suicide cults/mass suicides/religious suicides	60
Simulated suicide/fake suicide	61
Assisted suicide	61
Extended suicide/murder-suicide	62
Iatrogenic suicide	63
Other fatal and non-fatal suicidal behaviours	63
Key points	66

CHAPTER SEVEN: METHODS OF CHOICE 67
Fatal suicidal behaviour	67
Non-fatal suicidal behaviour	69
Key points	72

CHAPTER EIGHT: INDIRECT SELF-DESTRUCTIVE BEHAVIOUR AND ANALGESIC ABUSE 73
Analgesic nephropathy	75
Cumulative doses of analgesics leading to analgesic nephropathy	77
The role of phenacetin and paracetamol (acetaminophen)	78
The role of aspirin (acetylsalicylic acid)	79
The role of non-steroidal anti-inflammatory substances	80
Psychocultural aspects of analgesic abuse	81
Psychological problems and analgesic abuse	82
Headaches, pain and analgesic abuse	86
Key points	91

CHAPTER NINE: RISK FACTORS AND CAUSES	93
Family dynamics and related issues	93
Poor problem-solving skills	96
Aggression	97
Extended suicide and murder-suicide	97
Stress	100
Depression and other psychological disorders	101
Prior suicidal behaviour and substance abuse	107
South Africa's historical legacy	107
Suicidal behaviour and somatic co-morbidity	108
Cancer	109
HIV/Aids	112
Key points	120
CHAPTER TEN: MANAGEMENT AND PREVENTION	121
Pain management and analgesic abuse	125
Stress associated with chronic disease	131
A functional model to understand and manage analgesic abuse	134
Somatic co-morbidity: HIV/Aids	143
Prevention of suicidal behaviour in South Africa	149
Prevention and the youth	156
Cultural and traditional role expectations	159
The value of the psychological autopsy: A South African adaptation	160
Discussion of the psychological autopsy	164
Prevention	170
General considerations	170
Basic issues around psychobiology and the prevention of suicidal behaviour	171
Suicide survivor programmes	172
An organisational system for managing and preventing suicidal behaviour	172
Ethics and suicide prevention	183
Key points	184

CHAPTER ELEVEN: THE DURBAN PARASUICIDE STUDY (DPS) 185
Origins, design and aims of the DPS 186
Problem areas 188
A conceptual model for the future and a national suicide
    prevention programme 190
Key points 193

CONCLUSION 195

Select references 197
Index 221

Figures and tables

Fig. 9.1	Suicide risk following treatment	105
Fig. 10.1	Summary flow chart of the management and prevention of suicidal behaviour	173
Table 10.1	Assessment of the person with suicidal behaviour	174
Table 10.2	Recognition of significant life events	175
Table 10.3	Consideration of special problems	176
Table 10.4	Specific problem-orientated treatment	177
Table 10.5	Additional components of treatment	179
Table 10.6	Prevention and control	181
Fig. 10.2	Reduction of the psychological pain and addressing risk factors	182
Fig. 11.1	A summary of essential features of the DPS	187

Acknowledgements

FIRST, I EXPRESS my gratitude to those individuals with suicidal behaviour who painstakingly shared their time and experiences with me. A special thanks to Gaylynn de Villiers and the other members of SOLOS (Survivors of Loved Ones' Suicide) for their input and many discussions about their brave struggles to deal with the pain of their losses.

I acknowledge the co-operation and support of my various colleagues and friends. The invaluable contribution and hard work with word-processing, typing and diagram presentation from my research assistant, Ruwaida Sheik, is much appreciated. I would also like to express my appreciation to my personal assistant, Prenisha Ramballi for her secretarial assistance and support in so many ways during the writing and production of this book. I am grateful to Heather Edgeworth for proofreading the original draft and for her many helpful suggestions in preparing the manuscript. I am beholden to my editor, Andrea Nattrass, for her indispensable assistance, which added immensely to the final product.

To the members of my DPS (Durban Parasuicide Study) Research Group: Basil Pillay, Brenda A. Bosch, Naseema Vawda, Shireen Noor Mahomed, Thirusha Naidu, Shantal Singh and the others, as well as my departmental office manager, Fatima Hassein-Moosa, go my sincere thanks for your valuable contributions and for directing the focus of our research output. I am extremely indebted to Cindy York for her hard work in painstakingly collating all the newspaper reports on suicide and for her other unstinting research assistance. Finally, I am grateful to my publisher, Glenn Cowley, for his patience and guidance throughout the project.

Foreword

THIS FIRST COMPREHENSIVE volume on suicide and suicide prevention published in South Africa is a milestone in the development of the field of suicide research and prevention, which is now becoming increasingly acknowledged for its importance, not only in South Africa but in many countries throughout the world. The enormity of the problem of suicide calls for action, not only from health-care workers and other professional helpers, but from people in all sectors of society. Politicians and other decision-makers need to realise that the problem of suicide can be effectively combated and that limited resources are best utilised when co-ordinated through a national strategy for suicide prevention. Above all, there is a need for increased public awareness of what everyone both can and should do to help. To state it simply: the prevention of suicide is everybody's business!

There is a great need for more knowledge in order to support new initiatives in suicide prevention. Even though there is much to be learnt from research and prevention experiences from abroad, every country needs to make its own analyses of the problem and find solutions that are adapted to local challenges and available resources. This volume brings an abundance of information on epidemiological data, risk factors and high-risk populations, associations and causative mechanisms. On the basis of these facts, some of which are quite unique to South Africa, follows a presentation of a series of suicide preventive strategies and methods adapted to local conditions and challenges. This knowledge can only be accumulated through hard work and dedicated efforts in suicide research over many years. With this volume, Professor Lourens Schlebusch, an internationally renowned suicide researcher actively involved in suicide prevention nationally and internationally for many years, has provided an invaluable toolbox for all those who work to combat suicide. Filled as it is with sober information on suicide and its causes, it will reduce the myths, taboos and social stigma still associated with suicide. The many practical and clinical approaches described will be highly welcome to clinicians and professional helpers as well as to the informed and interested general readership.

This volume gives a full account of the many destructive implications of suicide in society. We must, however, never forget that the most profound and tragic consequences concern the individual and his or her family. In this book, Professor Schlebusch has managed to find a balance between, on the one hand, the scholarly and accurate description of suicidal behaviour that is needed to get to grips with the magnitude and severity of suicide as a public health problem and, on the other hand, a portrayal of the tragedy that suicide imposes on the individual person.

Lars Mehlum MD
Professor of Psychiatry and Suicidology and Director of the Suicide Research and Prevention Unit, University of Oslo
President of the International Association for Suicide Prevention

Abbreviations

AFRO	sub-Saharan Africa
Aids	acquired immune deficiency syndrome
AN	analgesic nephropathy
ARDS	Adult Respiratory Distress Syndrome
BAC	blood alcohol concentration
CNS	central nervous system
DALY	disability adjusted life year
DPS	Durban Parasuicide Study
ESRD	end-stage renal disease
GBD	global burden of disease
HBM	Health Belief Model
HIV	human immunodeficiency virus
HPA	hypothalamus-pituitary-adrenal
IASP	International Association for Suicide Prevention
ICU	Intensive Care Unit
ISDB	indirect self-destructive behaviour
MMPI	Minnesota Multiphasic Personality Inventory
MVA	motor vehicle accident
NIMSS	National Injury Mortality Surveillance System
NSAID	non-steroidal anti-inflammatory drug
OTC	over-the-counter
PAC	pituitary-adrenocortical
SADTR	South African Dialysis and Transplantation Registry
SAM	sympathetic-adrenal medullary
SANDF	South African National Defence Force
SOLOS	Survivors of Loved Ones' Suicide
WHO	World Health Organization

Introduction

[A]ll mankind is of one author, and is one volume... No man is an island, entire of itself... any man's death diminishes me, because I am involved in mankind.
(John Donne, *Meditation XVII*)

MOST PEOPLE ARE not aware of how widely pervasive suicidal behaviour has become in the world and in South Africa, and how exponential the problem is. The truth of the matter is that it has reached critically wide-ranging proportions. This lack of awareness is partly due to attitudes in many quarters where suicidal behaviour is either a matter of social taboo or constructed as self-harm used to manipulate others or to escape from reality. Suicidal behaviour, therefore, is sometimes not given the serious attention it merits. It may even be seen by some as a shameful or cowardly act. The person considering it might, accordingly, not be encouraged to discuss his or her suicidal thoughts and emotions openly with a health-care professional, or even with a friend or family member. Consequently, many people who feel depressed and hopeless (typical triggers to acting on suicidal thoughts) imagine themselves to be even more alone and isolated than they actually are. Opportunities are then frequently missed to help prevent the ensuing tragedy. The subsequent social stigma often also makes recovery difficult for those who survive either their own suicidal behaviour or that of a loved one. Furthermore, cutting edge research on stress and life-threatening conditions has revealed inordinately high levels of stress associated with suicidal behaviour in many South African communities (Schlebusch, 1998a, 2000a, b, c, 2004; Schlebusch & Bosch, 2000). While this to a large extent cuts across all ethnic, gender and age groups, a disturbing shift in clinical populations has been perceived in that increasingly more young and black South Africans are adversely affected.

Much of the relevant literature in South Africa is epidemiological, or simply descriptive, in character. A major issue, however, relates to the trustworthiness of statistics regarding suicidal behaviour. Accurate South African statistics are difficult to obtain, but studies reflect annual rates of up to 10% or more (17.2 or higher per 100 000 of the population) of all unnatural deaths to be suicides, with up to twenty times or more non-fatal suicide attempts. More detailed figures are presented in Chapters four and five. The problem is serious, more so because available figures reflect an incomplete representation as suicidal behaviour has been under-researched in the past, especially among certain groups. For example, lower rates were reported for fatal suicidal behaviour in the majority black population compared to other major ethnic groups (whites, Coloureds and Indians). These earlier findings are contradicted by contemporary research which shows that suicides generally, and suicidal behaviour among black South Africans more specifically, is a neglected and increasingly serious problem (Schlebusch, 2004).

In addition, the majority of reports base their figures on official statistics and on data recorded from mortuaries and in-patient hospital populations. These figures do not reflect comparative national samples of suicidal behaviour. Examples of such omissions include:

- suicidal behaviours not reflected in official records;
- sub-intentioned suicidal behaviour, which is often reported as accidental or not intended because it is not always possible to determine whether it involved significant self-destructive ideation;
- those cases seen at a general practice level; and
- sub-lethal, suicide-like gestures that might actually be serious suicidal behaviour.

Consequently, it can be assumed that available figures probably distort the true picture of the prevalence of suicidal behaviour in the community, reflecting only a part of the problem. The accuracy of statistics is further clouded by different cultural perceptions of suicide, and the fact that reliable figures for many areas in South Africa (especially rural ones) are unavailable.

Another particularly disturbing problem that may further cloud accurate statistics of suicidal behaviour is the relationship between violence and health-risk behaviours that result in premature death or injury. There is a real need within the South African context to investigate this issue further. Of late a dramatic increase in traffic-related injuries as well as interpersonal and gender-based violence and crime has been witnessed across the entire social spectrum (Suffla, Van Niekerk & Duncan, 2004). This is occurring almost to the point where, for many people, the situation has become characteristic of moral atrophy in that they now accept a culture of violence and lack of respect for the law. In 1990 it was pointed out that South Africa was ravaged by widespread violence (McKendrik & Hoffman, 1990). This violence occurs across the entire spectrum, including violence against children, rape, domestic violence, violence in schools, political violence and crime generally (McKendrik & Hoffman, 1990). Both the direct and indirect emotional injuries of such violence have been well described, especially the resultant trauma-producing behaviours that can take many forms, including suicidal behaviour (Schlebusch & Bosch, 2002).

We are, therefore, faced with an ongoing need for greater accuracy and more knowledge in this area, and there has been a call for more action to combat such self-destructive behaviour. These are important considerations that are not readily taken into account when explaining suicidal behaviour in South Africa, as also the fact that research on suicide prevention programmes has languished as a minor endeavour. Prevention of suicidal behaviour is discussed in Chapter ten. For now, it is sufficient to mention that although the issue of health education and disease prevention has received considerable attention in recent years, the prevention of suicidal behaviour continues as a relatively neglected area in mental health. The need to educate professional health-care workers and the general public on preventing suicide is critical. The price of neglecting such a need is too high to pay. Fortunately, knowing the facts is a crucial step towards solving the problems, and I hope that the information contained in this book will make a difference by helping to educate readers about suicide and suicidal behaviour.

There are also financial implications to be considered. If we take into account the spiralling health-care costs facing South Africans, then the need to prevent suicidal behaviour, a behaviour that in the index patients invariably leads to a spate of hospital admissions and attendant expensive medical and psychological procedures, becomes more acute. This high health-care cost does not take into account post-hospital treatment and management of the devastated family members or loved ones who often are left with pressing financial difficulties. It is, therefore, clear that apart from the enormous cost in human suffering, we cannot continue to ignore the financial ramifications of suicidal behaviour.

TYPES AND VARIANTS OF SUICIDAL BEHAVIOUR

An extensive review of the literature around nomenclature, classification and definitions in suicidology and suicidal behaviour is not intended here. Although it is necessary to clarify conceptual and other issues if we are to make sense of what suicidal behaviour is about and how it affects us all, an in-depth analysis of terminology in this book could deteriorate into a semantic debate, which is something that I wish to avoid. There have been many publications to improve clarity regarding these issues both internationally (Farberow, 1980; Hawton & Van Heeringen, 2000; Kerkhoff, 2000; Kreitman, 1977; Lester, 2000; O'Carrol et al., 1998; Shneidman, 1985; Wasserman, 2001a), as well as in South Africa (Schlebusch, 1990a). Suffice it to say here, that although terms may overlap, the value of understanding the essential differences between suicidal types within a South African context has long been argued (Schlebusch, 1990a, 1992a, b). It is, however, appropriate for us to look at certain basic explanations of some concepts, since not all suicidal behaviours are alike and clarity on this issue is a neglected area of research in South Africa.

Nomenclature embodies a set of logically and commonly defined terms used to facilitate communication and to provide an accepted terminology to describe and record clinical, pathological and associated observations (O'Carrol et al., 1998; Schlebusch, 1990a). Classification, by contrast, is an attempt to introduce some order into a discussion of the nature, causes and treatment of a maladaptive behavioural phenomenon in order to delineate its variations. It implies a scheme that is aetiologically and/or therapeutically valid or theory-based, and that provides a basis for studying causal patterns and management of the behaviour so classified, as well as allowing for systematic arrangement of items in categories (O'Carrol et al., 1998; Schlebusch, 1990b, c). A definition is an accurate explanation or description of a word, term or concept by its properties.

Desirable as it may be to have commonly accepted terminology, classification and unequivocal definitions, it remains an elusive goal. A primary example is defining suicidal behaviour which, at first glance, appears to be one of the most patently self-evident terms. However, the matter is not that simple as the concept of suicidal behaviour is not free from ambiguity. This was succinctly revealed in a letter to me from an esteemed colleague, a certain Professor of Paediatric Surgery who is known for his wit and superb command of language. On hearing of a southern African suicidology conference that I convened in 1992, he sent me the following missive:

> Laying no claim to expertise in philology or etymology, I am nonetheless impressed by the neologism 'Suicidology'. I am not in the least surprised that there is a society to study it. It fully deserves one. Not only does it contrive to mix Greek and Latin roots, anathema to us pedants, as the etymological equivalent of pulmonia or renectomy, but it sounds so perfectly awful. There must be better words to describe the study of automortification. May I suggest that at the next AGM of this indubitably august and learned body, assuming of course that a quorum survives their morbid interest, that you propose a constitutional amendment changing the society's name to 'A Society to Examine and Research Intentional Self-killing' which would at least give it an interesting (and entirely Greek) acronym.

With this in mind, a brief clarification is offered here of the various types or forms of suicidal behaviour, some of which are referred to in this book. This explanation is based more on the terms' characteristics rather than on psychiatric, psychological or other diagnostic criteria. This attempt to provide examples of suicidal behaviour's various manifestations does not negate the fact that there is a need for a standard terminology, nor is it an attempt to construct a classification or to provide comprehensive, all-embracing definitions. The idea is merely to emphasise that suicidal behaviours in South Africa (as well as all over the world) are complex, wide-ranging, multidimensional and multifactorial events with different behavioural characteristics, and to put the terms and data used in this book into perspective. In doing so, I have drawn from the work of the many experts in suicidology as listed in the Select references.

To start with then, *suicidal behaviour* occurs in different forms that involve a degree of severity that can range from a person wishing him- or herself dead to actually killing him- or herself. Despite much conceptual confusion around it, in the final analysis suicidal behaviour implies attempting or hastening in one way or another the death of the person who engages in such behaviour. In this book the term *suicidal behaviour* is used in a broad sense to denote a wide range of self-destructive or self-damaging acts in which people engage, owing to varying degrees of levels of distress, psychopathology, motive, lethal intent, awareness and expectations of the deleterious consequences or outcome of the behaviour. In a sense then, suicidal behaviour is considered here as just that: a form or variation of behaviour with a suicidal connotation. It is not a diagnosis in itself of a psychological or mental disorder, although it can be associated with conditions such as depression, schizophrenia and other disorders. It also includes, amongst others, aspects of psychological, neuropsychological, biological, biochemical, social, cultural, interpersonal, existential, philosophical and other variables.

Suicidal behaviour is further divided into *fatal* and *non-fatal* suicidal behaviours. These concepts can be refined upon consideration of various co-morbid factors that determine the outcome of the suicidal behaviour. Given this, *fatal suicidal behaviour* refers to self-committed, completed suicidal behaviour that embodied the victim's intent or aim to die and where that person managed to achieve that predetermined goal. As opposed to this, *non-fatal suicidal behaviour* refers to self-inflicted suicidal behaviour that did not succeed in ending the victim's life, and which embodies several manifestations such as those seen in *attempted suicide* and *parasuicide*. In this book the term *attempted suicide* refers to non-fatal suicidal behaviour where there is a fortuitous survival of the intended suicide. In such an instance the person tried but failed to end his or her life. By contrast, the term *parasuicide* in this book refers to non-fatal suicidal behaviour without the intention to die; it is more a cry for help. In such an instance the behaviour is used as an inappropriate problem-solving skill in the form of self-harm. In this sense then, the difference between attempted suicide and parasuicide is really the intent to die or not, although both have non-fatal outcomes. However, as is so often the case, sometimes I use the terms interchangeably in this book.

Suicidal ideation (frequently described as a person's thoughts about killing him- or herself) forms part of the process of suicidal behaviour and is likewise a discreet and complex phenomenon. Suicidal ideation as meant here, is not restricted to just thinking about committing suicide; it can also include a person writing or talking about and/or planning his or her suicidal behaviour.

In another step towards attempting a clearer perspective of the continuum of suicidal behaviours, other examples are mentioned briefly. The first is *assisted suicide*, which has been in the headlines of late and provides much food for thought. It means helping someone, who has indicated fatal suicidal intention, to end his or her life. This is not necessarily the same as *euthanasia*, which embodies mercy killing by directly administering a procedure to end someone's life. Other types of suicidal behaviours referred to in this book include:

- *extended suicide*: where one family member decides to commit suicide, but before doing so kills other members of his or her family;
- *murder-suicide*: in which an individual kills him- or herself after he or she has murdered others without prior intention of committing suicide (as is the case in extended suicide);
- *suicide pacts*: where there is a mutual agreement between people to kill themselves, usually at the same time and place;
- *cultural suicide*: suicidal behaviours that are culture-specific or culture-related;
- *religious suicide*: suicidal behaviour within a religious context;
- *rational suicide*: where a person is guided by a rational philosophy of life that includes a belief in the right to die and the right to carry out the suicide;
- *collective or mass suicides*: as in whole groups who commit suicide;
- *protest suicide*: as in the case of a detained labour activist who reportedly jumped to his death in protest against fatal police beatings (*The Natal Mercury*, 7 May 1991: 5);

- *iatrogenic suicide*: as caused by the lethal side effects of certain medicines, especially when taken by the elderly;
- *political suicides*: as seen in certain suicide attacks, some of which are referred to as suicidal terrorism;
- *simulated suicide*: when an individual pretends to be dead by his or her own hand by vanishing from known circles or by assuming a different identity;
- *pseudo-suicide*: here an individual might swallow a small amount of a harmless substance claiming it was poison;
- *imitative suicide*: the so-called 'Werther effect' or 'copycat' suicide that can occur when suicides are over-dramatised or romanticised, especially in the media;
- *silent suicide*: for example, when a bedridden, depressed elderly person dies from non-compliance with essential medical treatment or from self-starvation (Leong & Eth, 1995);
- *fake suicide*: when a person has been murdered and the act made to look like a suicide;
- *pre-emptive suicidal behaviour*: when a person attempts suicide to avoid the fearful prospects of a disease such as Aids; and
- other forms of *self-destructive behaviour* that can sometimes be seen as a variant of suicidal behaviour and which can be direct or indirect.

It is disconcerting that self-destructive behaviour appears to be a common occurrence in South Africa. *Direct self-destructive behaviour* involves deliberate self-harm. However, in the case of *indirect self-destructive behaviour* survival is usually left to fate, chance or to significant others. Examples include certain types of driving behaviour leading to road accidents that are victim precipitated, substance abuse, living a high-risk lifestyle by engaging in unprotected, promiscuous sexual behaviour with the full knowledge of the potential high HIV/Aids risk factor. This kind of behaviour can involve unconscious suicidal tendencies or 'a death wish'. In such a case, the person sometimes seems to be either unaware of or denying the fact that his or her behaviour can be a form of suicidal behaviour, in the sense that it is self-injurious or self-destructive, although there is not an immediate suicidal outcome but rather a long-term, cumulative effect that can result in premature death.

Clearly there is some overlap between the various types of suicidal behaviour mentioned here, aspects of ascertainment of such behaviours and how they are interpreted. However, although these different types of suicidal behaviours may have certain common characteristics, there are also differences between them that are related *inter alia* to the act itself, its precipitators, intention, the type of person and/or population involved, and the cultural, religious and socio-political context in which it occurs.

A MAJOR PUBLIC HEALTH RESPONSIBILITY

Preventing and managing suicidal behaviour is an important public health responsibility. With this in mind, questions urgently begging to be answered are:

- What additional knowledge is required?
- To what end should we apply this knowledge in order to address the problem effectively?
- Where should our focus be?
- Who should be informed?

Such considerations endorse the need for a book such as this one, which brings together an updated body of knowledge on suicidal behaviour in South Africa. In this book I discuss suicidal behaviour in South Africa against a backdrop of the global situation with a view to updating relevant data, offering prevention and management solutions and suggesting further research needs.

I have taken as my broad theme some of the most pressing multifactorial issues and vantage points to combating suicidal behaviour in South Africa. In addition to exploring the causes behind the individual who succumbs to such despair, I also examine and update current statistics that offer clues to the circumstances surrounding suicidal behaviour and question the misconceptions associated with such behaviour. Although more research is required, I make recommendations on how to address these problems. It is my hope that everyone who reads this book will be better equipped to deal with the issues, so that we will no longer treat suicidal behaviour differently from any other health-care problem. The important thing is to recognise that although ignorance can be manufactured, it also usually can be remedied by further study.

Whatever face it presents, suicidal behaviour is always a tragic event. This tragedy is poignantly captured in the true story told in Chapter one. Tormented by conflicting pressures, a young woman's husband committed suicide by shooting himself. Her story is emblematic of all decent humanity's striving to remain human in a world so frequently sorrowfully divided by the pain of suicidal behaviour. There are millions of people like her all over the world.

CHAPTER ONE

The agony of a survivor

[handwritten annotation: Fallbeispiel: ... at Hintergründe. Frau erzählt ihre Geschichte von ? und den Selbstmord ihres Mannes]

THIS CHAPTER IS based on true events. However, since confidentiality is essential to good clinical practice, I have altered aspects of the case (such as places, names, dates and other particulars) to preserve the anonymity of those involved. I have chosen to start with this story and to relate it in some detail and length in an attempt to illustrate, from the outset, the pain of those who are left behind following a suicide.

***

My husband had been a successful manager for a leading retail furniture group, but when my construction company started to grow rapidly and I suggested that I needed to take on somebody to help me manage the business, he asked if he could join me. We discussed it at length and I finally consented, the agreement being that we would see how it worked; if it didn't, he would return to the retail world. The business continued to grow and we went from two staff members to twelve.

We won a R500 000 tender that we thought could well be the making of the company. As we needed bridging finance we approached a financial institution. They required security and my parents agreed to use a policy of theirs as surety. There was never any doubt in my mind that the business was going to be a wonderful success.

We had to submit costs each month to the main contractor, who in turn would send them to the developer for payment. We had outlaid a considerable sum, but our first payment, due at the end of November, did not materialise. Our annual shutdown was due and we had salaries and bonuses to pay – and nothing was going to come in for weeks!

Phone calls and a visit to the main contractor's office were to no avail. He claimed the developer hadn't paid him, but in January the developer told us that the main contractor had been paid on 10 December 2001.

The situation became really stressful. I was suffering from terrible headaches and nausea and was swallowing migraine tablets every day. One day I felt particularly ill and decided it was time to see the doctor.

I suffer from a gynaecological problem and had been told I wouldn't fall pregnant again, unless I underwent fertility treatment for a second time – we already had a four-year-old son. We were stunned, therefore, when I was told that I was over four months pregnant! I had experienced a problematic delivery before and it would be necessary to have another caesarean section – it would cost us R13 000 at least.

Our beautiful little girl was born on 15 April 2002 and we were ecstatic.

After three weeks, however, I had to return to work and continue the ongoing fight for our money, but it seemed increasingly clear that we would never be paid. I now began taking anti-depressants as it was getting harder and harder to keep on top of things. Aggressive phone calls started from people to whom we owed money, and then the lawyers' letters arrived. Tensions were running high at home owing to the lack of money. To try to cut costs we moved out of the simplex we were renting and into a one-bedroom flat. Our son was sleeping in our bed and our daughter in the cot next to the bed – it was not conducive to a perfect marriage.

By August the stress was immense, but Charlie had done little to find a job, despite my desperate pleas. One night a few harsh words about something ended in an argument, with Charlie saying that he would not come into the company the next day. He said that he would look for a job. He also mentioned that he felt I no longer loved him, but instead of heeding the adage about marriage: 'never go to bed on an argument', I stormed out of the room.

The next morning I got up as usual, but Charlie pretended to continue sleeping. By the time I was ready to leave with the children, Charlie still showed no signs of stirring, so I left the flat without even saying goodbye.

The whole morning I felt that I should SMS him and tell him that what he had said wasn't true; I *did* love him! Time, however, flew by and, before I knew it, it was time to pick up my son from pre-school.

I decided to take him to my mother's place, as I had not settled the argument with Charlie. Just before getting to my mother's block of flats my cell phone rang, but I was unable to get to my bag in time to answer the call. As I pulled into the parking, it rang again. It was my factory manager. He asked me to meet him at the factory. When I asked why, he simply replied that he needed to talk to me. Warning bells rang and so I listened to the message that had just been left by the previous caller. It was the supervisor of my block of flats to say that I should get to the flat immediately.

I went into the missed calls register and phoned the number that came up. My supervisor answered and asked me to hurry up and get home. When I asked him what the matter was, he replied that Charlie was dead. My immediate thoughts were that he had overdosed on my anti-depressants, tranquillisers and sleeping tablets. 'Has he taken an overdose?' I asked.

'No, he's shot himself,' came the reply.

I went numb. I phoned my parents to let them know what had happened and then phoned my best friend and asked her to meet me at the flat. The next phone call was to my former next-door-neighbour, an ex-policeman named Bert. I asked if he could come to the flat – without him I don't know what I would have done. He organised forensics, photographers, the mortuary, etc. It seemed to take forever . . .

When I arrived at my flat, I found the supervisor, the chair-person of the body corporate and Inspector Ntuli, a policeman who was taking a statement from my domestic worker, who had found Charlie when she went to put the ironing away. He had shot himself in our bedroom while lying on our bed.

Inspector Ntuli tried to stop me from entering the bedroom, but I just pushed past him. If I didn't see this for myself I would never be able to believe what I had been told.

I was met by the most gruesome sight. Charlie was lying on his back with his right hand on his chest, clutching my gun. He had shot himself in the right temple. My husband was lying centimetres deep in blood. I had never seen so much blood in my life! The thought of how on earth I was going to clean up the mess kept going through my mind.

It seemed unreal. I just stood there and stared at his lifeless body and all that blood . . .

The rest of the day is a blur. I do, however, remember phoning my mother-in-law. On her asking how I was, I answered that I was not too good, and then blurted out that Charlie had committed suicide. My flat was soon full of friends; I am not sure whether I contacted them or somebody else did. My mother-in-law and sister-in-law were soon downstairs, but did not come up to the flat. I went down to them and my mother-in-law kept repeating the word 'Why?' Meanwhile, friends had contacted a cleaning company to come in and help clean up, and I was desperate to get hold of my priest. The detectives were in and out of the bedroom, laughing and chatting on their cell phones with no regard to how we were feeling.

We finally got hold of the priest who arrived just before the body was removed. As we gathered together in the lounge to say the Lord's Prayer, the body was brought past, swinging to and fro in the body bag as they turned the corner into the entrance hall, blood dripping onto the carpet, leaving a trail behind the numerous people required to carry the dead weight. This scene often comes back to me in the form of flashbacks.

The next moment the cleaning people arrived. I looked up to see my mattress being carried out the door. Next we heard a loud ripping sound and half of my bedroom carpet was taken out. Someone explained to me that it was impossible to get bloodstains such as these out of the bed or carpet. They would have to be incinerated.

Once all the police work was over, friends started to pack a bag for me, as I was to go to my parents' flat to sleep. It was then that we discovered that Charlie had actually taken all my pills and returned the boxes to the make-up bag in which I stored the medication. I searched, but there was no note; I was to learn later that only one in four people who commits suicide leaves a note. The only thing that was around was a pair of used earbuds in the bedroom rubbish bin.

My next thought was what was the right thing to do with regard to my son. He was very young and his dad was his best friend, hero and soulmate. My daughter had turned four months that day – she would never know her father.

I phoned the clinical psychologist we had visited in the past as well as a counsellor at Childline. Both of them gave the same advice: 'Tell your son the truth! If you lie to him he is bound to overhear phone calls and other conversations and will doubt anything else that you tell him because you lied to him in the beginning.'

What a horrible task. When I got to my parents' place I called Timothy aside and told him what had happened as gently, yet as truthfully, as I could. I told him if he had any questions he must feel free to ask and I would do my best to answer them.

From there on, exactly what happened and when it happened is not absolutely clear in my mind. Later, friends and a cousin took me back to the flat as we had noticed on the Friday that there was still blood on the wall and the bedside furniture. Try as we might, the blood would fade and then again dry to a brownish stain. A good friend actually ended up painting the bedroom and the bedside furniture as no amount of scrubbing could remove the blood. My cousin ripped up the rest of the carpet that was a stark reminder that the other half had had to be incinerated.

Someone was required to identify the body at the mortuary, something I felt was my duty. It ended up being a group of us who went, including Charlie's father. We were required to fill out forms and then were taken to the viewing room. The top half of Charlie's body was pushed into a glass, box-shaped protrusion in the wall. I remember standing there and looking at the hole in his head and asking out loud, 'Why, Charlie, why?' His yellow complexion reminded me of how quickly the blood had drained from his feet and hands and how yellow they had looked when I saw him on the bed.

At the time, I remember saying how fortunate I was that I had a business to run and a child to get to school. I was forced to get up on the Monday morning and keep going. If I had worked for somebody else, I am sure I would have taken compassionate leave and not left my bed.

Although Charlie and I belonged to different religions, it was agreed that the funeral be held at the church I attended. My mother-in-law mentioned that she thought Charlie would have wanted a 'happy' funeral, nothing morbid, so I was on a mission to give him the ultimate send off.

I organised for his favourite song to be played as the coffin was brought into the church, found suitable poems to be printed in the leaflet for the service, and had a hundred copies of a photograph of him with both his children on his lap, printed for the cover. Charlie was a keen league tennis player and so the club was notified and his team players were appointed as pallbearers. I also went through his cell phone, that had old friends' numbers listed on it and let them know. He had been friendly with his ex-boss and when it was decided he would fly up from Cape Town, I asked him to do Charlie's eulogy. Charlie's parents had also asked a friend of the family to read the eulogy that Charlie's father had written.

Along with many of our friends, I inserted a notice in the paper. On the second day, much to my horror, there was a notice from his ex-wife, Nora, stating how she would miss him. I couldn't believe that a woman he despised and had had nothing to do with for ten years would do this. They had only been married for eleven months, during which time she had had numerous affairs. She had destroyed Charlie's self-esteem and left him a very hurt man. On the day of Charlie's suicide, his mother had said she could have understood it if he had done something like this when he was still involved with Nora, but not now!

I was devastated. How dare she be so two-faced and insensitive to how I felt? As I knew where Nora was working, I managed to get her cell-phone number. When I could not get her on her cell, I left a very strong and abusive message with her secretary, telling her in no uncertain terms what I thought of her and what she had done. I also requested that she leave my family alone; I wanted nothing to do with her. Little did I know this was the start of the huge rupture that would occur between me and my in-laws, who had constantly berated Nora, mocked her and spoken of their distaste for her.

I found out that Nora would not have known a thing if it wasn't for my sister-in-law telling her the news of Charlie's suicide. A few of my friends, trying to protect me, called Nora to tell her to keep away. Then I got a phone call from my sister-in-law to say that she was the one who had told Nora. To say that I was hurt and angry is an understatement. My sister-in-law did apologise to me on the next occasion I was there, but during the course of the visit who should walk in, but Nora. She behaved like a long-lost friend. I was seething!

The day of the funeral arrived. Apart from very close friends and family, I could not say who was there. The church was, however, filled to capacity; there was standing room only. Charlie's mother had asked to view the body before the coffin was taken into the church. They had cleaned him and made him up well. There was no blood to be seen, and I bent over and touched his cheek. It was a shock to feel how cold he was. Without any thought, my family sat on the right of the aisle and Charlie's family sat on the left.

When I had asked for Charlie's favourite song to be played as they brought the coffin into the church I had no idea of the impact it would have. The church had an excellent sound system and I was overwhelmed when the song filled the building – apparently there were very few dry eyes. Apart from knowing it was a moving service and the priest's words were kind and gentle, the only other thing I can remember is that not a word about my family, children or myself was mentioned in Charlie's father's eulogy. It was as if we did not exist. My mother also commented on this later, and it was really upsetting for me.

We followed the coffin out of the church and watched as they loaded the coffin into the hearse and drove off. I was hugged and kissed by so many people – many I hadn't seen or heard from in years. We then went up to the hall for tea. I stood on the veranda and someone gave me a cup of tea. I took no notice of what was going on around me. I have heard this numbness spoken of as God's anaesthetic; although I was oblivious to much that was going on around me, I managed to go through the motions. This occurred for a long time after the suicide.

Next we were invited to tea at Charlie's parents' house. I can remember just wanting to be alone, but felt it my duty to be there. Three friends escorted me. The only place that was available to us to sit was at the dining room table, so this is where we headed. I did not move from there until we left some time later. As the crowd thinned, I said my farewells and left for home. This was to be the start of a very long, emotional roller-coaster ride!

'Why?' was a question everybody asked, including me, and to which I did not have the answer. I was angry with Charlie for leaving me to handle all that was going on at the time, totally alone, and at the same time depriving his four-month-old daughter and four-year-old son of a father, and me of a husband and best friend. How dare he make such an important decision on his own, leaving behind no explanation?

Then the 'if onlys' started. If only I had sent him that SMS that morning telling him I loved him, it might have made a difference. What else could I have done to change what had happened? I should have sorted out the argument before going to bed. If only I had taken my son home instead of taking him to my mother's place, I might have been able to stop him . . .

I had suffered from depression before Charlie's suicide, but now I was in a very deep, dark pit! The hurt, the raw pain, the disbelief, the anguish, added to everything else, left me torn apart. It is common, apparently, to feel suicidal yourself and I will vouch for that. In a second my life had been turned upside down. I was now a widow, single parent, breadwinner and all that my family had to pivot around. The responsibility was overwhelming.

The day following the funeral I had reason to drop in at my mother-in-law's house. She said, 'Glenda, we have to talk.'

'What about?' I asked.

First she brought up the telephone conversation with my sister-in-law with regard to Charlie's ex-wife, Nora. She wanted to know how I could have spoken to Martha like that and said she had never expected such foul language from me. I told her that Martha was an adult and could fight her own battles; it had nothing to do with her.

Then she asked, 'What have you said to your parents? They never phoned once to offer their condolences and they totally ignored us at the funeral.'

The next question really floored me. 'What was wrong with you yesterday? Everybody here was asking about you.'

I had lost my husband to suicide and I had just come from his funeral – surely I wasn't expected to be my normal gregarious self. I was deeply disturbed and in shock!

I left there feeling crushed. The one person who I had thought would understand and support me the most was lashing out in anger at me and I could not understand it.

I then started on a mission to try to answer that never-ending 'Why?' question that played on my mind. I tried every bookstore and library in town to find books on suicide. I managed eventually to find one, which was very old and outdated. While going through the archives at the local library, a librarian got chatting to me and mentioned that a close friend of hers had lost his wife to suicide and that I should phone him. She later gave me his number and I did contact him. It was a relief to hear that everything I was going through he had been through, and that I was not alone on my journey through grief.

I continued to search for answers and eventually got a friend in America to send me some books, and a couple of the larger bookstores were able to source some books for me on suicide. I trawled the Internet and discovered hundreds of support groups that existed overseas for those bereaved by suicide. A lot of literature expressed the view that it was worthwhile joining a support group. I started with Lifeline and continued my search, following up on all suggestions that were given to me as to where to find a support group. My search was fruitless! Nobody could tell me of an existing support group I could attend.

I was lucky in that I was going for counselling with the most helpful psychologist. She understood my frustrations and when all the roads she had suggested came to a dead end, she agreed, despite a very heavy schedule – sometimes consulting from 6h00 to 20h00 – to help me establish a support group.

In the interim, a woman from my church had given my name to a woman that had also lost her husband to suicide and also been left with small children. When I received her phone call it was like manna from heaven. Here was somebody that knew what I was going through, had been there, done that, got the T-shirt, and she was extending a hand of support to somebody new to this horrible journey of suicide grief. She made arrangements to meet me for coffee that Saturday morning and it was the start of a wonderful friendship, one where she carried me through what seemed to be the roughest times, guiding me and supporting me, as she knew the road well.

I did a lot of research into how I could find suicide survivors and was given the name of a man who had run a bereavement support group, but had left Pietermaritzburg to live in Cape Town. He was able to give me a few names and numbers of people who had lost people to suicide and had attended the group he had run.

It was at this stage that my psychologist set up a time and place for us to meet with a few of the people I had managed to get hold of and were interested in starting a support group. Thanks to her, the seed was planted for SOLOS (Survivors of Loved Ones' Suicide). We decided when to meet again and I arranged the venue.

The group went from strength to strength and we learnt from our mistakes along the way, as we had nobody to tell us exactly what to do. With the help of a friend, I was able to get professionals to speak at the meetings and each gathering helped to put another piece into that huge unfinished puzzle. My psychologist was always prepared to help out with the group and it was nice to have a professional on board.

I put our story out to newspapers and magazines, even asking for interested parties to contact me with regard to starting up support groups in the various provinces. We managed to get a small group up and running in the Cape, but the woman who was going to do all the initial work in Gauteng, never managed to get things off the ground. It is a lot of hard work and takes tenacity to keep things up and running. The moment you let things slide a little, as I have during my 'all fall down' phases, things are inclined to fall apart.

The group provided a place where we all felt safe in the knowledge that each one of us had lost somebody to suicide. There is a terrible stigma attached to suicide and many people have been honest enough to tell us that they actually do not know what to say, and fear that they may upset us. If only the public could be educated to know that it is all right to speak of our loved ones; all we want to do is talk about them and acknowledge their lives and the memories we still treasure.

After collecting a whole lot of information on 'survivors' – as we are internationally referred to – for the members of the group and myself, I thought I would make copies for my mother-in-law, as they might be of help to her, too. When I arrived at her house, she came out onto the veranda. Within moments the conversation turned into a barrage of abuse. She said that Charlie would still be alive if he hadn't married me and she called me a murderess. She said that my father-in-law had had things to say about me. I said I would like to speak to him about this and so she immediately called him at his work. He was not available so she left a message for him to phone back urgently. I had had enough abuse and so climbed into the car and immediately headed for my father-in-law's workplace. He was very cool towards me and when I asked him what he had said about me, he replied that he had said nothing. I told him that is not what I had heard and that I could have his wife up on criminal charges for what she had just said to me.

He turned around and said, 'That's exactly how you operate.'

I couldn't believe what he had said; we had never exchanged angry words before and to this day I have no idea what he was alluding to.

Each time I had visited my mother-in-law I had been subjected to a barrage of abuse and, via friends, I heard of the terrible and untrue things that were being said about me. I was down, and felt I was being kicked in the teeth. It was time to keep a low profile with regard to my in-laws; they obviously blamed me for Charlie's suicide. I had read numerous articles that documented that in the case of a spouse committing suicide, the remaining spouse often bore the brunt of the blame. Members of the support group backed this up as well, but it was of no comfort to me. I was hurt. Up until Charlie had committed suicide, I had been the person my mother-in-law turned to for advice; she wouldn't even choose a new pair of glasses without my being present.

The next time I tried to contact my in-laws was when I had my daughter baptised. I was told that they were unable to attend the baptism. This also caused pain. On the day of the baptism I kept looking to the back of the church, just in case. I thought that my sister-in-law might at least make an effort, but there was nobody from their side of the family at all. I was devastated. They couldn't make an effort to attend their son's only daughter's baptism, but were planning on attending their other granddaughter's baptism.

That day I SMSd the family and said I would have nothing more to do with them. I had had my share of abuse from them. Any association with them seemed to be destructive and always set me back.

Nevertheless, the questions lurk, 'Why can Charlie's parents not understand how much I am suffering, and how great the impact of his suicide has been on my life? Why can it not be acknowledged that I was part of his life – in many more ways than they were?'

True, no mother or father expects to lose a child before they themselves die, but there were times when Charlie didn't see his parents for months on end. I was always the one to push him to visit or phone on birthdays, and Mother's and Father's Day. The last Mother's Day that Charlie was alive, I had bought my mother a copy of the book *Chicken Soup for the Mother's Soul*. When I purchased the book I decided to buy a copy for Charlie's mother as well. Boy, did he get acknowledged for this. It was never suggested that I might have had a part in the gift. Charlie got all the credit for something he was not responsible for.

Until recently, I have never kept a journal as such, but I did keep all my e-mails and computer correspondence on the initial stages of my journey through my grief. I received lots of correspondence in response to my letters and articles in the newspapers. The following are a few extracts from e-mails I received. I am sure all those who have gone through the death of somebody by suicide can identify with them:

> Our eldest son, who was nineteen, committed suicide in May 1996. Although it was 'the end of the world' for us, as it is for most remaining family members, we have come a long way in healing, growing and stepping away from blame, shame, resentment and guilt.

> ... it's hard working on your own grief, questions, sadness and so on, when there are children who require your attention, often when you *just want to be alone*. It's the hardest thing I've ever done. My daughter took up *all* my energy and also used me as the target of her anger at the world. She matured very quickly, and today has worked through the loss of her 'hero'.

> On 17 November 2000 my husband left home and never returned. He was found in his car the following day. I'm devastated by my loss and tortured by my actions that might have contributed to my beloved's pain and his reason for taking this decision.

> I too am a survivor of suicide, my husband dying two and a half years ago. Your concept of starting a support group is an

excellent idea – those around you give the best support they can, but they cannot comprehend the overwhelming sense of tragedy, the many unanswered questions, the anger, the hurt ... well I could go on and on.

All the e-mails contained a similar thread and spoke of the pain, anger and anguish experienced by those left behind when a loved one commits suicide.

I had read of the difficulties of anniversaries, special holidays, birthdays and the like and therefore prepared myself for my first Christmas and New Year alone. Christmas Eve and Christmas Day I spent with friends and my mind was kept pretty occupied. New Year's Day I spent with my immediate family and I was seemingly coping, but the next day all the wheels fell off and I simply could not get out of bed on 2 January. The tears flowed uncontrollably. All I wanted was to be with Charlie. The loneliness eats away at you and there are times that you are in a room with twenty other people, but feel alone.

Until the funeral, everybody is there for you, the phone rings non-stop and visitors are always around. The post is bulging with sympathy cards and nobody can do enough for you, but once the funeral is over it takes very special people to even so much as make a phone call or bring up the deceased's name. Everybody continues with their lives, and expects you to do the same.

The unanswered questions have remained an issue and my search for answers is perpetual. Did the ingestion of my medication play a role in Charlie's irrational decision to shoot himself?

Those lone earbuds in the bin in the bedroom also baffled me. Surely somebody who is thinking of shooting himself doesn't care whether or not his ears are wax free? I also phoned the policeman friend of mine to ask if the gun was fully loaded – did it contain all five bullets or had Charlie played a game of Russian Roulette? Bert answered that Charlie had fully loaded the gun.

He had loaded the gun, replaced the box of bullets in its original location, and climbed back into bed, pulling the duvet up over him. How long had he lain there? What was going through his mind? He was the most gentle, kind person, someone who wouldn't hurt a fly. How could he choose and carry through such a violent manner of killing himself?

My son's way of dealing with the loss of his father was to become absolutely impossible. He had been 'daddy's boy' right from birth. Charlie was the first one to hold him and owing to my post-natal depression, it was he who bonded with him. Every night they would snuggle together on the couch and recite all the television adverts out loud. On a Saturday afternoon Charlie played tennis. If it was a home game, Timothy toddled along with dad, even if I was going to meet up with him later. Sunday morning was either the beach or the tennis club with dad. They played ball together, laughed at *Mr Bean* together, rumbled and tumbled together – Charlie was Timothy's closest friend, the ultimate dad. As the saying goes, 'Anybody can be a father, but it takes somebody special to be a dad.'

Timothy had never been an easy child, suffering from constant colic for the first nine months of his life. Charlie, however, had the patience to deal with him and when I felt I needed time out, Charlie took over. His love for his son was unconditional and it took something really dramatic for him to get angry with him.

How could he have left a little person whose life revolved around him and who was the apple of his eye? Even if I was not enough to live for, he had his son and a beautiful baby daughter of whom he was so proud. So often you hear of the person who commits suicide writing in the suicide note that he or she feels the people being left behind would be better off without him or her. How could Charlie think this? There were no insurance policies that would cover all the debts that were accumulating; my parents had had to forfeit all their retirement money, and we were almost destitute. Together we could have fought and got through it all, but here I was left alone, severely depressed and almost non-functional, trying to support two elderly parents, a disabled brother and two tiny children.

All these thoughts go whizzing through your mind and that emotional roller-coaster ride starts again. In one hour you go through phases of anger, sadness, disillusionment, denial, bargaining with God, hopelessness, anguish . . . When people speak of the phases of grief, you think you will slowly go through a single phase at a time. This is not the case. In one day I can go through every stage ten times, and then some.

Regardless of the circumstances, life goes on. Timothy went into Reception last January. It was routine for Charlie and me to drop him off in the morning, together. That first day was dreadful and very lonely, a big reminder of Charlie's absence.

It is so true when the literature talks of everybody grieving differently and their relationship with the deceased affecting the grieving process. Charlie and I were husband and wife, best friends, parents, work partners, co-breadwinners – we did everything together and spent almost twenty-four hours a day, seven days a week together. His presence was so obvious in every sphere of my life; therefore his absence is overwhelming.

CHAPTER TWO

Suicide in history, the arts and religion

THE PHENOMENON OF suicidal behaviour has been discussed for thousands of years although its history as a subject of scientific research is more contemporary. Suicidal behaviour, from a historical perspective, was not examined scientifically until 1897 when the pioneer Emile Durkheim (a sociologist) published *Le Suicide*, his revolutionary book on suicide in which he held that occurrences of suicide increase as a society's values break down. The word 'suicide' first appeared in literature in the mid-seventeenth century (Shneidman, 1985), and 'suicidology' (derived from 'suicide') has both Latin and Greek origins. Many Greek and Latin phrases were used to convey a person killing him- or herself, for example, 'haireo thanatou', Greek for 'to seize death', and 'vulnero me ut moriar', Latin for 'wounding myself in order to die'. According to the *Oxford English Dictionary* the word was first used in 1651, but the exact date of its first use is open to question and some claim that it was used as early as 1642 (Shneidman, 1985).

This book is not the place for a major review of the literature on the history of suicidal behaviour as it probably constitutes one of the most extensively developed areas of research in mental health worldwide. Instead, by way of illustration, I will offer a few brief examples and comments in terms of suicidal behaviour in history, literature, art and religion.

HISTORY AND THE ARTS

Throughout the centuries people from all walks of life have resorted to suicidal behaviour. It has impacted on history, the arts and culture, and the suicidal deaths of the more famous are well documented (Dolce, 1992; Schlebusch, 1992b; Shneidman, 1985, 2001). A few examples are sufficient to illustrate the phenomenon.

Cleopatra, the last Egyptian queen of the Ptolemy Dynasty (69–30 BC) chose to die from the bite of a poisonous snake rather than to surrender to the Roman Empire.

Shakespeare is a playwright famous for his tragedies involving suicide. One of the most romanticised suicides in all his writings is the double suicide of Romeo and Juliet, while his most famous soliloquy is probably 'To be or not to be' by Hamlet, although in this play it is Ophelia who actually commits suicide by drowning. This tragic event was depicted in a famous painting, *Ophelia*, by Sir John Everett Millais in 1851. In this painting the flowers floating on the surface of the water were carefully chosen for their symbolic meanings, that is, poppies (death), daisies (innocence), roses (youth), violets (faithfulness and early death) and pansies (love in vain). Shakespeare's plays had a significant influence on such Pre-Raphaelite painters (Beckett, 1994).

The Dutch painter Vincent van Gogh, who sold only one of his paintings in his lifetime, shot himself in 1890. In an 1889 self-portrait he vividly portrayed the mental anguish he suffered.

The suicides of Adolf Hitler and his bride of short duration Eva Braun at the fall of the Nazi government are well known. Ironically, with the rise of Hitler, many artists were discredited in Germany: their work was seen as 'degenerate art' because it did not support the Nazi Aryan ideology. Paintings by such masters as Van Gogh, Picasso and Matisse were ripped from their frames and randomly hung amongst those of asylum inmates, the first exhibition of 'degenerate art' being held in Munich in 1937. In 1938 Ernst Kirchner, already depressed by political events in Germany, was so distressed at his art being labelled 'degenerate' that he committed suicide a few months thereafter (Beckett, 1994).

The British writer Virginia Woolf drowned herself in 1941. Ernest Hemingway (author of *For Whom the Bell Tolls*) committed suicide by shooting himself with a hunting rifle. Marilyn Monroe, one of Hollywood's best known actresses, was found dead from an overdose. The American poet, Sylvia Plath, whose autobiography *The Bell Jar* documents her attempted suicide as a teenager, took her own life in 1963. The Japanese writer, Yukio Mishima, committed hara-kiri in 1970. In a thought-provoking book, Shneidman (2001) deals with thirteen writers on suicide and provides a unique insight into related issues around literary, historical, sociological, biological, psychiatric and psychological considerations as well as on survivors and volunteers.

Many well-known South Africans have committed suicide. Examples include poet and author Eugene Marais; a cabinet minister towards the end of the apartheid era; the poet Ingrid Jonker; and the Afrikaans singer Johannes Kerkorrel (Barron, 2005; Schoonakker, *The Sunday Times*, 2001a). Other examples of suicidal behaviour reported in the South African press are mentioned in Chapter six.

Depression is one of the most common psychological disorders associated with suicidal behaviour. Throughout history, stretching back to the beginning of recorded time, depression has affected people of all types and all ages. It is a disease with many consequences, one of the most serious being suicidal behaviour.

A perusal of early writings reveals evidence of depression in many individuals. Both King Saul and Job, from descriptions of their behaviour in the Old Testament, suffered from serious depression. Although early Egyptian writings mention suicide, they lack the precise terminology for depression, and yet it was recognised and treated in a manner reminiscent of modern psychotherapy. Historically, depression was considered to have a single cause, and was referred to as melancholia. The ancient Greeks thought that of the four 'humours' or fluids produced by the body and influencing temperament and behaviour, an excess of one, black bile, caused melancholia. Although ancient Greek literature also describes the concept of divinely inspired depression, Hippocrates noted that the origins of psychiatric problems stem from natural rather than supernatural causes and offered an early catalogue of melancholic symptoms. Galen, a physician of the Roman era, mentions depression, describing it as a melancholic state. Melancholia was seen predominantly as a religious problem in the Middle Ages, often caused by demonic possession.

In addition to the 'To be or not to be' soliloquy on suicide in Shakespeare's *Hamlet*, the works of William Cowper, Edgar Allan Poe, Fyodor Dostoevsky, John Milton and William Blake all depict depression.

Throughout the ages, mood disorders leading to suicidal behaviour have often been linked with creative, imaginative minds.

Modern history, however, has provided ample evidence that depression is not the prerogative of any specific group (Schlebusch, 1990b).

THE COPYCAT EFFECT

One of the problems concerning the depictions of suicide in many popular novels and dramas is that the writing tends to romanticise suicidal behaviour, thereby placing vulnerable people at risk for seeking suicide as a glamorous type of demise.

A compelling example of this may be found in the so-called 'Werther effect' that developed from a book by Goethe published in 1774, *The Sorrows of Young Werther*. It tells of the hero, a young man named Werther, who commits suicide after a love disappointment. Its publishing sparked off several similar suicides, thereafter sometimes called the 'Werther effect' or 'copycat effect'.

Some people committed suicide while dressed as Werther, and others committed suicide in the same manner as the young hero and had a copy of the novel that was open on the actual page that described the suicide. The book was written by Goethe in part to purge himself of his own suicidality, but he was surprised by the effect that the book had on others (Phillips & Cartensen, 1988). As long ago as 1897 Durkheim acknowledged that suicide may be affected by imitation. The underlying premise is that if suicidal behaviour receives inappropriate publicity, it can be contagious amongst the vulnerable. Although this highlights the responsibility of drawing undue attention to suicide (especially as reported in the media), it usually takes more than dramatising or romanticising suicide to trigger it. As discussed at various points in this book, biochemical, psychological, socio-cultural and other variables can be aetiologically involved.

SUICIDE AND RELIGION

Most religions do not condone suicide (Oosthuizen, 1988). In the time of St Augustine in the fifth century, the Catholic Church condemned suicide as a sin; it was officially banned by the Council of Braga in AD 563 when it was declared by the Catholic clergy that it broke the sixth commandment of 'Thou shalt not kill' (Dolce, 1992). The rationale is that the suicidal person has not given life to him- or herself, but received it from the Creator, and thus has no right to destroy it (Oosthuizen, 1988).

Although most of the world's religions express themselves to a greater or lesser degree against suicide, there are certain circumstances in which exceptions are sometimes made. Examples of these circumstances include:
- to avoid an execution or to avoid falling into the hands of enemies alive;
- when a person is terminally ill;
- as a heroic deed;
- to destroy a person's enemies;
- to protect a person's fatherland;
- as martyrs for the sake of evoking faith;
- in collective or mass suicides; and
- as in the case of the Rain Queen of the Venda people in South Africa, to make way for a successor (Oosthuizen, 1988).

Throughout history whenever social upheaval, political oppression and religious persecution were the order of the day, whole groups were driven to commit collective suicide (Colt, 1991). Classical Greek and Roman history reflects many examples of entire towns and armies that chose suicide instead of surrender (Colt, 1991). The history of the defence of Masada is an example. In the year AD 73 a group of Jews in Palestine opted for death instead of surrendering to the Roman legions (Colt, 1991).

Five definite suicides are mentioned in the Bible. Three of these, namely that of Samson who brought down the pillars of the building, which fell on him (Judges 16: 29–30), Saul who threw himself onto his own sword (Samuel 31: 4–5), and Ahithophel who hanged himself (2 Samuel 17: 23), are ascribed mitigating circumstances. The other two are Zimri, who died when he went into a fortress that he set on fire (1 Kings 16: 18), and Judas, the man who betrayed Jesus and who subsequently hanged himself (Matthew 27: 5).

Other examples of suicide that gain respect include:
- the actions of the samurai in Japan, referred to as seppuku or hara-kiri (self-disembowelment), which was performed to protect a person's honour;
- Hindu widows who cast themselves on their husbands' burning funeral pyres when the husband's body was cremated (a custom called suttee that is now illegal); and

- the practice in some ancient religions to fast to death in order to be freed from the contamination of the world (Oosthuizen, 1988).

One of the most dramatic examples of a collective religious mass suicide occurred in 1978 when the religious group, The People's Temple, founded by the Reverend Jim Jones, formed a colony in a remote area of Guyana; Jones later instructed his followers to commit suicide (Killduff & Javers, 1978). Although most people died from ingesting cyanide (in a cold drink) it is believed some were lethally injected, while others died from gunshot wounds or alternative causes. One woman slit her throat and those of her three children, but some individuals survived (Maaga, 1998). There are other examples such as the Branch Davidians, The Solar Temple and Heaven's Gate (Maaga, 1998). A few examples of suicide cults, mass suicides and religious suicides that have been reported in the South African press are noted in Chapter six.

Of late, religious fundamentalism has been associated with numerous suicide attacks, sometimes referred to as political suicides (Dingfelder, 2004). The emotional effects of indirect trauma often produce behaviour which can take the form of, for example, acts of political suicides, which spread fear and anxiety to people even if they are far removed from where the actual events occur. These effects can be delayed for weeks or even years, or surface immediately. They are varied and can result in emotional blunting and severe psychosocial disorders (Schlebusch & Bosch, 2002).

There are various religious understandings of suicide in Africa. For some, a person who is mentally ill is considered to have been bewitched through black magic, and when such a person 'has no strength' he or she hangs him- or herself and becomes an evil spirit or a roaming ghost, not going to the kingdom of the ancestors (Oosthuizen, 1988). Metropolitan Durban (a busy harbour city on the east coast of South Africa) and its immediate surroundings, are unique in representing most of the world's major religions, namely, Christianity, Hinduism, Islam, Judaism, Buddhism, Jainism, Zoroastrianism, Confucianism, Taoism and others. Long-term studies on suicidal behaviour in this region are discussed in more depth in Chapter eleven.

Throughout history, writers have had (from a religious perspective) different views on suicide (Oosthuizen, 1988). For example, David Hume, the well-known sceptic British philosopher of the eighteenth century, maintained that if there is a God, then we should be grateful that He arranged life in such a way that we may leave it when we wish to do so; Nietzsche's nihilistic approach emphasised in *Zarasthustra* that freedom to bring about one's own death should not be condemned, but praised; and others maintain that when a person has ruined his or her life, real repentance can only be expressed through suicide. In the Bible, Samson, who died by his own hand, was praised as a hero of faith in that his suicide simultaneously destroyed the enemies of his people (Hebrews 11: 32–33). This phenomenon is also seen in contemporary examples, such as in certain suicide attacks so frequently reported in the media. In the past, in times of religious persecution, women committed suicide in order to avoid rape and were praised for this by theologians in the early church. Others committed suicide during political turmoil, such as at the time of the Nazi regime, because they feared that they might give away their comrades to avoid being martyred (Oosthuizen, 1988).

A South African study makes the point that the decline in religious fervour, along with the technological explosion and the increased emphasis on material prosperity, has affected thinking with regard to religion and suicidal behaviour across cultures in South Africa (Heuer, 1988). Heuer observes that the growing acceptance of suicide in classical Roman life might have been due to the decline of religious belief, especially with regard to an afterlife. This, according to Heuer, usually follows the trend of religious belief degenerating into some disguised form of cultural expression.

KEY POINTS

- The history of suicide goes back to ancient times.
- Depression has been established as an important factor contributing to suicidal behaviour.
- Although it is an important consideration, it usually takes more than dramatising or romanticising suicide to trigger it.
- Many talented, creative people have taken their own lives, but suicide does not occur exclusively among such people; individuals and groups of people from all walks of life have committed suicide.
- Religions generally frown upon suicide, although various religions over the centuries have condoned suicide in specific circumstances.

CHAPTER THREE

Trends within an international and African context

SUICIDAL BEHAVIOUR IS an increasingly serious worldwide problem (Bertolote, 2001; Hawton & Van Heeringen, 2000; Lester, 2000; Wasserman, 2001a). This trend has been observed in both developed and developing countries, including South Africa (Schlebusch, 2004; WHO 1999a).

THE GLOBAL SITUATION
The World Health Organization (WHO) and other researchers show that globally approximately one million people die from suicide every year (Bertolote, 2001; Hawton & Van Heeringen, 2000; WHO, 1999a), and that by 2020 this will increase to approximately 1.53 million people per annum (Bertolote, 2001). There are about ten to twenty times more non-fatal suicide attempts per year, although in some regions non-fatal suicide attempts could be up to forty times more frequent than fatal suicidal behaviour (WHO, 1999a). Consequently, the estimated universal fatal to non-fatal suicidal behaviour ratio ranges from about 1:10 to 1:40. In 2000, the estimated global figures suggested one death by suicide every forty seconds and one attempt every one to three seconds (WHO, 1999a). By 2020 this is estimated to increase to one death every twenty seconds and one attempt every one to two seconds (Bertolote, 2001). South African figures have been calculated separately and are reported in Chapter four.

On average, these statistics point to more people globally and annually dying from suicide than from war, or from other causes of death such as violence, homicide and traffic accidents. However, in the sub-Saharan Africa (AFRO) region, adult and child injury mortality rates from both intentional causes (homicide and violence) and unintentional causes (road traffic accidents and other injuries) are very high (Matzopolous, Norman & Bradshaw, 2004). The AFRO region (one of the six WHO regions of the world) is itself subdivided into two sub-regions according to levels of mortality, namely AFRO D and E, with South Africa falling into AFRO E (Matzopolous, Norman & Bradshaw, 2004).

Further, figures show that globally an increase has been observed in suicide rates from 10.1 per 100 000 to 16 per 100 000 of the population between 1950 and 1995. This constitutes approximately a 60% increase in 45 years. During the same period suicide rates increased by about 49% for males and 33% for females (Bertolote, 2001; WHO, 1999a).

Suicidal rates generally have shown a positive relationship with age, in that they tended to increase in older people, but when actual numbers and frequency are considered in relation to age from a worldwide perspective, suicides have now tended to move from the elderly towards younger people, which is sometimes referred to as the 'ungreying' phenomenon (Bertolote, 2001). More suicides globally (53%) today are committed by people in the 5 to 44 year age group than in the older age groups, with most suicides occurring in 35 to 44 year olds for both males and females (Bertolote, 2001; WHO, 1999a). This downward trend in the age of clinical populations in both absolute and relative terms means that for the younger age groups, suicide is among the top five causes of death for both men and women. During the latter half of the twentieth century, the predominance of male suicide rates over females ones globally, seems to have remained relatively constant, with only a minor increase from 3.2:1 (in 1950) to 3.6:1 (in 1995) and with a predicted 3.9:1 in 2020. Rural China is the exception to this, where the female rates tend, on average, to be higher than those of males do (Bertolote, 2001; WHO, 1999a).

Researchers caution that reported data must be interpreted with care when making cross-national, cross-cultural and even cross-regional comparisons, because of variations in the reliability of international and regional data (Bertolote, 2001; Cantor, 2000; Cheng & Lee, 2000; WHO, 1999a). There are differences in reported rates by different investigators, and between reported rates per 100 000 of the population and the actual number of suicides in a particular country or region. Differences also occur because of the hidden burden of suicidal behaviour and because of cultural and other influences. Not only do major variations occur in suicide rates between countries and regions, but in countries with small populations a few more or less suicides can greatly alter the picture, thus giving an inflated impression of increases or decreases in suicidal behaviour. There are excellent reviews of such findings (Bertolote, 2001; Cantor, 2000; Cheng & Lee, 2000; WHO, 1999a); space does not allow for a detailed discussion of these global variations, so only a few additional points are mentioned here. For example, considerable differences have been reported between some Asian and Western countries, and between certain countries and regions within these areas (Bertolote, 2001; Cantor, 2000; Cheng & Lee, 2000; WHO, 1999a). Figures indicate that the lowest suicide rates occur in the eastern Mediterranean region in countries that mainly follow Islamic traditions. This also applies to some central Asian countries that were formerly part of the Soviet Union, whereas some of the highest suicide rates (that is, over 30 per 100 000 of the population – which constitutes almost twice the global average suicide rate of 16 per 100 000) occur in parts of Europe, especially eastern Europe and some countries in the Baltic region. Globally speaking, it is noteworthy that almost 30% of all suicides occur in only two countries, namely, China and India, where the large populations of each of these two countries probably also have a bearing on the high suicide rates (Bertolote, 2001; WHO, 1999a). One of the most striking trends in the Western world has been the increase of suicide in young males, especially in countries in the New World, western Europe and Scandinavia (Cantor, 2000).

THE AFRICAN SITUATION
This book deals specifically with suicidal behaviour in South Africa and, consequently, only a few comments on other parts of Africa are offered here. Comparatively speaking, some of the highest suicide rates in the regions of Africa, the Americas, South-east Asia and the west Pacific have been reported in island countries, including Mauritius, Cuba, Sri Lanka and Japan (Bertolote, 2001; WHO, 1999a). Although, as mentioned, we must be careful when making cross-cultural, cross-regional and cross-national comparisons, it is interesting to note that in the past, despite numerous

published studies on suicidal behaviour, there was a paucity of related work on black Africans, partly because suicidal behaviour has been claimed to occur less frequently in these communities (Schlebusch, 1988a). With regard to more traditional black African societies, there are even fewer published reports on suicidal behaviour.

In most African societies, according to earlier studies, the rate of suicide was usually reported as being less than 1 per 100 000 of the population per year (Jacobsson, 1985; Schlebusch, 1988a). With minor exceptions, this situation seemed to have prevailed for some time (Schlebusch, 1988a). For example, a few decades ago suicide was reported as rare in Uganda (Orley, 1970) and in Nigeria (Prince, 1968). This view was upheld by others at the time also in respect of Senegal (Collomb & Zwingelstein, 1968). However, some later studies (in the 1980s), albeit few, reported higher figures, namely reports from Buzoga in Uganda, which gave figures closer to those of Western countries (Jacobsson, 1985; Schlebusch, 1988a).

More contemporary data on suicidal behaviour in Africa remain equally variable. In a 1980s review of the literature, in sub-Saharan African countries suicide rates are reported as 1 per 100 000 in Nigeria and other west African countries and 8.5 per 100 000 in Buzoga (Uganda) in east Africa (German, 1982). As in the case of later studies in Uganda, one study on suicidal behaviour in a general hospital in western Ethiopia reported a suicide rate in 1985 of at least 3 to 11 per 100 000 inhabitants per year (mean 4.5) (Jacobsson, 1985), which is higher than has usually been reported elsewhere in black Africans (Schlebusch, 1988a). Likewise, suicide rates in 1990 of 10.6 (for males) and 5.2 (for females) per 100 000 for Zimbabwe, and 20.6 (for males) and 6.4 (for females) per 100 000 of the population in 1996 for the island of Mauritius, have been reported (Bertolote, 2001).

Although further research is required, recent reports indicate that the problem of suicidal behaviour in Africa is more serious than was generally known. For example, a newspaper article quotes an appeal from a Botswanan government minister to people who want to commit suicide not to use the country's trains to do so, but rather to use trees (*The Independent on Saturday*, 21 February 2004: 6). Further, as noted earlier, deaths from both intentional and unintentional causes in the AFRO region are high. A recent comparison of injury mortality and disability adjusted life years (DALYs) with estimates from a global burden of disease study (GBD 2000) revealed interesting statistics (Matzopolous, Norman & Bradshaw, 2004). This comparison indicates age-standardised death rates per 100 000 for South Africa in 2000 as:

- total intentional death rates of 87.8 – with homicide and violence being 72.5 and suicide and self-inflicted death being 15.3;
- total unintentional death rates of 70.0 – with road traffic accidents being 43.0 and other unintentional injuries being 27.0; and
- total injuries of 157.8.

For the AFRO region the GBD 2000 age-standardised death rates per 100 000 were:

- total intentional of 60.4 – with homicide and violence being 53.8 and suicide and self-inflicted death being 6.5;
- total unintentional of 79.1 – with road traffic accidents being 34.0 and other unintentional injuries being 45.1; and
- total injuries of 139.5.

The world GBD 2000 age-standardised death rates per 100 000 people were:

- total intentional of 28.7 – with homicide and violence being 14.0 and suicide and self-inflicted death being 14.5;
- total unintentional of 58.2 – with road traffic accidents being 21.6 and other unintentional injuries being 36.6; and
- total injuries of 86.9.

As discussed in the next chapter, South Africa, which is part of the AFRO E region, appears to have higher suicide prevalence rates than the reported overall AFRO and world averages. Once again, however, such comparisons need to be interpreted with due circumspection, given the cautions expressed earlier and the fact that compared to many African countries, considerably more South African research data on suicidal behaviour are available.

KEY POINTS

- Globally and annually, more people die from suicide than in war.
- From 1950 to 1995 there was about a 60% increase in suicide rates globally.
- Recent research has indicated that globally about a million people die annually from suicide, and the expectations are that by 2020, the figure will have increased to one and a half million.
- A cause for concern is the 'ungreying' phenomenon of ever-younger people committing suicide.
- In general, more males than females take their own lives.
- Most concerning for the people of Africa is that suicide rates are significantly higher than was previously believed.

CHAPTER FOUR

Trends within the South African context

COMPARED TO MANY other parts of the world, and as discussed later in this chapter, the incidence of suicidal behaviour in South Africa is inordinately high (Schlebusch, 2004; Schlebusch & Bosch, 2000). With the exception of a few studies, there is unfortunately no past reliable database on the extent of the burden of suicidal behaviour in South Africa and indeed the whole Africa region. Research-based limitations of clinical and epidemiological trends, therefore, prevent an accurate analysis of such data (Schlebusch, 2004). As a result, only general trend analyses are possible (Schlebusch, 2000a, 2004). Prudence is needed in interpreting the figures reported in this book as they are based on the results of studies that are not necessarily representative of the entire suicidal population in South Africa. Furthermore, suicidal behaviour can be hidden, and real figures may be even higher as the existing figures may well record a bias because of under-reporting. It also needs to be emphasised that because of different sample sizes reported in the research quoted and for the years surveyed, results are not that readily comparable across years and ethnic groups.

Remarkably divergent suicidal behaviour prevalence rates were reported in South Africa in earlier research (Schlebusch, 1988a, 1992a, 1995a; Schlebusch & Bosch, 2000). Several reasons accounted for this, for example:
- inconsistent and inadequate reporting of suicidal behaviour particularly among the black African population;
- major historical, socio-political and economic events and changes affected not only the mental health of the nation, but also the gathering of accurate statistics, many of which relate only to academic hospitals;

- the hidden burden of suicidal behaviour;
- cultural considerations; and
- a lack of representative sampling that included figures based on research influenced by pre-1994 apartheid policies (that involved the legal segregation of ethnic groups).

Despite these shortcomings, available data show that in South Africa suicidal behaviour is a significant public health concern. As a result, research and service delivery in this area have lately attracted considerable interest (Schlebusch, 2004).

Certain worrying trends about the gravity of the situation are clearly discernable. The earlier findings are now contradicted by contemporary research (Burrows et al., 2003; Schlebusch, 2004; Schlebusch, Vawda & Bosch, 2003), which shows that suicidal behaviour amongst black South Africans is a serious problem that is increasing. It has also been argued that this increase should be viewed as a genuine escalation of the problem rather than simply as a reflection of improved recording practices over recent years in post-apartheid South Africa (Mkize, 1992; Schlebusch, 2004; Schlebusch & Bosch, 2000; Schlebusch, Vawda & Bosch, 2003).

FATAL SUICIDAL BEHAVIOUR

Research-based data on fatal suicidal behaviour in South Africa is available from the Durban Parasuicide Study (DPS), which is discussed in more detail in Chapter eleven; ad hoc studies; and from the South African National Injury Mortality Surveillance System (NIMSS). The gathering of information for NIMSS commenced formally at the beginning of 1999 and is collated from existing investigative procedures at mortuaries, state forensic laboratories and courts (Burrows et al., 2003). It is a collaborative effort between different research groups and government bodies in South Africa. NIMSS provides and disseminates descriptive epidemiological data about non-natural deaths that are all subject to medico-legal investigations in terms of existing legislation (Wyngaard, Matzopoulos & Van Niekerk, 2002). The fourth NIMSS report, published in 2003 (Matzopoulos, Cassim & Seedat, 2003), contains information on deaths in 2002 that was gathered from thirty-four mortuaries across the country, representing between 35% and 40% of all non-natural deaths in the country. Data were captured from both rural and urban mortuaries, although the mortality profile reflected a higher urban than rural representation. The previous (third) NIMSS report contained data on deaths in 2001 from thirty-two mortuaries in six of the nine South African provinces (Matzopoulos, 2002; Prinsloo, 2002a). Much of the most recent data on fatal suicidal bahaviour reported here is drawn from these NIMSS reports.

South African suicide rates have in the past been reported to range from 6 per 100 000 (or lower in some studies) to 19 per 100 000 of the population (or higher in some studies or for males), depending on when and where the sampling was done and which ethnic group was surveyed (Schlebusch, 2000a, 2004). For example, the mean South African suicide rate for 1949 to 1958 was reported to be 8.65 per 100 000. In Durban the rate was higher at 14.66 per 100 000 per annum (Meer, 1976). Breetzke (1988) mentioned that in the 1980s in the Cape Town area the suicide rate was significantly lower for blacks (0.7 per 100 000 of the population) than for Coloureds (3 per 100 000 of the population), whereas for whites it was 14 per 100 000 of the population. The study also found that an unusually high proportion of whites (35.0%) left suicide notes as opposed to only 14.0% of Coloureds and blacks, but in all ethnic groups approximately similar numbers of males and females left notes. Another South African study reported suicide notes in 8.4% of a large sample of parasuicidal patients seen (Deonarain & Pillay, 2000). Of this group 8.6% were females and 7.8% were males, and the main precipitating factors for the suicidal act were interpersonal conflicts between spouses, partners or family members. Generally speaking, suicide notes are usually left by about 15% of patients (Stengel, 1983). An analysis of a large sample of suicide notes found that men more often noted love or romantic problems as a motive for their suicides whereas older people more frequently tended to be motivated by an escape from pain (Lester et al., 2004). This supported the view that intrapsychic rather than interpersonal problems tend to motivate the suicides of older people.

In 1988 overall suicide rates were reported as 5.6 per 100 000 of the population (Levin, 1988). In a different study an ethnic breakdown of reported suicides rates in 1989 reflected rates of just under 4 per 100 000 for blacks, 16 per 100 000 for whites, 4.5 per 100 000 for Coloureds and 7.1 per 100 000 for Indians (Levin, 1992). Another

Cape Town study reported a suicide rate in 1993 to 1994 for whites of 20 per 100 000, while the black and Coloured suicide rates were below comparable American baseline rates of 13 per 100 000 (Lerer, Knobel & Matzopoulos, 1995). By comparison, an eastern Cape study noted an increase in black suicide rates from 2 per 100 000 to 11.6 per 100 000 over a twenty-year-period from 1971 to 1990 in Umtata (Mkize, 1992). An analysis of suicide patterns in the Pietermaritzburg city area, in the KwaZulu-Natal province near Durban, found suicide rates for blacks over a nine-year-period between 1982 to 1996 to be 14 per 100 000 of the population (Wassenaar et al., 2000). This study noted that the overall suicide rate increased gradually from 1989 and peaked in 1995 at 18.24 per 100 000 of the population.These findings are consistent with other contemporary data that dispel the myth that suicide is as rare in black South Africans as previously thought (Schlebusch, 2004; Schlebusch, Vawda & Bosch, 2003; Vawda, 2005). Not only do more recent studies show considerably higher suicide rates for blacks than earlier studies cited, but they also reflect an actual increase in suicidal behaviour in South African blacks (Schlebusch, 2004). This is further demonstrated by other reports that in the late 1990s in South Africa, 43.3% of all suicides were amongst blacks (WHO, 1999b). A recent press article highlights various studies that show the high suicide rate amongst South African blacks (Horner & Fredricks, *The Sunday Times*, 2005).

In addition, rates for certain types of fatal suicidal behaviours appear to be higher than the international average. For example, Townsend (2003) reported murder-suicide rates for 2000 to 2001 in Durban, to be 0.89 per 100 000 as opposed to a global average of 0.22 per 100 000. Although research on murder-suicides in South Africa has been limited, there appears to be an increase in both extended suicide and murder-suicide. For example, press reports have shown an average of almost two such incidents or more per month since the beginning of 2005 (Premdev, *The Sunday Tribune Herald*, 2005). In one case in the western Cape thirteen people died in family killings at the hands of their partners. Reports show that one woman is killed by her intimate partner every six hours in South Africa, which is the highest rate in the world, although all the partners do not go on to commit suicide (Goldstone, *The Mercury*, 2005). Unless action is taken, the warnings of human rights groups are that the current trends in family violence are set to continue (Ngalwa, *The Sunday Tribune*, 2005). This is discussed further in Chapter nine.

Compared to the statistics for the general population, there are some occupational groups in which suicide figures have been much higher. For example, in 1990 and 1991 the South African Police Services (SAPS) in the western Cape reflected suicide rates of 58.14 per 100 000 in 1990 and 24.91 per 100 000 in 1991 (Pieterse, 1993). Other research depicts countrywide police suicide rates as 203 per 100 000 in 1994 and 1995 (Rossouw, 2000). Rossouw also emphasises that although there was an overall decrease from an estimated 149 per 100 000 in 1996 to 135 per 100 000 in 1997, police suicide remains a very worrying problem. Across the country's nine provinces, this study reported the highest police suicide rates in 1997 to be in two provinces, the Northern Cape (36 per 10 000) and the Free State (29 per 10 000) (Rossouw, 2000). More contemporary research quotes studies reflecting police suicides per 100 000 as ranging from 110 in 1999 to 130 in 2000, with high-risk areas (provinces) being the Northern Cape, Mpumalanga, North West and Gauteng (Pienaar, 2003). Suicidal ideation in members of the SAPS of 8.64% has been reported, although studies quoted indicate this figure to be as high as 10.58% in uniformed police members with the highest level being in black police members (Pienaar, 2003). Researchers point out that internationally suicide by members of the police force is frequently higher than by the general population (Pienaar, 2003; Rossouw, 2000). In South Africa the number of police suicides has been reported as being five times that found in police services in some other countries (Pienaar, 2003).

Another example of high suicide rates reported in 1992 in a specific occupational group occurs in the South African National Defence Force (SANDF) (Brink, 1992). Reports indicate that at least 300 members of the SANDF committed suicide between 1994 and 1999, with statistics showing that in 1999, on average, four soldiers committed suicide every month (*The Independent on Saturday*, 1 April 2000: 8). A recent press report states that three South African soldiers were killed and four were wounded when a colleague shot them in Burundi, after which the soldier shot himself. They were a part of the South African contribution to the United Nations' peace mission (*The Independent on Saturday*, 21 May 2005: 1).

Occupational groups aside, in South Africa in 1990, the overall suicide rate was 17.2 per 100 000 of the population (WHO, 1999b), which is higher than many other African countries and the reported world average of 16 per 100 000 mentioned in Chapter three. Finally, at a recent conference NIMSS figures showed that of the large metropolitan areas surveyed in South Africa (Cape Town, Johannesburg, Pretoria and Durban) the suicide rates for Durban were 14 per 100 000, which was second only to 15 per 100 000 for Johannesburg, giving Durban the second-highest suicide rate in the country (Naran, *The Sunday Tribune*, 2005). Suicide prevalence rates amongst people with chronic disease are discussed in Chapters eight and nine as there are no clear-cut figures in this regard.

Although comparative figures must be interpreted with caution for reasons already mentioned, there appears to have been a gradual increase in the overall suicide rates reported. For example, contrary to the rates per 100 000 mentioned, it was reported in 1988 that suicides accounted for less than 1% of non-natural South African deaths (Levin, 1988), whereas a few years later another investigation found that approximately 7% of all non-natural deaths in Cape Town during 1993 to 1994 were due to suicides (Lerer, Knobel & Matzopoulos, 1995). Another study examined a dramatic increase in fatal suicides during 1990 to 2000 among young professional Coloured males in Paarl (a fairly large town in the southern Cape) (Laubscher, 2003). Nationwide, in 1999, fatal suicidal behaviour accounted for about 8% of all non-natural deaths in South Africa (WHO, 1999b), but the figure rose to about 10% by 2000 (Burrows et al., 2003; Prinsloo, 2002b), with a similar picture of 9.69% found in 2002 (Matzopoulos, Cassim & Seedat, 2003), and as reported in 2003 (Schlebusch, 2004, 2005a). The most recent NIMSS figures for 2003 reveal that 11% of all non-natural deaths in South Africa are suicides (Matzopoulos, 2004).

GENDER DISTRIBUTION
Suicides in South Africa vary considerably across gender, age and ethnicity. However, as with the international figures quoted in Chapter three, studies have consistently shown that in South Africa more males than females commit suicide. That said, in the last decade the male to female ratio seems to have increased in this country (Schlebusch, 2004). A Durban study reported that between

1982 and 1987 the male to female suicide ratio in South African Indians was 3:1 and for whites it was 4:1 (Gangat, 1988). A Pietermaritzburg study compared data covering a ten-year-period from 1982 to 1992 for that magisterial district (Wassenaar & Naidoo, 1995), with national South African data that covered the period 1984 to 1986 (Flisher & Parry, 1994). Both studies excluded black suicides because of unreliable and fragmentated data for this group due to the apartheid political system that prevailed at the time. The comparison showed higher national rates per 100 000 of the population, which were 19.52 for white males and 5.14 for white females, with an average rate of 12.33. National rates for Indians were 10.97 for males and 3.42 for females, with an average of 7.19. Compared to this, the Pietermaritzburg figures were 12.11 for white males and 12.86 for Indian males, and 2.45 for white females and 3.10 for Indian females. The average for the area was 7.28 for whites and 7.98 for Indians (Wassenaar & Naidoo, 1995). A follow-up Pietermaritzburg study for the period 1982 to 1996 that did include blacks found the mean regional rates per 100 000 to be 13.48 for blacks, 15.5 for whites and 14.9 for Indians (Wassenaar et al., 2000). The male to female ratios were 5.8:1 for blacks, 5.3:1 for whites and 4.3:1 for Indians. Interestingly, black females had the lowest rate of 1.96 per 100 000, followed by white females with 2.45 per 100 000 and then Indian females with 2.8 per 100 000. Overall, South African rates of 24.5 per 100 000 for males and 6.9 per 100 000 for females have been reported more recently (Matzopoulos, Norman & Bradshaw, 2004).

Results from a 1999 report show that in South Africa nationally, male suicides continue to predominate with 79.2% being males (WHO, 1999b). This situation also prevailed in 2001 when nearly five times more males than females committed suicide nationally, the male to female ratio being 4.7:1 with males making up 82.4% of suicides (Donson & Van Niekerk, 2002). This persistent male suicide predominance is also reflected in 2002 national suicide statistics (Matzopoulos, Cassim & Seedat, 2003).

AGE DISTRIBUTION

South African figures are consistent with the gobal situation of a shift in suicides from the elderly towards younger people (Bertolote, 2001; WHO, 1999a). This tendency for younger people to commit suicide is documented in several studies. A Cape Town study reported that about two-thirds of all suicide victims between 1993 and 1994 were younger than 34 years old (Lerer, Knobel & Matzopoulos, 1995). In the Pietermaritzburg study already mentioned (Wassenaar et al., 2000), the highest male suicide rates were in the 25 to 34 year group while for females the highest rate was in the 15 to 24 year age group, although patterns of suicides reflect considerable gender and cultural variations.

According to more recent data, suicides for all races during 1999 to 2000 also tended to occur in the younger age groups (15 to 34 years), except for whites amongst whom fewer suicides occurred in the 15 to 24 year age group with a fairly even spread across the rest of the age spectrum (Burrows et al., 2003). By the end of the 1990s the average national life expectancy in the country was 62.3 years for males and 68.3 for females and the average age of people who committed suicide was 36.3 years (WHO, 1999b). In 2001 the average age of non-natural deaths surveyed was 32.8 years while the highest percentage of suicides ocurred in the 20 to 34 year age group (46.5% of all suicides), although children as young as 10 years committed suicide and comparatively speaking there was a decrease in suicides between the ages of 35 to 64 years (Donson & Van Niekerk, 2002; Prinsloo, 2002b). According to the most recent NIMSS figures, the average age of suicide victims in 2002 was 35 years, with the highest percentage in the 25 to 29 year age group, followed by the 20 to 24 year age group and then the 30 to 34 year age group (Matzopoulos, Cassim & Seedat, 2003).

Other common causes of death include homicide in the 15 to 24 year age group (56.3%), homicide in the 25 to 34 year age group (56.3%), homicide in the 35 to 44 year age group (46.4%) and homicide in the 45 to 55 year age group (38.1%). This was followed by transport-related deaths in the 45 to 54 year age group (30.8%), and in the 55 to 65 year age group (32.9%) (Matzopoulos, Cassim & Seedat, 2003). The most common cause of death in the under 14 year age group was transport-related (38.9%). A further breakdown by age is given in Chapter seven, which discusses methods used in suicidal behaviour in South Africa.

ETHNIC DISTRIBUTION
Figures reported in 1999 show that the ethnic distribution for suicidal behaviour was: 43.3% black, 38.4% white, 15.9% Coloured

and 2% Asian (Indian) (Schlebusch, 2003; WHO, 1999b). Research data extracted from the NIMSS for 1999 to 2000 show that for Asians, blacks and Coloureds, suicide was the third major contributor to deaths after homicide and unintentional causes, and that for whites, suicide was the second leading cause of death after unintentional causes (Burrows et al., 2003). The same study also reported that although blacks accounted for the largest number of cases in all manner of unnatural deaths, this was least so for suicide during the period researched, and that suicide rates varied considerably across race and age groups. They were twice as high for whites as for Asians, and four times as high as those for Coloureds and blacks. According to a 2002 report the highest percentage of suicides was amongst whites (26.7%), followed by Asians (18.0%), blacks (7.6%) and Coloureds (6.8%) (Prinsloo, 2002b). Further available figures show that by 2001 in certain regions of South Africa, for example, Cape Town, whites were more likely to commit suicide than to be murdered. In all of the non-natural deaths surveyed at the time, 26.7% of whites committed suicide compared with 18.3% who were the victims of homicide. In violent deaths 80.5% were males, the majority of whom were black (Padaychee, *The Sunday Times*, 2003; Prinsloo, 2002b). Interestingly, in the early 1990s it was reported that in the metropolitan area of Cape Town, white women (as opposed to black and Coloured women) were also more likely to die from suicide than from homicide (Lerer, 1992). In this study, black and Coloured homicides predominated overall as compared to suicides for the three ethnic groups sampled.

The reported overall average crude South African death rate in 1994 was about 4.9 per 1 000 of the population per annum (Ntuli et al., 2000). Between 1999 and 2000, the number of non-natural deaths was estimated to range from 65 000 to 80 000 (Burrows et al., 2003). The figure rose to between 68 930 and 80 000 per annum by 2001 when it accounted for 12% to 15% of more than 500 000 annual deaths from all causes (Prinsloo, 2002a). By 2002 non-natural deaths numbered between 70 000 and 80 000 (Matzopoulos, Cassim & Seedat, 2003). In the last few years between 8% and 10% of all South African non-natural deaths have been due to suicide. This means that there is a significant loss of lives as a result of suicide in relation to the population of the country, which in 2000

was estimated at 43 291 441 excluding HIV/Aids-related deaths (Ntuli et al., 2000). Indications are that between 6 893 and 8 000 South Africans die of suicide annually (Schlebusch, 2004). This represents up to:
- 667 deaths by suicide every month;
- 154 per week;
- 22 every day; and
- virtually 1 every hour.

With an overall average household size of 4.4 in 1996 (Ntuli et al., 2000), it means that a vast number of South Africans are directly affected by fatal suicidal behaviour. If we include the index patients' nuclear family members, this means more than 35 000 people annually or about 96 per day are immediately involved. This is the proverbial 'tip of the iceberg' as many thousands more (extended family members, friends, work colleagues, and so on) experience the psychological anguish of being exposed to fatal suicidal behaviour.

NON-FATAL SUICIDAL BEHAVIOUR
Accurate statistics are not available regarding the real occurrence of non-fatal suicidal behaviour as there has been no systematic data collection in this domain in South Africa. Information concerning this self-destructive phenomenon is thus mostly derived from ad hoc research (Schlebusch, 2004; Schlebusch & Bosch, 2000). For example, a 1950s South African study reports only 2 attempted suicides by black Africans out of 252 attempted suicides in Cape Town (Walton, 1951). One of the few early investigations in the 1980s on parasuicide in black as a category in its own right, in the Ga-Rankuwa/Medunsa catchment area near Pretoria, indicated a parasuicide rate of approximately 11 per 100 000 of the population (Pelser & Oberholzer, 1987). According to this study, however, investigations indicate that since suicidal behaviour is not necessarily reported to hospitals unless the consequences are perceived to be life-threatening, the figures probably represent an underestimate. More recent research shows that as for suicide, the picture for non-fatal suicidal behaviour is equally alarming, since for every suicide it is estimated that there are at least twenty (or more) non-fatal suicide attempts (Schlebusch, 2000a, 2004).

Again, as for suicides, in some occupational groups such as the police services, higher non-fatal suicidal behaviour rates than those for the general population have been reported. For example, studies conducted in the western Cape in 1990 and 1991 show non-fatal suicidal behaviour rates of 24.91 per 100 000 in 1990 and 49.83 per 100 000 in 1991 (Pieterse, 1993). Studies show that between 10% predominantly black patients (Deonarain & Pillay, 2000) and 12% (Bosch, McGill & Noor Mahomed, 1995) of patients of all race groups (20.2% white, 15.3% Coloured, 52% Indian and 12.5% black) who are referred for psychological/psychiatric help in general hospitals are non-fatal suicide attempts in the hospitals where the research was done. In some metropolitan centres the high incidence of non-fatal suicidal behaviour among black South Africans seen in general hospitals has raised concern (Deonarain & Pillay, 2000; Schlebusch, 2004) as there has been, according to recent research (Schlebusch, Vawda & Bosch, 2003), an increase of up to 58.10% over a ten-year period.

As noted earlier, the South African ratio of fatal versus non-fatal suicidal behaviour is thought to be up to 1:20 or higher depending on where the research sample was drawn from (Schlebusch, 2000a, 2004). This figure is comparable to global reported ratios of 1:20, which in some cases can be as high as 40:1 (Bertolote, 2001; Schlebusch, 2000a; WHO, 1999a). Consequently, based on the suicide figures quoted on pages 49 and 50, it is estimated that between at least 137 860 and 160 000 or more South Africans engage in non-fatal suicidal behaviour annually (Schlebusch, 2004). This represents:
- 13 333 non-fatal suicide attempts every month;
- 3 077 per week;
- 438 every day; and
- 18 or more per hour in South Africa.

Given the average household size of about 4.4, it means that up to 700 000 or more members of households are directly affected by non-fatal suicidal behaviour annually, or about 1 900 or more daily. This tragic situation excludes figures for non-fatal suicide attempts that are not reported. Again, merely the tip of the iceberg is seen.

With regard to age in non-fatal suicidal behaviour, earlier (between 1988 and 1995) general hospital-based studies in Durban identified the peak age as the 20 to 29 year group – about one-third of all admissions for suicidal behaviour; and the second-most at-risk age, as between 10 and 19 years (Bosch, McGill & Noor Mahomed, 1995; Schlebusch, 1992a, 1998a). More recently, a study reported a mean age of 25 years for non-fatal suicidal behaviour in a large Johannesburg general hospital sample involving mainly black patients (Deonarain & Pillay, 2000). In the younger age groups, childen as young as 4 years have presented with non-fatal suicidal behaviour in general hospital samples, and in one study in 2000 the age peaked at an average of 9 years (Noor Mahomed, Selmer & Bosch, 2000). Most of these studies found that generally more women (about two-thirds) than men (about one-third) engage in non-fatal suicidal behaviours (Schlebusch, 2004).

SUICIDAL BEHAVIOUR IN HOSPITAL

There is a paucity of South African data on fatal suicidal behaviour in general hospitals. In addition, surprisingly scant attention has been paid to patients who commit suicide in acute psychiatric units in South Africa. A number of studies on suicide outside the mental health setting within the general hospital have been done elsewhere in the world, normally on medical, surgical, or other non-psychiatric patients (Schlebusch et al., 1986). The suicide of a person while he or she is in in-patient care is a shattering event for both staff and patients. In contrast to the welter of studies on suicidal behaviour generally, there are comparatively few South African studies on psychiatric in-patients who commit suicide, although the reported suicide rates for psychiatric in-patients vary from two to six times those in the general population (Schlebusch et al., 1986).

One of the few large South African studies, as part of the ongoing research programme discussed in Chapter eleven, reported specifically on the prevalence of suicides in a general hospital psychiatric in-patient unit (Schlebusch et al., 1986). The total admissions over the study period were 6 961, during which time nine patients committed suicide, giving an average suicide rate of 1.4 suicides per 1 000 admissions. Twice as many males as females committed suicide. The mean age was 39.2 years and most suicides occurred in young adults and adolescents. Most patients were unemployed, with a history of previous parasuicides and psychiatric hospitalisations.

This suicide rate at the time was comparable to studies on psychiatric in-patient suicides in other countries, which ranged from 0.8 to 3.8 per 1 000 admissions (Schlebusch et al., 1986). The study cites various international rates of 1.9 per 1 000 admissions and 4.5 per 1 000 in an in-patient year in state psychiatric hospitals (Schlebusch et al., 1986). Our research showed a relationship between the acuteness of the distress of patients admitted and the likelihood of suicide. For example, the average duration of stay (during at least part of the study) was between six and eleven days per admission. This indicates a high turnover of acute patients. It was also shown that the suicide rate was higher in acutely ill psychiatric patients than in chronic ones. The role of somatic co-morbid factors, physical ill-health and prevalence rates of suicidal behaviour in chronic disease patients is discussed in Chapter nine.

CONCLUSIONS
The high suicide prevalence rates, and the equally high estimated fatal to non-fatal suicidal behaviour ratios in South Africa indicate that the situation has reached serious proportions (Schlebusch, 2003, 2004, 2005a). The figures presented here exclude those people who are indirectly affected, such as family members outside the nuclear family, friends, school and work colleagues, and the community at large. The impact should be measured not only in terms of the adverse psychological effects, but also as related to other wider issues such as the repercussions for the country's health-care delivery system and the economy. What is even more alarming is that these figures are based on various national and regional samples in which suicidal behaviours were recorded, and most likely reflect only a part of the true extent of the problem.

KEY POINTS

- Recent studies reveal a significant increase in suicides.
- Suicide rates are higher in certain occupations.
- Almost five times more males than females commit suicide. However, approximately twice as many women as men engage in non-fatal suicidal behaviour.
- Early studies of suicide in South Africa seem to have under-represented the number of fatal suicides because prevailing conditions made the collection of accurate data impossible. This is particularly true of suicide in the black population.
- The average age for South Africans who engage in suicidal behaviour has decreased significantly.

CHAPTER FIVE

Children and adolescents

AS IS THE CASE for adults, it is difficult to get accurate, reliable statistics on child and adolescent suicidal behaviour in South Africa. Based on the available research findings, we can arrive only at an informed estimate of the nature and size of the problem.

FATAL SUICIDAL BEHAVIOUR

Known rates of fatal suicidal behaviour in young people are a cause for great concern (Burrows et al., 2003; Donson & Van Niekerk, 2002). In Chapter three I discussed the 'ungreying' phenomenon in terms of which suicides have now tended to move from the elderly towards younger people (Bertolote, 2001; WHO, 1999a). Earlier studies quoted indicate that suicide in South Africa accounts for up to 1.2% of all deaths of children aged 14 years and younger, and that in the white and Indian populations suicide is the third-leading cause of death in this age group (Madu & Matla, 2003). According to the NIMSS findings the youngest suicide in 2001 was committed by a 10-year-old (Donson & Van Niekerk, 2002), but more suicides occurred in the 15 to 19 year old group than in the 10 to 14 year old group (Prinsloo, 2002b). NIMSS data from 2002 reveal a similar trend, the highest fatal suicidal behaviour rate being in the 15 to 19 year age group, followed by the 10 to 14 year age group (Matzopoulos, Cassim & Seedat, 2003). As in the case of non-fatal suicidal behaviour of young people in South Africa, suicide rates also tend to reflect that in the 10 to 19 year age group more females (12%) than males (7%) commit suicide (Bradshaw, Masiteng & Nannan, 2000). This means that on average 9.5% of non-natural deaths in young people in South Africa are because of suicides. This rate, disturbingly, is as high as the adult suicide rate. Compared to the reported adult suicide rates that reflect more male than female suicides, it is noteworthy that more young females than males in South Africa commit suicide. The meaning of these findings requires further research.

Other leading causes of death in this young age group are:
- injuries (the most common overall, but especially for males in the 15 to 19 year age group);
- infectious diseases (the most common in the 10 to 14 year age group);
- tuberculosis, which is the most common disease, followed by Aids in the case of young females; and
- epilepsy.

In 2002 the leading causes of death in the under 14 year old age group were transport-related (38.9%), followed by non-transport-related (30.8%), whereas in the 15 to 24 year group it was homicide (56.3%) (Matzopoulos, Cassim & Seedat, 2003). Collectively speaking, gender-based violence, sexual risk-taking behaviour, alcohol abuse and high levels of general violence are some of the most important aetiological factors that affect the health of South African youth (Bradshaw, Masiteng & Nannan, 2000). These statistics have significant implications for suicidal behaviour. Transport-related deaths remain high in South Africa across the age spectrum, but young children are particularly vulnerable as pedestrians and passengers (Sukhai & Van Niekerk, 2002).

NON-FATAL SUICIDAL BEHAVIOUR
Although divergent statistics are quoted, they clearly indicate that the problem of non-fatal suicidal behaviour in the young is very serious. The DPS findings noted that the child and adolescent age group was the second-most at-risk age group for non-fatal suicidal behaviour after young adults. The DPS is more fully discussed in Chapter eleven. One study reported in 1999 that suicidal behaviour amongst youth constituted about 10% of referrals to clinical psychologists at Letaba Hospital in the Limpopo Province (Mhlongo & Peltzer, 1999). Several other studies presented at South African suicide conferences have noted that during the last few decades, up to about one-third of all non-fatal suicidal behaviours involved children and adolescents (Schlebusch, 1988a, 1992a, 1995a; Schlebusch & Bosch, 2000). As mentioned in the previous chapter, some researchers found that in very young children the age peaked at 9

years, the age range in suicidal children studied being 4 to 12 years (Noor Mohamed, Selmer & Bosch, 2000).

More recent research that was hospital based noted a sharp rise in suicidal behaviour in blacks generally, and found that 24.5% of the total sample of suicidal behaviour patients admitted to the hospital where the study was undertaken were black youths aged 18 years and younger (Schlebusch, Vawda & Bosch, 2003). These findings, along with a male to female ratio of 1:2 for the adolescent group, were comparable to a similar ratio reported in the earlier DPS studies, and are very different from the 5:1 male to female ratio in fatal suicidal behaviour mentioned in the previous chapter. Such findings have important implications for school-based suicide prevention programmes (as discussed in Chapter ten).

Likewise, South African non-hospital-based studies have reported wide-ranging figures. For example, in 1995, a Durban study found that up to 4% of primarily Indian schoolchildren expressed suicidal ideation to their school counsellors (Pillay, 1995a), while a 1992 Cape Town study of high school students found that 7.8% of them had attempted suicide, that 19.0% had seriously considered it, and that 12.4% admitted that they had told someone of their intentions to commit suicide (Flisher et al., 1992). Research into another high school sample conducted amongst black youths in the eastern Cape region, reported in 1995 that up to 47% of those surveyed had suicidal ideation (Mayekiso & Mkize, 1995). Of these, 18% reported definite plans to commit suicide, while 5% indicated that they would kill themselves if they could, and a further 24% had thoughts of self-harm but felt they would not act on these. A 1998 study among secondary high school pupils in the Limpopo Province, reported parasuicide rates of 17% for boys and 13% for girls (Peltzer & Cherian, 1998). A more recent 2003 study in the Limpopo Province conducted among black secondary school adolescents (only 4.5% were from other ethnic groups) in and around Polokwane, reported even higher suicidal behaviour prevalence rates, with a male preponderance in those sampled (Madu & Matla, 2003). According to this research, 37% of the learners thought of taking their lives, 17% had threatened to do so or had informed others about their suicidal intentions, 16% had made plans to commit suicide, and 21% had made attempts. These cohorts represent a group that is not usually seen in hospitals, but who may seek help and utilise counselling services at their schools.

CONCLUSIONS

Although death is not supposed to be a common occurrence in children and adolescents, statistics reflecting death by suicide as well as problems with other suicidal behaviours and/or ideation in this age group appear to be inordinately high. Suicidal behaviour in this age group is a morbid health event that results in personal suffering and considerable implications for health-care facilities in South Africa (Schlebusch, 1985a, b, c). The data discussed in this chapter yield certain consistencies that serve to endorse the need to identify appropriate patient profiles to prevent and manage suicidal behaviour in the youth. In many cases of threatened or non-fatal suicidal behaviour, parents and other adults often do not take the behaviour seriously, either because they consider it only a gesture or because they want to avoid publicity and social embarrassment. Given the research findings we have discussed in this chapter, the severity of the problem in young people in South Africa should not be underestimated.

KEY POINTS

- About one-third of the reported cases of suicidal behaviour in South Africa involve children and adolescents.
- Statistics reveal a grave situation, with estimates of up to 9.5% of unnatural deaths of children and adolescents in South Africa being the result of suicidal behaviour.
- Contrary to the case for adults, more young females than young males are likely to commit suicide.
- Recent hospital-based research indicates that a quarter or more of the patients who were admitted because of their non-fatal suicidal behaviour were black youths aged 18 years or younger.

CHAPTER SIX

Reports in the South African press

Nachalany

THE SUSCEPTIBILITY OF individuals vulnerable to suicidal behaviour who learn about suicide through mass media publicity has received considerable attention (Colt, 1991; Schmidtke & Schaller, 2000; Schmidtke, Schaller & Wasserman, 2001). There is a significant body of knowledge about the imitation effects of media coverage of suicidal behaviour on potential victims. These imitation effects need to be correlated with other factors, for example, exposure to other approaches to suicidal behaviour that can be risk factors and influence vulnerable people, as well as the age, gender and personality variables of the individual likely to be so affected (Schmidtke & Schaller, 2000; Van Heeringen, Hawton & Williams, 2000).

Copycat suicide or the 'Werther effect' are terms used when referring to the phenomenon of imitating the suicidal behaviour of others. As mentioned in Chapter two, soon after Goethe published his novel *The Sorrows of Young Werther* in the eighteenth century, there was a spate of young people in Europe who committed suicide in such a way as could be linked to the suicide of the novel's hero, Werther. This resulted in the book being banned in several countries. In addition, authors have written about various other examples of the imitation of suicidal behaviour throughout history, for example, during times of religious persecution, political oppression, social upheaval and so on (Colt, 1991).

The copycat phenomenon raises issues around the responsibility of the media in reporting suicidal behaviour as well as in preventing it. Such controversy will not be explored here, except to emphasise that there appears to be an increasing tolerance of suicidal behaviour and the concept of suicidal transmission is becoming extremely relevant (Bille-Brahe, 2000). Information technology as well as media development have brought about expanded opportunities to influence peoples' attitudes about and towards suicidal behaviour, thereby enhancing the contagious effects of such behaviour (Bille-Brahe, 2000). The media and the press can play a proactive role in helping to prevent this by not sensationalising coverage about suicidal behaviour and by providing information about available help.

I have chosen to present a random sample of reports from selected publications in summarised form. The articles appeared during the period 1997 to 2005, and represent only a fraction of similar articles that were published during this time. They were selected from more than 169 articles that tell the story of how frequently suicidal behaviour is reported in the press. They are mentioned here also to illustrate the many sub-types of suicidal behaviour that occur and the detail of some of the facts revealed.

SUICIDE PACTS

- A 46-year-old Japanese dentist and a 25-year-old woman committed suicide at the dentist's home after having met on an Internet site that provides information on how to kill yourself (*The Sunday Times*, 29 October 2000: 14).
- In an apparent suicide pact, two girls (aged 16 and 17) killed themselves in a car in Sussex after a party at a friend's house. The two girls grew up in South Africa and were apparently distraught about emigrating (*The Sunday Times*, 24 December 2000: 3).
- A mother and her 40-year-old daughter, both white, killed themselves together. They were the last remaining members of the family of the late Bobby Locke, a South African golfing legend. Both signed their wills two weeks previously, stating that should anything happen to them, their dog was to be put down and the ashes to be sprinkled over their graves. The two lived together and were described as inseparable and reclusive (Jorden, *The Sunday Times*, 2000).

SUICIDE CULTS/MASS SUICIDES/RELIGIOUS SUICIDES

- Members of the Solar Temple Cult either committed suicide or were murdered: in Canada in 1994 five people committed suicide or were murdered; in Switzerland in 1994 forty-eight died; in France in 1995 sixteen were murdered; in Canada in 1997 five were murdered (Trench, *The Sunday Times*, 1997).

- Thirty-nine members of a cult called Heaven's Gate killed themselves, believing this would lead to a better existence on a passing comet. The cult was busy writing a screen-play about their lives. A member who left the cult a week before the suicide received a videotape with farewell messages on it. The group was described as polite and hard-working (*The Mercury*, 2 May 1997: 9).
- Members of the Movement for the Restoration of the Ten Commandments barricaded themselves into their church before dousing it with fuel and setting it alight. The building was razed to the ground. Those inside were burnt beyond recognition. Cult followers believed that sacrificing their lives would assure them a place in heaven as they feared the world was coming to an end (*The Mercury*, 20 March 2001: 1).

SIMULATED SUICIDE/FAKE SUICIDE
- A 54-year-old male left a suicide note at his home for his wife and two sons. He left his clothing alongside a river, thinking he would be thought of as having drowned, then he moved to a neighbouring province to live with his 34-year-old mistress (*The Mercury*, 18 April 2003: 3).
- Siblings tried to disguise murder as suicide. A man who assaulted then suffocated his wife and tried to make her death look like suicide, has been charged with murder. His sister has been charged with defeating the ends of justice for the part she played in covering up the murder (Mkhwanazi, *The Mercury*, 2005).
- A man was taken to hospital after an alleged suicide attempt following a murder. He was not arrested and discharged himself from hospital, but then disappeared. He left a note stating that he was afraid that he would be blamed for the murder (Zondi, *The Daily News*, 2005).

ASSISTED SUICIDE
- A 74-year-old with motor neuron disease travelled from England to Zurich (Switzerland) to receive help from a charity called Dignitas, which assists with suicide for people with terminal or distressing illness. He was given a fatal dose of barbiturates (*The Mercury*, 21 January 2003: 5).

- The Dutch health minister favoured allowing doctors to prescribe suicide pills for patients although doctors would not actually participate in the suicide. The ruling would apply to very old people who were tired of life, even if they were physically healthy. This went further than current legislation that allows doctors to end the lives of those who are terminally ill (*The Mercury*, 16 April 2001: 2).

EXTENDED SUICIDE/MURDER-SUICIDE
- A 43-year-old black male killed himself by poisoning himself and cutting his throat. This was after hacking his wife, seven children and grandson to death with an axe in a fit of rage. The man left a tape recording in which he said that he could not die and leave his children alone (*The Mercury*, 30 April 2004: 10).
- A 31-year-old black male killed himself by grabbing electric cables above a train after killing his former girlfriend. Police suspect that he killed the woman because she ended their relationship (*The Mercury*, 22 February 2000: 3).
- A 40-year-old unemployed Indian male drove a car into the harbour with his daughter (14) and niece (18) inside. The two girls survived as they managed to escape from the car and were pulled to safety. A relative could not provide an answer as to why he might have done this and the girls and wife were too traumatised to talk (Vernon & Nel, *The Mercury*, 2000).
- A black male shot his wife and then himself after a family dispute (*The Mercury*, 5 February 2001: 4).
- A 60-year-old black male murdered seven people in a two-hour spree starting at 02h00. He arrived at his brother and sister-in-law's house at dawn and told them about the killings. He then left and committed suicide by shooting himself next to the bodies of his two wives whom he had killed. He left a will detailing how his estate should be divided among his four surviving daughters (Dumisane, *The Sunday Times*, 2000).
- A woman smothered her aged mother in an old age home to end her pain and then committed suicide by jumping from the seventh floor of the building (Mthembu, *The Daily News*, 2005).

- A 40-year-old man shot and killed his pregnant wife after an argument with her. He then shot his wife's daughter and his wife's 5-year-old son, who survived. After this he shot himself in the head and died on the way to hospital (Lee-Ann, *The Mercury*, 2000).
- There has been a spate of violent deaths in schools. One of the most recent was the killing of a 31-year-old woman teacher by her ex-boyfriend, in front of one of her pupils. The man then shot himself (Carvin, Angela & Zoubair, *The Mercury*, 2004).
- A 56-year-old male shot and killed his daughter (21), critically wounded his wife (53), and then shot himself. The incident took place after an argument with his daughter over her university exam results (*The Mercury*, 28 June 2001: 3).

IATROGENIC SUICIDE
- Parents of a 17-year-old boy who committed suicide have blamed the lack of information about the side effects of acne medication for his death. The boy was said to be doing well at school and related well to teachers and peers. The use of the drug has been linked to suicide in Britain and in America. A growing number of parents complained about the side effects of medication for acne that include suicidal behaviour in their children (Kalideen, *The Mercury*, 2002).

OTHER FATAL AND NON-FATAL SUICIDAL BEHAVIOURS
- A 73-year-old white male drove his car off a mountain pass to avoid being shot by two hijackers who were in the car with him. It was described as a 'do or die stunt' in which the victim hoped that if the accident resulted in his death, the hijackers would also die. No one died and the hijackers fled the scene (Loewe & Majekula, *The Star*, 2004).
- Two black male security guards were playing a form of Russian Roulette while on night shift. After severely injuring his 20-year-old colleague in the game, the other, a 21-year-old, shot himself in the head, killing himself. A third colleague witnessed the incident (Comins, *The Mercury*, 2003).
- A man shot himself in a pub over losing a R2 bet while playing Russian Roulette with a group of friends. He was described as a pleasant family man, was in his early 30s and

worked in the finance industry in Springs. The manager of the pub said that carrying guns had become a way of life and that he thought they should be banned (Nwandiko, *The Independent on Saturday*, 1999).

- A 67-year-old woman poured paraffin over herself then set herself on fire with matches. Her family managed to put the fire out with water and blankets and she was hospitalised in a critical condition. Since the death of her sister a year before, she had had a history of depression (Carvin, *The Mercury*, 2004).
- A well-known national (Springbok) rugby player apparently went to his ex-girlfriend's house, told her that he couldn't live without her, then slit his wrists in the kitchen. His family doctor said that his breakdown was a culmination of a long period of stress (Schoonnakker, *The Sunday Times*, 2001b).
- A Centurion high school has been rocked by the suicide of a 16-year-old boy – the third suicide at the school in four months. No suicide note was found (Hosken, *Pretoria News*, 2004).
- A 24-year-old black male described as 'distraught' over the death of popular South African black female diva Brenda Fassie, committed suicide by taking an overdose of tablets. He left a suicide note for his mother stating that he could not live without Brenda Fassie (Venter, *The Mercury*, 2004).
- A 41-year-old male e-mailed his suicide note to his ex-wife pleading with her to take care of his champion show dog worth R60 000. There is now a custody battle with the dog's breeders and the deceased's ex-wife over the dog (Sukraj, *The Sunday Times*, 2004).
- A woman who was forced into an arranged marriage that she was opposed to, committed suicide one month before the wedding. She wished to marry a man who was of a different faith and so had outraged her father. In her suicide note she said that her family did not care about her (*The Sunday Times*, 23 July 2000: 3).
- A Catholic priest committed suicide after allegations of two counts of sexual molestation (one with a minor) and after being shunned by peers. He was issued with a decree of suspension, became depressed, but had refused therapy (Nzama & Leeman, *The Mercury*, 2003).

- In one month three KZN police members took their own lives. The reasons are thought to be high levels of stress and uncertainty regarding their professional future. In 2000, the police suicide level was almost eleven times that of the general population and higher than the global average of 1.6 per 10 000. In 2001, 2 out of every 10 000 police officials committed suicide. Police suicide is said to be ignored, misunderstood, misrepresented, often not reported because of the stigma and under-researched (Ramsamy, *The Independent on Saturday*, 2001).
- A Belgian of Congolese origin set herself alight as a protest at not being allowed to open a shop (*The Mercury*, 12 October 2004: 7).
- A girl received a suicide SMS from a popular 15-year-old male friend before he killed himself. A suicide SMS to family and friends is an emerging trend; it is easier to say something shocking in an SMS. Sending an SMS provides the sender instant gratification as there is an immediate response. Constant SMSing can lead to communication gaps and maladaptive ways of forming relationships (Booyens, *You Magazine*, 2004).
- A 15-year-old boy was convicted of inciting someone over the Internet to murder him. The boy pleaded guilty and the 17-year-old who had stabbed him, admitted to attempted murder (*The Sunday Times*, 30 May 2004: 15).
- Many Grade 12 learners have called a toll-free suicide help line. Most callers were black and Coloured pupils who felt under pressure from parents who had told them they had to do well because of the sacrifices they had made for them. Teachers also called to get tips on how to handle depressed or suicidal pupils (Khan, *The Daily News*, 2004).
- Three high school students committed suicide within two weeks around the matric examination period. One suffocated herself with a plastic bag, another hanged herself and the third died from an overdose (Nkosi, *The Mercury*, 1999).
- A 17-year-old girl hanged herself at home after writing her own funeral arrangements for a bus for her school friends to attend the funeral. She said in the note her reason for suicide was due to the loss of her boyfriend who had been shot dead (Nyembezi, *The Independent on Saturday*, 1998).

- Firearm-related deaths in South Africa over the past ten years are more than five times the number of Americans killed in Vietnam and twice the number of people killed by the tsunamis in Asia. Gunshot wounds, road accidents, alcohol and suicide were some of the most common reasons for premature death in South Africa (Ajam, *The Independent on Saturday*, 2005).
- A video analyst for the South African rugby team committed suicide after an uproar following his handing pictures of the infamous 'Kamp Staaldraad' to the media. At the time of his death the man was teaching and coaching rugby at a Durban school (Van de Berg, *The Sunday Times*, 2005).
- A 31-year-old woman was sentenced to fifteen years in prison for being convicted of corruption. Her husband jumped to his death from a sixth-floor window while being questioned by the authorities (Broughton, *The Mercury*, 2005).

Throughout this book there are several additional references to press reports on suicidal behaviour in South Africa. Sources such as these can provide important statistics that are not always reflected in other research data. The South African press is certainly very alert to the consequences of the tragedy of suicidal behaviour and, in my experience, often work closely with health and academic authorities in presenting the facts and indications of warning signs.

KEY POINTS

- The media need to exercise great responsibility when it comes to reporting on suicidal behaviour.
- Despite the phenomenon of copycat suicide, it usually also takes the presence of other risk factors in an individual to trigger suicidal behaviour.
- The examples given here are a small sample of the regular reports concerning suicide that have appeared in various press publications in recent years.

CHAPTER SEVEN

Methods of choice

SEVERAL REGIONAL, ETHNIC, gender and age differences have been found by those investigating the methods of choice used in fatal suicidal behaviour as well as in non-fatal suicidal behaviour.

FATAL SUICIDAL BEHAVIOUR
A comprehensive international review quotes selected South African studies that found firearms, hanging and swallowing poison to be common methods in suicidal behaviour (Lester, 2000). A 1995 Cape Town study showed that firearms and hanging were the method of choice in 68% of suicides early in the 1990s (Lerer, Knobel & Matzopoulos, 1995), while another study in Cape Town examined the link between suicide, homicide and high blood alcohol concentration (BAC) levels in women who were victims of homicide and suicide (Lerer, 1992). Significantly, elevated BAC levels in the homicide victims were found. In this study, drug overdose was the method of choice in 34% of the suicide victims, while other methods used included firearms, hanging, gassing, drowning, jumping, cutting and burning. In some occupational groups (for example, the South African Police Services) up to 90% of suicides were committed with a service pistol, which is probably also associated with the availability of these methods (Rossouw, 2000).

According to figures at the end of the 1990s for South African fata suicides, hanging was the most frequently employed method (36.2%), closely followed by shooting (35.0%) (WHO, 1999b). Other methods included poisoning (9.8%), gassing (6.5%) and burning (4.1%). Research in 2001 found hanging (42.3%) and the use of firearms (29.4%) were the major methods of choice in suicides, while poisoning, drugs and pesticides were preferred by 13.6% of suicides, and gassing accounted for 7.1% (Donson & Van Niekerk,

2002). Other methods employed included sharp objects, asphyxia, electrocutions, drowning and falls (jumping off high areas). According to the same report, seasonal trends indicated that the ingestion of poison peaked in March (11.5%). Hanging as a method peaked around July (9.7%), while the use of firearms was highest in April (9.9%). Although there was a noticeable decrease in May, suicides appeared to increase towards the end of 2001. A March 2005 press report highlights the fact that the number of firearm-related deaths in South Africa over the past ten years is five times the number of American soldiers killed in Vietnam, and nearly twice the number of people killed by the recent tsunamis in Asia or those who perished in the Bosnia-Herzegovina war (Ajam, *The Independent on Saturday*, 2005). Press reports quote NIMSS figures that show gunshot wounds, road accidents, excessive use of alcohol and suicide topped the list for causing premature fatalities in South Africa in the major metropolitan areas (Cape Town, Johannesburg, Pretoria and Durban). Durban has the highest number of suicides by hanging and, as pointed out in Chapter four, it also has the second-highest suicide rate in the country. Durban is where my research team and I are involved in the DPS work on suicide discussed in Chapter eleven.

An analysis of sex distribution in a 2002 report showed that males accounted for 82.4% of suicides, in which the major choice of methods were hanging (46.4%) and firearms (31.4%) (Donson & Van Niekerk, 2002). In females, most suicides were as a result of poisoning (35.1%) and hanging (22.7%). Hanging was the method of choice in the largest percentage of suicides among Asians, blacks and Coloureds, while in whites the use of firearms accounted for the largest percentage. Among victims aged 10 to 54, hangings predominated, whereas in the 30 to 34 year age group the use of firearms was highest. In the 25 to 29 year age group, the use of poisoning was most common. In the 40 to 44 year age group gassing peaked as a method. The highest number of burns and jumping was found in the 25 to 29 year age group.

This NIMSS report also revealed that in terms of the day of the week, 18.3% of male suicides and 16.1% of female suicides occurred on Mondays. More than 40% of suicides occurred over weekends, that is, 43.5% of male suicides and 43.7% of female suicides. In terms of time of day, most suicides were committed between 07h00

to 20h00. Female suicides peaked at 08h00 and at 16h00, while most male suicides also occurred at 08h00. Suicide did not have any major seasonal variations over the year (Donson & Van Niekerk, 2002). According to 2002 NIMSS findings:
- hangings, firearms, poisoning, gassing and burning remain common methods of choice for suicide;
- the peak months for suicide are November and December with peak time of death being 07h00 to 08h00 and 17h00 to 18h00; and
- that peak time occurred most commonly on Sundays, Mondays and Saturdays (in that order) (Matzopoulos, Cassim & Seedat, 2003).

Interestingly, the three leading external causes of death overall (that is, not only suicides) were: firearms (29%), sharp force injuries (14.5%), and motor vehicle pedestrian fatalities (11.5%) (Matzopoulos, Cassim & Seedat, 2003). Other causes of death included: blunt force injuries, unspecified motor vehicle injuries, burns, hanging, passenger vehicle deaths, driver vehicle deaths and drowning.

One of the few South African studies on suicidal behaviour in family practice, found that the most common method used was overdose (63.63%) (Cassimjee & Pillay, 2000). This was followed by hangings (21.21%), all of which were fatal except for one case; firearms (9.09%), all of which were fatal except in one case; and laceration of wrists (6.06%). Of the overdose patients, 60.06% used medication as their method of choice. A further breakdown showed that 30.30% used over-the-counter (OTC) substances and 30.30% used prescription substances. Some of these overdoses resulted in non-fatal suicidal behaviour. In a study on in-patient hospital suicides, jumping from high-rise buildings near the hospital was the most common suicide method (Schlebusch et al., 1986).

NON-FATAL SUICIDAL BEHAVIOUR
Although methods used in non-fatal suicidal behaviour are diverse, findings from a large DPS study are in keeping with other studies which found that overdose of medication is one of the most common methods, especially in young people (Bosch, McGill & Noor Mahomed, 1995). The authors emphasised that patients

probably used the substances as a result of their availability. This has also been noted in other South African investigations that implicated availability in the choice of method (Schlebusch, 2004). One earlier investigation in KwaZulu-Natal found that almost three-quarters of a sample of young self-poisoners used medicines belonging to family members in the same household (Pillay, 1988), whereas more recent findings point also to the use of common household poisons such as paraffin, turpentine, insecticides and various other household substances (Schlebusch & Bosch, 2000; Schlebusch, Vawda & Bosch, 2003). A survey of largely black non-fatal suicidal behaviour in Johannesburg found that 61.9% of the patients surveyed took overdoses, 24.7% ingested poisons, 4.2% took detergents and 9.2% tried other methods such as hanging, gassing and cutting (Deonarain & Pillay, 2000). Likewise, in a study in Letaba in the Limpopo Province, 73% of suicide victims (who were mainly black youths) had ingested harmful substances (Mhlongo & Pelt-zer, 1999). Another survey in the same province, involving mainly black youths, found that 69.3% had poisoned or drugged them-selves, whereas 24.4% used other lethal methods such as stabbing or hanging (Madu & Matla, 2003).

The use of certain common methods of non-fatal suicidal behaviour emerged as a serious cause for concern, especially amongst blacks in the cohort of hospital-based patients recently studied by members of the DPS group (Schlebusch, Vawda & Bosch, 2003). In 40.4% of the patients seen, these methods included self-poisoning by using household utility liquids such as paraffin and various poisons. This is particularly problematic because of the easy access the patients had to such substances, but also because the methods used implied serious intent. Additional research in this regard requires more intense input from health professionals in South Africa in terms of designing effective prevention strategies. The same study reported that other potentially lethal methods such as hanging and throat laceration accounted for 7.5% of the sample studied, which showed that these methods are not only applicable to fatal suicidal behaviour. Similar findings in several other studies quoted here, confirm the lethal intent in young patients who are sometimes not viewed as serious in wanting to die and whose behaviour is treated merely as a suicidal gesture.

The DPS research (discussed in more depth in Chapter eleven), which spans some 26 years, has collectively shown that the overall choice of method in non-fatal suicidal behaviour tends to be 90% overdose and 10% self-injury. In the case of overdose, a wide variety of substances is ingested, but OTC analgesics (painkillers), prescription-only benzodiazepines (tranquillisers) as well as antidepressants are most commonly used, followed by household poison and utility products. Over the years I have argued strongly for better control of accessibility to such substances (Schlebusch 1987, 1991, 1992b, 1995b, 2004). This also applies to OTC analgesics, which are common substances of abuse in South Africa and which feature frequently in suicidal behaviour. The abuse of OTC analgesics also leads to a variety of neuropsychological problems and serious self-destructive diseases such as analgesic nephropathy (AN) resulting in end-stage renal disease (ESRD) (Schlebusch, 1991; Schlebusch, Lasich & Wessels, 1985). This last form of self-destructive behaviour is discussed in more detail in Chapter eight.

Research shows that the choice of method used (especially medicinal substances and poisons) for all age groups is strongly influenced by a number of factors such as:
- accessibility to the method;
- knowledge or, conversely, lack of knowledge of the lethality of the method;
- experience and familiarity with the method;
- meaning, symbolism and cultural influence associated with the method used in suicidal behaviour; and
- the potential suicidal person's state of mind (including the presence of a mental disorder) and level of intent at the time (Schlebusch, 2004).

The DPS research also supported the views that:
- a prior history of a mental disorder, especially depression, and psychological or psychiatric treatment for suicidal behaviour increased the risk;
- with repeated attempts, more severe and lethal methods may be used; and
- there appears to be more recklessness in order to secure help, as the ongoing non-fatal suicidal behaviour does not get the desired effect from significant others on whom the suicidal behaviour is supposed to impact.

In terms of seasonal breakdown, most non-fatal suicidal behaviour tends to peak over weekends and towards the end of the year, especially in youths who are faced with examination and other pressures, but also because of the pending festive period. Some studies do show a fairly even spread of suicidal behaviour during the year with a slight peak at the beginning of the year when new challenges need to be faced (Deonarain & Pillay, 2000).

A whole range of methods other than those discussed here are used in suicidal behaviour (both fatal and non-fatal). For example, in a recent incident a man drove his car into the path of a speeding train at a level crossing (Rondganger & Hoskins, *The Daily News*, 2005), and in Durban several incidents have been reported where people have driven their cars into the bay in attempts at drowning themselves.

KEY POINTS

- There is great concern over the role of household utility products such as paraffin and poison, firearms and the high use of prescription and over-the-counter (OTC) medications in fatal and non-fatal suicidal behaviour.
- People wishing to commit suicide in South Africa employ a variety of methods. The method chosen, however, depends on various factors.
- Hangings, firearms, poisoning, gassing and burning are common methods used to commit suicide.
- In cases of non-fatal suicidal behaviour, most individuals resort to overdosing.

CHAPTER EIGHT

Indirect self-destructive behaviour and analgesic abuse

It was Apollo, Apollo my friends
Who brought into reality these pains upon pain, which are
   my misfortune.
But my own hand, itself, struck the blow;
I alone, no one else did it.
(Sophocles, *Oedipus Rex*)

The desire to take medicine is, perhaps, the greatest feature which distinguishes man from other animals.
(William Osler)

CERTAIN BEHAVIOURS THAT often result in serious injury or premature death are not generally viewed as suicidal behaviours, even if in one way or another they hasten the demise of the person who engages in them. A landmark book by Farberow, published in 1980, defines and systematically examines the many and diverse manifestations of such indirect self-destructive behaviours (ISDB). These include:
- the uncooperative behaviour of the patient who suffers from physical disease (including dialysis patients, as discussed in this chapter);
- substance abuse (alcohol, cigarettes, other drugs, and so on);
- self-mutilation;
- driving behaviour and motor-vehicle accidents;
- gambling;
- certain types of criminal activity; and
- certain stress-seeking behaviours and high-risk sports (Farberow, 1980).

ISDB is said to be distinguishable from direct self-destructive behaviour on the basis of, amongst other factors, time and awareness (Farberow, 1980). In ISDB the effect is long term (even over many years) and the person is unaware of the consequences of the behaviour, or does not care about its effects and/or does not consider the behaviour to be suicidal. Analgesic abuse fits into this category of ISDB, especially where it leads to chronic disease and a need for dialysis or renal transplantation, although other diseases also can be implicated. Although not everybody agrees with me on this, I consider analgesic abuse to be important to a discussion on suicidal behaviour in South Africa. This is because of the clear association between substance abuse (especially analgesics and alcohol and the latter's role in violence and traffic accidents) and suicidal behaviour in this country, as is evident from the data that have been discussed in this book (see also Chapter nine).

The complex concept of ISDB has a long history going back to the work of Durkheim in 1897, Freud's thoughts on the death instinct, Menninger's (1938) work and others (Farberow, 1980). Some authorities have used the term 'sub-intentioned death' in discussing indirect suicide and covertly self-destructive behaviours (Shneidman, 1985). I have discussed the question of risk-taking and stress and the effect on health and its relation to suicidal behaviour in *Mind Shift*, a book that deals specifically with stress (Schlebusch, 2000c). Suffice it to mention here, that stress and risk-taking have implications for ISDB. What I propose to do in this chapter is to give an overview of the link between stress, suicidal behaviour and specifically the abuse of analgesics (painkillers), especially OTC analgesics (and also the analgesic properties of certain other substances) in South Africa as a form of ISDB, which in some instances lead to chronic diseases.

A series of DPS studies based on work done when I developed a psychonephrology service in the late 1980s, confirmed the high prevalence of the abuse of analgesics in the general South African population. This abusive behaviour resulted in end-stage renal disease (ESRD) as a consequence of analgesic nephropathy (AN) (Bosch & Schlebusch, 1991; Schlebusch, 1990a, 1991, 1998a; Schlebusch & De Marigny, 1987). These patients required renal dialysis or renal transplantation. At the time, I reported that although the physiopathogenesis of AN had been well researched, there was a need for further research into the psychopathogenesis of AN and of the analgesic abuser. These DPS studies also confirmed that psychological, psychiatric and medical hazards associated with OTC analgesic abuse have been insufficiently publicised amongst the general consumer. Most of the warnings regarding the dangers of their abuse appear either in the scientific literature or in small print in package inserts, and do not seem to reach the 'at-risk' general public at a sufficiently intense level to alter the course of this eminently preventable ISDB, with its high costs in terms of health care and human suffering. To some extent, this situation still prevails today.

A wide variety of analgesics (painkillers) is available in South Africa, both on prescription and OTC. More than a decade ago, a professionally edited index of ethical medicines listed numerous analgesics that were available in South Africa at the time, including syrups and, in some cases, 'extra strength' and topical analgesic products (MIMS Medical Specialities, 1991). By 2004, the relatively easy availability of analgesics had increased further and they are sold under a variety of proprietary names (MIMS Medical Specialities, 2004).

ANALGESIC NEPHROPATHY
The abuse of analgesics is a major public health problem frequently associated with physical diseases such as AN and others mentioned in this chapter, as well as with problems such as rebound analgesic-related headaches and psychological disorders. Although analgesic abuse in psychiatric patients appears to have been only recently considered a serious problem, AN has been a recognised clinical condition for the past three decades. Certain OTC or non-prescription analgesics have been available for over a century, but the initial accounts of analgesic abuse, leading to AN resulting in ESRD, originated from Switzerland only in 1953 (Spuhler & Zollinger 1953). Initially AN was thought to occur mainly in Switzerland, Scandinavia and Australia, but similar reports subsequently followed from Britain, western Scotland, the United States of America, Canada, Germany, Malaysia, South Africa and countries elsewhere (Gault & Wilson, 1978; Henrich, 1988; Murray, 1973; Schlebusch, 1991; Segasothy et al., 1988). The syndrome of AN was initially described as chronic interstitial nephritis, but papillary necrosis was later recognised as the

characteristic underlying pathology. Reasons frequently given for analgesic abuse include headache, depression, pain and various psychiatric and psychological problems (Schlebusch, 1991). It is frequently difficult to obtain a history from such patients since most deny analgesic abuse, whereas others appear either genuinely to underestimate the amounts taken (Van Gelder, 1990), or lack the knowledge to appreciate the consequences of such health-risk behaviour (Schlebusch, 1990a).

Significant differences have been noted in the incidence and prevalence rates of AN between different geographic regions (Alfrey & Chan, 1992; Burkart, Hamilton & Buckalew, 1989; Henrich, 1988; Kincaid-Smith, 1978; Murray, 1981). These remain difficult to explain (Schlebusch, 1991). Such regional differences occur within countries as well as between them. Some studies conclude that 5% to 7% of all patients with chronic renal failure have a history of analgesic abuse (Anandan & Matzke, 1981; Schlebusch, 1991), whereas others have reflected figures of 2.5% for Europe and as high as 25% for countries such as Australia, for new patients with ESRD accepted for dialysis (Kincaid-Smith, 1978). It has been reported that in countries such as Sweden, Denmark and others, better control of the sale of combination analgesics has reduced the frequency of AN (Alfrey & Chan, 1992).

In South Africa, contemporary press and scientific reports continue to highlight concerns over the abuse of analgesics (Allers, 2003; Keeton, *The Sunday Times*, 2004). In addition, these reports stress the need for tighter local control of such drugs, given the fact that in many countries other than South Africa, consumers cannot buy any products over the counter that contain codeine (which is a relative of heroin). South African AN figures ranging from 7% to 33% have been reported in the past for patients on a chronic renal failure treatment programme (Furman, 1987; Parsoo et al., 1983; Schlebusch, 1991; Schlebusch & De Marigny 1987; Seedat, 1990; Seedat & MacSearraigh, 1984). In my research I have quoted various studies regarding AN prevalence in South Africa, and have confirmed a regional variation in this country, as well as significant ethnic differences in local ESRD aetiology (Schlebusch, 1991). For example, hypertension as well as the abuse of certain traditional herbal remedies play a significant role in the lives of many black South Africans. In addition, a significant incidence of post-transplant analgesic dependence in patients who formerly suffered from AN has also been noted in certain South African centres (Furman et al., 1976; Schlebusch, 1991).

High South African AN figures ranging between 21.5% and 33.0% have previously been reported in Durban, on the country's east coast with its high levels of humidity which have been implicated in the onset of the problem and as a partial explanation for its local prevalence (Schlebusch, 1991; Seedat & MacSearraigh, 1984; Seedat et al., 1984). More recently, however, a lower percentage of AN in new patients on dialysis has been noted. This appears to be consistent with reports by the South African Dialysis and Transplantation Registry in 1990 (SADTR, 1990), which reported a decrease in AN figures for South Africa as a whole for all new patients registered, that is, 4.0% in 1989 compared to 9.6% in 1988 (SADTR, 1988), and 6.6% in 1987 (SADTR, 1987). Although these later figures appear to indicate a decline in the percentage of new AN patients in South Africa, the numbers have been at the high end of the range, not only in terms of new AN patients and patients on treatment, but also in terms of continued general public abuse (Allers, 2003; Keeton, *The Sunday Times*, 2004), and as a choice of method in suicidal behaviour involving overdoses (Schlebusch & Bosch, 2000).

CUMULATIVE DOSES OF ANALGESICS LEADING TO ANALGESIC NEPHROPATHY

Those at risk of developing AN are individuals who consume analgesics frequently or abuse them as part of self-medication (Alfrey & Chan, 1992). The relative risk of these individuals developing ESRD is approximately four times greater when compared to people who either do not or only occasionally consume analgesics (Burkart, Hamilton & Buckalew, 1989), or who adhere to medical instructions in the use of analgesics (Schlebusch, 1991). Reported quantities of analgesics ingested by patients with analgesic kidney disease vary. Such amounts include:
- a range from 1.0 kg to 15.3 kg over a 3 year to 23 year period (Segasothy et al., 1988);
- at least 1 g daily for 3 years, and 2 to more than 15 preparations taken from 4 years to 45 years (Murray, 1973);
- 1.3 kg to 25 kg over a 2 to 35 year period (Kingsley et al., 1972);
- heavy consumption for 5 years to 20 years (Gault & Wilson, 1978);

- 3 kg to 15 kg over a 3 to 20 year period (Gault et al., 1968); and
- 20.3 kg over a 12 year period (Knapp & Avioli, 1982).

It is estimated that the threshold dose for increased risk of AN is 2 kg to 3 kg of the index analgesic (that is, the substance being abused that causes the problem). This is approximately the equivalent of taking 4 to 6 tablets or powders containing 300 mg of the index analgesic per day, for 3 to 5 years, before AN develops (Burkart, Hamilton & Buckalew, 1989; Henrich, 1988; Seedat & MacSearraigh, 1984). Although AN can develop over such a short period, it usually takes longer and involves larger quantities of analgesics.

THE ROLE OF PHENACETIN AND PARACETAMOL (ACETAMINOPHEN)

Phenacetin has been in use since 1887. Its sedative, analgesic and mood-altering properties (sometimes even used to increase work productivity), along with its extensive use in the European influenza pandemic between 1918 and 1919, contributed to the popularity of phenacetin as a constituent in combination (mixture) compounds, whilst its easy OTC availability initially caused its abuse to go undetected (Henrich, 1988). Early reports associating AN with the abuse of combination products containing phenacetin resulted in its removal (as it was considered to be the primary offending agent in the development of AN) from OTC analgesics in many countries between 1961 and 1975, and even from prescription substances in some countries in 1986 (Henrich, 1988; Van Gelder, 1990). In certain countries phenacetin was replaced with acetaminophen (paracetamol) in combination products.

Despite this, the incidence of AN did not decline as expected, which suggests that combination compounds, even without phenacetin, are aetiologically important in promoting AN (Anandan & Matzke, 1981; Henrich, 1988). As early as 1970, researchers stressed that more careful analysis had revealed that implicating phenacetin as a causative agent in AN might have been premature (Wenger & Einstein, 1970). Studies have shown a decline of AN in some countries upon removal of phenacetin from OTC analgesics, but point out that a ban on phenacetin in others did not reduce the incidence of AN there (Burkart, Hamilton & Buckalew, 1989). Other studies show that compounds containing aspirin, phenacetin or acetaminophen (the principal metabolite of phenacetin) lead to a higher incidence of AN than when each of these substances is taken individually (Henrich, 1988; Van Gelder, 1990). In some countries, approximately two-thirds of analgesic ingestion is the result of self-medication and about 80% of the over 400 available analgesics consist of compound products (Henrich, 1988). In countries where acetaminophen has been reported to be the causative agent in AN and ESRD, the drug is still commonly used (Segasothy et al., 1988).

Acute renal failure following acetaminophen poisoning from self-induced overdose has been reported (Davenport & Finn, 1988), as has AN and ESRD when acetaminophen has been taken in large doses over a prolonged period (Segasothy et al., 1988). In countries where compound analgesic consumption is very high, and where phenacetin has been replaced in popular preparations with either acetaminophen or other substances, the newer analgesic combinations may also be nephrotoxic if abused (Burkart, Hamilton & Buckalew, 1989). South African researchers have voiced concern about the casual use in South Africa of acetaminophen and its role in analgesic kidney disease (with or without other active ingredients) and about the often vague reasons given by patients for its excessive consumption (Schlebusch, 1991; Seedat & MacSearraigh, 1984).

THE ROLE OF ASPIRIN (ACETYLSALICYLIC ACID)
The medicinal effects of the bark of the willow (*salix alba*) – the source of salicin, which can be converted to salicylic acid – have been known for centuries. Over the years, several authors have summarised the historical development of aspirin and the salicylates and their uses (Dixon et al., 1963; Jeffreys, 2004; Smith & Smith, 1966). Some 400 years ago Hippocrates wrote about the pain-soothing effects of willow bark and leaves. The synthetic manufacture of aspirin was accomplished in the early 1890s by the chemist Felix Hoffman in Germany (Jeffreys, 2004; Wenger & Einstein, 1970). Aspirin tablets as we know them today, were introduced in the United States of America in 1915 and by 1970 some 20 million pounds of the substance were consumed there per annum, that is, about 44 million tablets daily (Wenger & Einstein,

1970). By the 1990s in South Africa some 500 tons of aspirin were sold annually (Faber, 1990).

Aspirin has been used chiefly for mild pain relief, but other effects can include:
- its ability to lower raised body temperature (primarily noted in patients with fever, thus affecting the body's 'thermostat', which is probably located in the hypothalamus);
- its anti-inflammatory effect, especially in rheumatic and immunological disorders (arthritis, rheumatic fever, etc.);
- its ability to act on cellular metabolism in connective tissue (which is a major reason for the pre-eminence of salicylates in the treatment of rheumatic fever and low-grade pain in arthritis); and
- a multiplicity of metabolic effects on body tissue (Jeffrey, 2004; Wenger & Einstein, 1970).

Aspirin was also found to inhibit platelet function and is currently known to prevent platelet aggregation and so, in low doses, may assist in preventing cardiovascular disease.

Although, like other analgesics, aspirin has unquestionable medicinal value and therapeutic effects if used correctly, various aspects of its toxicity are known following prolonged ingestion and abuse. Amongst others, these include:
- idiosyncratic reactions in sensitive individuals; and
- symptomatic abdominal intolerance (for example, heartburn, nausea, vomiting, abdominal discomfort including ulceration, etc.) (Schlebusch, 1991).

Despite negative effects such as these and an increasing focus on its pharmacology and toxicity, in recent years the use of aspirin has increased enormously worldwide and it has been described as a wonder drug with many advantages if it is used appropriately and responsibly (Jeffreys, 2004).

THE ROLE OF NON-STEROIDAL ANTI-INFLAMMATORY SUBSTANCES

The abuse of non-steroidal anti-inflammatory drugs (NSAIDs) has also been reported to cause adverse renal consequences and nephrotoxicity (Henrich, 1988; Van Gelder, 1990). Although the bulk of AN cases have been associated with papillary necrosis due to combination analgesic abuse, there is evidence that the NSAIDs may also be associated with the lesion, although less frequently so. The increasing recognition that abuse of NSAIDs can contribute to acute renal failure is due, amongst other reasons, to the considerable number of people who have a potential therapeutic indication for the drugs, making the population potentially at risk a significantly large one (Henrich, 1988). Some of the commonly recognised clinical syndromes of nephrotoxicity with NSAIDs include renal insufficiency, interstitial nephritis, and hyperkalaemia as well as sodium and water retention. The syndrome can also occur because of a number of drugs in various chemical groupings of NSAIDs (Van Gelder, 1990). In addition, reports of anaphylactic reactions (an abnormal response of the body to a foreign substance) associated with the abuse of NSAIDs are cause for concern (Henrich, 1988).

PSYCHOCULTURAL ASPECTS OF ANALGESIC ABUSE

Psychoactive drugs came into the history of humankind as substances that were used to alter consciousness. The reaction that they produce reflects both the chemical actions of the drugs on humans as well as their psychological and cultural aspects (Room, 1989). Understanding the pharmacology as well as the cultural context of substance use is, therefore, an important aspect in appreciating their use and abuse (Room, 1989). Drugs have a variety of use-values within different socio-cultural contexts, for example, as medicines, beverages, foodstuffs, solvents, sacred or sacramental objects, carriers of symbolic meanings, value for trading, economic and fiscal resources, and so on (Room, 1989). Experts have pointed out the great variations in this regard as well as the complex interplay between the patterns of psychoactive drug use and the users in different societies and cultures (Room, 1989; Schlebusch, 1991). Nevertheless, it has been argued that almost any drug is potentially toxic when abused (Schlebusch, 1991). A vast international literature is available concerning the biomedical, psychological, cultural, social and other mechanisms underlying drug use and abuse.

In South Africa acute and chronic diseases as well as psychological and behavioural complications are commonly reported in relation to drug toxicity involving the abuse of analgesics, herbal medicines, alcohol and other drugs. Local cultural factors, as well as intensity of advertising, could partly explain some of the marked regional variations in the reported incidence of analgesic abuse, both in South Africa and elsewhere. Furthermore, not only are patterns of analgesic ingestion sometimes culturally and socio-economically related, but genuine underestimation by patients of actual amounts ingested, and lack of knowledge of the dangers of analgesic abuse might offer additional explanations of why these substances are abused (Van Gelder, 1990). Given this, the roles, lifestyles and patterns of medicinal use are all important when taking a patient's history, as is the exploration of the patient's belief systems and illness behaviour (Schlebusch, 1985d, 1990a, 1996; Schlebusch & Ruggieri, 1996).

In addition, South Africa is both a developed and a developing country, where professional health care from a First World perspective is often practised in a Third World context (Schlebusch, 1990a). The country's population (aptly nicknamed the 'rainbow nation') consists of a complex, multi-ethnic society characterised by variations in lifestyles and in the pathological basis of diseases. As a result, specific psychological problems unique to different patient cultural groups (and usually not documented) should be considered when providing psychological and mental health-care services for patients at risk of substance abuse and suicidal behaviour.

PSYCHOLOGICAL PROBLEMS AND ANALGESIC ABUSE
My interest in the psychopathological origins and consequences of prolonged ingestion of OTC analgesics was fuelled not only because analgesic abuse leads to renal papillary necrosis and chronic renal insufficiency, but also because of the common occurrence of analgesic and other substance abuse in South Africa in the general population, and its relation, in particular, to suicidal behaviour. As my work in this area evolved, it became increasingly clear that analgesic abuse is a major problem with regard to:
- the potential renal patient population;
- psychiatric patients;
- suicidal behaviour involving analgesic poisoning, which accounts for a significant number of overdose patients being admitted to academic hospitals (Schlebusch, 1988a, 2004); and

- the general public, who are at risk of becoming medical or psychiatric casualties as a result of their analgesic abuse (Schlebusch, 1991).

In addition to its causal link with somatic disease, several studies have reported on the association between psychiatric and psychological problems and analgesic abuse. For example, in a number of local studies (Furman, 1987; Kingsley et al., 1972; Schlebusch, 1991; Schlebusch, Lasich & Wessels, 1985; Seedat & MacSearraigh, 1984; Van Gelder, 1990), and international studies (Alfrey & Chan, 1992; Anandan & Matzke, 1981; Gault et al., 1968; Gault & Wilson, 1978; Kincaid-Smith, 1978; Murray, 1973; Murray, 1981; Wenger & Einstein, 1970), the AN syndrome has been characterised as part of a long-standing psychological problem associated with:
- psychological dependence on analgesics;
- emotional instability;
- anxiety;
- depression;
- habituation to and dependence on other drugs (alcohol, nicotine, laxatives, diuretics, caffeine, etc.);
- somatoform disorders;
- lack of psychological coping skills; and
- the inability to deal effectively with stress.

Also cited as part of this issue are:
- complex, immature or inadequate personalities;
- conditioned pain behaviour;
- high pain verbalisation;
- lifestyle problems;
- neurosis;
- the need for a 'psychic lift';
- substance-seeking behaviour;
- a belief in the mood-altering properties of analgesics; and
- seeking feelings of well-being.

Secrecy and deception about analgesic abuse and persistence in analgesic abuse despite warnings about the hazards are common. Neuropsychological and intellectual impairment can often be detected, as well as psychosocial (often socio-economically related) problems and occupational impairment. In addition, abnormal familial attitudes toward analgesics, family histories of analgesic and other substance abuse, family histories of other psychiatric disorders as well as marital and sexual problems are sometimes found. Previous psychiatric histories, personality disorders, chronic insomnia, chronic pain (especially headache, migraine and backache) where the analgesics are consumed to relieve the pain, and the practise of polypharmacy have been reported. My research has also shown that the denial of and resistance to discussion of analgesic abuse commonly preceded an eventual admission of it (Schlebusch, 1991; Schlebusch & De Marigny, 1987). Most of the patients also fitted the criteria for depression.

Other research has been done on analgesic abuse by individuals with psychological and psychiatric problems without AN or ESRD (Allers, 2003; Fritsche et al., 2000; Jacobsen & Hansen, 1989; Juang et al., 2000; Kaplan & Sadock, 1995; Marazziti et al., 1999; Radat et al., 1999; Radat et al., 2002). In particular, certain somatoform disorders, cognitive disorders, substance-related disorders, mood disorders and anxiety disorders appear to be implicated. Analgesic abuse has also been aetiologically implicated in dementia and neuropsychological deficits (Wells, 1985). Jacobsen and Hansen (1989) argued that analgesic abusers in many instances most likely also tend to abuse analgesics in order to deal with the distress associated with having specific psychiatric disorders.

In some of my studies, as part of a series of investigations on the psychopathology of analgesic abuse, I reported findings specifically on the neuropsychological deficits found in AN, on the association between analgesic-related substance abuse acting on the opiate receptor sites in the brain and substance-induced cognitive disorders, and on the pain-behaviour of analgesic abusers (Schlebusch, 1991). My findings took into account the poor pain tolerance and excessive pre-morbid complaints of headache in these patients and neuropsychological deficits seen in uraemia (Bosch & Schlebusch, 1991; Schlebusch, 1982).

These results showed several lines of aetiological evidence pointing to an association between headache (often described as migraine, but which was not typical of this disorder), psychopathologically based habitual analgesic consumption, substance-related disorders, and opiate-like-induced cognitive disorders. Although most patients claimed to use analgesics initially for headaches, some often continued to abuse analgesics in the absence of headaches, which reflected a psychological problem and substance-seeking behaviour. Their 'headaches' seemed to be more often associated with tension or stress.

Research on analgesic abuse typically shows that most patients claim to abuse analgesics because of persistent headaches of varying descriptions, often mentioning migraine, although the symptoms and pathophysiology described by them are not always characteristic thereof. In addition, headaches and pain, significant in patients with various somatoform disorders and hypochondriacal tendencies, are some of the most common general medical complaints frequently used to explain away work absenteeism or lack of engagement in undesired activities, and represent a prominent symptom in many psychiatric disorders, including anxiety-related disorders and depression. Given the above, my further investigations into the pain behaviour of analgesic abusers as well as the type and onset of the headaches that they complain of, revealed interesting findings, including:

- a psychological and physical dependence on analgesic intake associated with continually increased dosage to control analgesic-induced side effects;
- childhood conditioning towards analgesic abuse; and
- pain-prone personality characteristics, which contributed to a predisposition to analgesic abuse (Schlebusch, 1991).

There is sufficient evidence to support the fact that opiate-related analgesics bind on specific receptor sites in the brain, and although the complexity of their actions is apparent there are no simple answers to the exact mechanisms of dependence (Lader, 1983). This is particularly worrying if we consider the vast quantities of active ingredients that analgesic abusers ingest, particularly opioid-like substances such as codeine phosphate as this is associated with substance dependence, neuropsychological deficits and substance-induced cognitive disorders. There are some authorities who argue that we should even add sugar and some spices to the list of abused psychoactive drugs (Room, 1989). It has also been suggested that because nicotine (smoking) appears to increase the clearance of caffeine from the body, it might contribute to the higher coffee consumption of nicotine smokers (Greden, 1985). Caffeine has a pharmacological half-life of about three-and-half hours, and a daily intake of 500 mg to 600 mg of caffeine represents a standard cut-off point; levels beyond this increase the risk of overt clinical manifestations of caffeinism (Greden, 1985; Schlebusch, 2000c). Although different symptom constellations frequently co-exist in caffeinism and sensitivity to different doses varies significantly, clinical manifestations of the disorder include:

- anxiety;
- psychophysiological manifestations (headache, tachycardia, diarrhoea, lethargy, tremulousness, epigastric pain, etc.);
- insomnia;
- withdrawal symptoms;
- depression;
- accentuation of stress; and
- miscellaneous medical issues (complications related to conditions such as gastrointestinal problems, etc.) (Greden, 1985).

Furthermore, inordinate levels of caffeine intake are often confounded with the abuse of other substances such as minor tranquillisers, sedative-hypnotics, alcohol and cigarette smoking – all of which may have clinical implications (Greden, 1985; Schlebusch, 2000c). The consequences of these various factors for health-risk behaviour, including non-treatment-adherence (non-compliance) behaviour can be serious. For example, the inverse relationship between non-treatment-adherence behaviour, cognitive disorders, exogenous variables, and endogenous toxins from a causal secondary or interactional stance, needs to be carefully considered in view of our present understanding of stress, health behaviour, abnormal illness behaviour, psychological coping mechanisms and suicidal behaviour (Schlebusch, 1991).

HEADACHES, PAIN AND ANALGESIC ABUSE
As already mentioned, most patients typically claim to abuse analgesics because of pain that includes persistent headaches of varying descriptions (Gault et al., 1968, Gault & Wilson, 1978; Murray, 1973; Schlebusch, 1991). It is often difficult, however, to

diagnose retrospectively, differentially the exact cause of their pain, as some individuals also tend to practice polypharmacy by using a variety of analgesics that could further contribute to causing headaches.

Although prevalence rates may vary, about 80% of the general population annually suffer from headaches (*Current Practice*, 1988; Thompson, 1985a), and about 10% to 20% present to physicians with headache as their primary complaint. Likewise, chronic pain is one of the most frequent medical complaints, and chronic low back pain is one of the most common causes of time lost from work (Thompson, 1985b). South African figures for prevalence rates of pain and headaches are not considered any different from those in other parts of the world (Lindegger, 1990). My research shows that, generally, the headaches these patients complain about, can be broadly grouped into psychogenic, cluster, tension headaches, vascular or migraine headaches with their many variants, and recurring or chronic headaches (Schlebusch, 1991).

Psychogenic headaches are, as the term implies, related to psychogenic aetiology (psychological causes). As mentioned, psychiatric disorders are frequently associated with headaches but when a diagnosis is made the link is frequently missed (Thompson, 1985a). For example, apart from the role of anxiety and stress-related disorders, headache is a common complaint in patients with somatoform disorders (especially pain disorders and hypochondriasis). These patients frequently seek numerous analgesic prescriptions as a result of their abnormal illness behaviour (Thompson, 1985a). Cluster headaches refer to headaches that typically occur in clusters of one or more daily, for several weeks. They tend to be short in duration (twenty minutes to two hours), unilateral (usually occurring on the same side), are without prodromata and may leave the patient euphoric after an attack (Thompson, 1985a).

It has been suggested on a theoretical basis that tension headache and common migraine can be conceived of as being on a continuum representing different ends of a spectrum, but it is clinically useful to differentiate between them for management purposes. Classic vascular headaches constitute about 30% of migraines (Thompson, 1985a). Migraine can be defined as a paroxysmal

disorder characterised by headaches (separated by pain-free intervals) that include at least two or more of the following symptoms:
- unilateral pain (hemicrania);
- nausea and vomiting;
- visual motor, dysphasic or sensory aura lasting about 30 minutes; and
- a family history in a first-degree relative of the index patient (*Current Practice*, 1988; Thompson, 1985a).

Migraine's common precipitating factors include:
- stress;
- anxiety;
- fatigue;
- relaxation after stress (commonly over weekends and holidays);
- bright flickering lights;
- missing regular meals;
- alcohol;
- dietary sensitivity;
- menstruation;
- menopause, with or without mood disorders (depression);
- the use of oestrogenic oral contraceptives; and other causes.

By contrast, tension headache can be defined as a generalised discomfort or pain that includes feelings of tightness, and of pressing or heaviness like a tight band, a skull-cap, or a squeezing weight (*Current Practice*, 1988; Thompson, 1985a). It can occur every day, does not usually prevent sleep, is worse when the patient is tired, stressed or excited, is unrelieved by simple analgesics; and may be accompanied by nausea, but not by vomiting. Psychological stress is often associated with prolonged contraction of head and neck muscles, resulting in constriction of blood vessels, leading to tension headaches (Schlebusch, 2000c; Thompson, 1985a). Apart from certain biomedical considerations, stress, depression and anxiety are often associated with tension headaches, which can be classified as episodic tension-type headache, or chronic tension-type headache, both with or without increased muscle tension (Kunkel, 1990). Symptoms common in migraine (for example, photophobia, photopsia, nausea, vomiting, anorexia, and so on) are usually absent in tension headaches, and patients with tension headaches do not necessarily take to bed in a dark, quiet room like the migraineur (Kunkel, 1990).

In addition, there are various other headaches such as:
- acute catastrophic headaches commonly indicating subarachnoid haemorrhage, encephalitis or meningitis, or other central nervous system (CNS) infectious processes, which require immediate admission to a neurological ward;
- headaches of recent onset in the elderly;
- headaches due to brain tumours or other intracranial masses;
- post-concussion or trauma-related headaches; and others (*Current Practice*, 1988; Thompson 1985a).

It is possible for some patients to present with two headaches, such as migraine and tension headaches, which can occur simultaneously. For many of the analgesic abusers that I studied, the term 'headache' could mean any ache from the neck upwards (Schlebusch, 1991). In the psychological evaluation of a headache it is, therefore, important to determine its exact location and to take a careful history, especially a drug history of both prescription and non-prescription substances (Thompson, 1985a). Furthermore, headaches can be a result of the abuse of certain substances (analgesics, alcohol, nicotine, caffeine, etc.) or a side effect of some, such as certain anti-depressants and a range of other medications (Thompson, 1985a). For example, one report noted a relationship between abuse of analgesics and tranquillisers, a particular personality type and headache and depression (Keller & Schwarz, 1983). Another study conducted as part of my research programme, found that people seek to control their psychological and physical states with the simultaneous abuse of alcohol, analgesics and/or benzodiazepines, because of difficulty in coping with life problems (Nattrass, 1995, 1996). This research also noted that suicide is not an uncommon occurrence in the substance abuser, as was graphically illustrated in the film *Leaving Las Vegas*, in which the protagonist kills himself by consuming excessive amounts of alcohol. Headaches are also some of the most common medical and neurological symptoms (Thompson, 1985a) and are associated with neuropsychological sequelae that require a careful differential diagnosis for appropriate management. Moreover, headache can also be conceived of as a subjective symptom of some other underlying problem, rather than a disease. Being a final common pathway for multiple factors that can interact synergistically, its aetiology is rarely unifactorial, but is often due to a complex combination of biopsychosocial factors (Thompson, 1985a). Finally, as part of the symptom complex, psychological stress can exacerbate headaches irrespective of the underlying aetiology (Schlebusch, 2000c; Thompson, 1985a).

The usual pattern of abuse may follow one of two directions:
- original medical prescription or self-treatment for pain in which patients themselves gradually increase the dose and frequency thereof for their own use, thus developing substance-seeking behaviour, causing them to visit several physicians or pharmacies to procure supplies or by procuring OTC analgesics at supermarkets or other outlets; and
- via introduction by peers and others (Schlebusch, 1991).

Although initial analgesic intake may be for pain relief, the analgesic action soon may be appreciated for its other effects, such as its mood-altering properties (Murray, 1973). Finally, as is evident from the discussion in this chapter, patients with chronic pain can tend to be either substance-dependents or substance-abusers (Maruta, Swanson & Finlayson, 1979; Steger & Fordyce, 1982), who engage in self-administered polypharmacy and excessive use of other substances such as alcohol, purgatives, tobacco, coffee and so on. In this respect, dependence on a substance can mean 'behaviourally dependent', or 'physically dependent' (neuro-adaptation), which includes a change in the biological system manifested by a withdrawal syndrome (Jaffe, 1989).

> **KEY POINTS**
>
> - Those who engage in indirect self-destructive behaviour do not generally view it as suicidal behaviour.
> - There is a complex relationship between drug abuse and self-destructive behaviour, which requires consideration of, *inter alia*, biomedical, cultural, social and psychological factors.
> - There is a high rate of analgesic abuse (particularly of OTC analgesics) in South Africa. This is frequently associated with psychological problems and abuse.

CHAPTER NINE

Risk factors and causes

Suicide: that mysterious route towards the unknown.
(Victor Marie Hugo, *Les Misérables*)

I HAVE INDICATED throughout this book that suicidal behaviour is a complex phenomenon and that risk factors for and the causes of suicidal behaviour are multifactorial and multidimensional. Worldwide it has been shown that these risk factors are wide ranging and include psychiatric, psychological, biological, sociological, genetic, cultural, somatic, personality, substance abuse, family dynamics, interpersonal problems, stress and other variables. Any of these factors can play a significant role in one way or another (Hawton & Van Heeringen, 2000; Wasserman, 2001b). In this chapter I focus more specifically on South African research findings.

FAMILY DYNAMICS AND RELATED ISSUES
Many South African studies have noted the role of family dynamics in suicidal behaviour. For example, one of the DPS investigations found a significantly higher prevalence of family conflict as a recent stressor among suicidal adolescents as compared to control subjects (Pillay, 1995a). In a study involving suicidal patients who were seen in general practice, the following causes were the most prominent: interpersonal problems, marital problems, partner-relational problems, family problems, financial problems, stress, examination problems at school or university, psychiatric disorders (especially depression) and incest (Cassimjee & Pillay, 2000). Such findings are in keeping with other reported studies that found family problems and interpersonal conflicts to be reasons often given for suicidal behaviours (Schlebusch & Bosch, 2000). A frequent problem involves feelings of loss of support because of

family change caused by parental separation, divorce and remarriage and adverse parent-child interactions. It was also found that (if inadequately managed) parental loss through divorce, but especially parental bereavement can be a risk factor in childhood suicidal behaviour as compared to controls without parental loss (Du Plessis & Schlebusch, 1992). Other critical aetiological considerations noted locally are associated with:

- family psychopathology (such as a history of family members' suicidal behaviour, substance abuse and other psychological disorders in family members);
- school-related and academic problems in young people (especially in a non-supportive or over-demanding family environment);
- exposure to family violence;
- a family history of suicidal behaviour; and
- child abuse (Noor Mahomed, Selmer & Bosch, 2000).

With regard to sexual abuse, a study of university students with suicidal ideation and behaviours reported that in 28.9% of those surveyed, 36.3% reported contact sexual abuse and 63.7% reported non-contact sexual abuse such as exposure to exhibitionism, sexual requests, and so on (Collings, 1992). This study also pointed to other research that found a significant association between child sexual abuse and later self-destructive behaviour. From a cognitive behaviour therapy point of view, it has long been known that dysfunctional cognitive schemata in children (that is, more unhappy than happy memories) can lead to vulnerability and to later onset depression and, as our research showed, to suicidal ideation and/or behaviour (Du Plessis & Schlebusch, 1992; Schlebusch, 2004).

Some researchers also found pathological levels of inflexibility and cohesion in the family functioning of suicidal adolescents (Pillay & Wassenaar, 1997a). Rigid problem-solving behaviour, over-controlling parenting styles and a lack of tolerance for developmental or role changes were characteristic features of such families. Similarly, these families were found to be over-involved in and over-protective of their children, allowing little or no room for individuation and normal developmental progression. Another investigation by the same researchers noted a significantly higher prevalence of family conflict as a recent stressor among suicidal adolescents compared to control subjects (Pillay & Wassenaar, 1997b). These authors explained that the conflicts were ongoing stressors, with the suicidal behaviour occurring at a threshold point in the crisis build-up, indicating the young person's inability to continue in the conflict-ridden environment. These studies also noted that the recognition of family risk factors for suicidal behaviour in young people is an essential feature in planning intervention and prevention programmes, which are discussed in Chapter ten. An interesting South African study involving black adolescents, showed a relationship between self-punitive wishes and dissatisfaction with father-adolescent relationships, mother-adolescent relationships, family interaction and the degree of family acceptance (Mayekiso, 1995).

Furthermore, various DPS researchers (Schlebusch, 1988a, 1992a, 1995a; Schlebusch & Bosch, 2000) have persistently cautioned that:

- as children grow up, the prevalence of suicidal behaviour and other self-destructive behaviour can increase dramatically during adolescence and early adulthood if risk factors are not timeously identified and addressed;
- young people's perceptions of suicidal behaviour may be a significant factor in this regard;
- interpersonal problems are major causative factors;
- the media can play a significant role in influencing perceptions about suicidal behaviour (because of the Werther or copycat effect and dramatisation of the suicidal act);
- family problems are often perceived as one of the main causes of suicidal behaviour; and
- unpremeditated, impulsive acts can be utilised (often in persons without a particular psychiatric morbidity) in the face of a predominantly interpersonal crisis, especially in the young (Bosch, McGill & Noor Mahomed, 1995). This has major implications for prediction and prevention and the need to develop appropriate, cost-effective therapeutic interventions.

I have pointed out that school-related and academic problems in young people can be significant risk factors for suicidal behaviour. What is perhaps less known in South Africa, is that reading impairment (which is internationally one of the most prominently investigated learning disabilities) has been associated with many psychopathological disorders and can serve as a co-morbid factor in suicidal behaviour, especially in young people at school. Identifying and treating learning disabilities (especially problems in reading) can be powerful preventors of subsequent psychological disorders and potential suicidal behaviours (Wood & Goldston, 2000).

POOR PROBLEM-SOLVING SKILLS
Various authors have noted that suicidal people are often poor at solving interpersonal problems (Schlebusch, 1992a, 1995a; Williams & Pollock, 1993). It is in this context that suicidal behaviour has been viewed as an inappropriate method of communication and problem-solving technique, especially by young people, when individuals feel unable to express their distress in a conventional manner. Typically, if other attempts to deal with their problems have been unsuccessful, they resort to more desperate calls for help. Furthermore, research data from the DPS group provide support for the hypothesis that (as part of a process) non-fatal (low intent) suicidal behaviour is increasingly being employed as a first-line, crisis-management strategy by people (especially younger individuals) who would not always be considered to have particularly overt psychological morbidity (Schlebusch & Bosch, 2000; Schlebusch, Vawda & Bosch, 2003). That is, they use suicidal behaviour as an inappropriate problem-solving strategy (Schlebusch, 2004).

The belief that people who threaten to commit suicide are not serious about it, or will not actually make such an attempt, does not accord with the facts. According to some authorities, at least 80% of suicides are preceded by either verbal or non-verbal behaviour cues that indicate the suicidal person's intentions (Sue, Sue & Sue, 2000). South African research has shown that more than two-thirds of people who engage in suicidal behaviour communicate their intent to do so within three months preceding the act and a significant number visit their general practitioners for treatment for a psychological disorder (usually depression) in the two weeks preceding the suicidal act (Schlebusch et al., 1986). This accords with other research which indicates that a substantial proportion of people who engage in fatal suicidal behaviour have had some contact with their medical health professional in the last twelve months of their lives, and that a significant number of individuals were in treatment at the time of their suicides (Pirkis & Burgess, 1998; Schlebusch et al., 1986). Nevertheless, a substantial number of people do not make any contact with either a specialised mental health professional or a general practitioner, which is an extremely worrying fact concerning risk factors for repeated suicidal behaviour (Sakinofsky, 2000).

AGGRESSION

Aggressive behaviour is common in both suicide and violence and the link between suicide and violence has been well researched. It is also evident from the South African data regarding methods of choice in suicidal behaviour discussed in Chapter seven. The overlapping themes include increased impulsiveness, emotional lability, disinhibition, decision-making and reasoning problems, and an underlying biological or genetic predisposition that could result in increased aggressiveness (Nock & Marzuk, 2000). As noted in Chapter three, injury is one of the major causes of death in South Africa, a problem of significant magnitude (Matzopoulos, 2002; Matzopoulos, Cassim & Seedat, 2003), which includes intentional and unintentional injuries (Matzopoulos, Norman & Bradshaw, 2004). Violence often plays a role in such injuries as it does in suicidal behaviour.

EXTENDED SUICIDE AND MURDER-SUICIDE

What is lacking in South Africa is more in-depth research on the causes of extended suicidal behaviour and murder-suicide. These have been well researched internationally, and have been referred to as possibly the most extreme examples of the link between violence and suicidal behaviour (Cheng & Lee, 2000; Nock & Marzuk, 2000). There has been an apparent escalation in 'crimes of passion' and family murders in South Africa, and the press has recently reported a number of family slayings that have struck this country. Of the few early studies in this regard, one looked at the role of personality disorders (especially the dependent personality) (Schlebusch, 1988b). Another emphasised the distinction between murder-suicide and extended suicide (Graser, 1992). In murder-suicide, the family murder occurs primarily as an act of murder and secondarily as a suicidal act, whereas in extended suicide it is the other way around: that is, the intention was there all along to commit suicide after first killing the family as part of the extended suicidal act.

It is well known that suicide risk increases in patients with an elevated degree of hopelessness (the link between depression, cognitive rigidity, problem-solving failures and suicidal behaviour) and, if violence and dysfunctional relationships are present in depressed patients, extended suicide becomes an additional risk (Van Heeringen, Hawton & Williams, 2000; Williams & Pollock, 2000). A recent South African study found work-related stress and post-traumatic stress disorder as well as the availability of and familiarity with firearms to be common in murder-suicide (Townsend, 2003). This study also observed similar patterns to those reported in many international studies, which tends to suggest that the characteristics of murder-suicide appear to be constant across cultures, and that murder-suicide is more akin to suicide than homicide. Additional causes cited in family killings include socio-economic pressures, transformation, the trauma resulting from child abuse and various psychological factors (Ngalwa, *The Sunday Tribune*, 2005).

I have emphasised before that two of the primary motives for suicidal behaviour include murderous impulses and escape from unbearable psychological pain (Schlebusch, 1988a). These motives may develop when love objects or social support systems are threatened, lost or become otherwise unobtainable. When a patient fears or experiences intolerable aloneness, severe hopelessness and intense self-contempt, murderous impulses can develop towards the love object that is threatened or unattainable. If a patient's immediate family is the love object in this instance, and is considered to be part of the self, suicidal behaviour can develop. Through the processes of introjection and projection, these murderous impulses may then be turned not only on the self, but also on the perceived love object, that is, the family, thus resulting in family murder as an extended suicide. The surviving children in a family murder are frequently the first to realise the full horror of these events, and are often the ones who call the neighbours or the police. The long- and short-term emotional effects of such experiences must be taken into account by subsequent psychological intervention (Schlebusch, 1988a).

Although various racial and language groups are generally represented in this phenomenon, I noted that an analysis of statistical data of the 127 family murders in South Africa in 1983 indicated that white, Afrikaans-speaking families predominated at the time, possibly because of the pending changes towards democracy and the abolishing of the apartheid system, causing the victims to fear an uncertain future (Schlebusch, 1988a). Other researchers found that in the 1980s perpetrators of murder-suicides were largely white (65%), black (29%) and Coloured (6%) (Roos, Beyers & Visser, 1992). Generally, murder-suicide can occur amongst all cultural and ethnic groups (Felthous & Hempel, 1995). Another South African study covering the years 2000 to 2001 found that in the province of KwaZulu-Natal (specifically the Durban metropolitan area) 88.4% of victims of murder-suicides were black and 11.6% were Indian, which probably reflects the major ethnic composition of the geographical study area (Townsend, 2003). A review of newspaper reports from 1997 to 2001 found that 59% of the perpetrators of murder-suicides were black, 27.7% were white, 19.8% were Indian and 2.4% were Coloured (Osborne, 2001).

Five press reports, ranging from the late 1980s to 2005 illustrate some of the dynamics described in this section. In the first, a young man, aged 18 years, committed suicide after shooting and killing his girlfriend's father, aged 43 years. During the incident he also shot and seriously wounded his girlfriend's sister, aged 16 years, and two visitors to their home. His actions followed a custody dispute and an argument with his girlfriend's father about her and their 5-month-old baby's whereabouts (*The Natal Mercury*, 5 August 1988: 2). The second article tells of a 45-year-old woman who was murdered by her husband, along with her 63-year-old mother and 7-year-old foster brother, because she refused to have sex with her husband out of fear that he was HIV-positive and would infect her. After a police stand-off, the husband then turned the gun on himself (Ndaba, *The Natal Mercury*, 2005). In a third article, a soldier warned his family by phone that he was going to kill himself. Before he did so, he shot several of his colleagues (Mthembu & Hosken, *The Daily News*, 2005). This incident is also referred to in Chapter four as an example of suicide in the South African National Defence Force. Interestingly, the soldier's brother had committed suicide some five years earlier by shooting himself.

In the fourth article, residents of an affluent neighbourhood were jolted when an 82-year-old grandmother allegedly took her own life after shooting her daughter and inflicting a critical injury on her granddaughter (Tse, *The Mercury*, 2005). Finally, perhaps one of the more infamous South African examples of a murder-suicide occurred in the early 1990s when a paedophile shot himself after he shot his lover shortly before being arrested for allegedly abducting and abusing six young girls, before selling them into sex slavery or killing them. The young girls were never found and the home of the perpetrators was demolished and rezoned for building a child protection facility (*The Independent on Saturday*, 2 July 2005: 7). Other press reports of murder-suicides and extended suicides are mentioned in Chapter six.

STRESS
Chronic and acute stress are critical co-morbid aetiological considerations in suicidal behaviour (Pretorius & Roos, 1995; Schlebusch, 1995b). The role of dysfunctional perceptions in stress-arousal associated with a range of psychological problems including suicidal behaviour, has been well documented in South Africa (Schlebusch, 2000c). Some authors have referred to the role of stress as precipitated by a conflict in social roles in young people from traditional backgrounds in a multicultural South African society, who have to cope with new roles and a more Western-orientated culture (Wassenaar et al., 2000). My own research has also emphasised the role of factors such as acculturation, socio-economic pressures, high crime and violence rates, a history of human rights violations with its resultant trauma as well as the process of transformation, all of which combine to create high stress levels that can act as suicidal triggers (Schlebusch, Vawda & Bosch, 2003).

Up-to-date retrospective analyses of risk factors in suicidal behaviour in South Africa have listed the following risk factors as some of the most common:
- repeated attempts in non-fatal suicidal behaviour lead to more severe and lethal attempts;
- recklessness to secure help increases as the non-fatal suicidal behaviour does not get the desired effect from significant others on whom the suicidal behaviour is supposed to impact;

Risk factors and causes

- interpersonal problems;
- marital problems;
- partner-relational problems;
- family problems;
- financial problems;
- stress;
- academic-related problems;
- psychological disorders (especially depression and substance abuse);
- incest;
- a history of suicidal behaviour in family members;
- exposure to family violence;
- a family member's suicidal behaviour;
- child abuse;
- school-related problems in younger children;
- chronic and acute stress, which are critical co-morbid aetiological considerations in suicidal behaviour in South Africa;
- problems with acculturation;
- socio-economic pressures;
- high crime and violence rates; and
- a history of human rights violations and transformation (Schlebusch, 2004; Schlebusch & Noor Mahomed, 2004).

All of the factors listed above produce high stress levels. In certain occupational sub-groups (for example, in the police services) post-traumatic stress disorder has also been found to be a predominant risk factor.

Elevated stress has also become a major risk factor in young black South Africans. For example, factors such as urbanisation, globalisation, increasing competitiveness in education and employment, rising expectations and a move away from traditional roles and value systems towards Western lifestyles and norms have all been cited as significant stressors in South African black youths who are suicidal (Vawda, 2005).

DEPRESSION AND OTHER PSYCHOLOGICAL DISORDERS

As noted in Chapter two, suicidal behaviour has a long history. The same applies to depression, which also afflicts people of all types and ages. For centuries, poets, philosophers and physicians have described depression and its associated behavioural manifestations. As knowledge has increased, so scientists and clinicians have penned more precise descriptions of depression.

International research has clearly identified various psychopathological conditions as co-morbid factors in the aetiology of suicidal behaviour (Hawton & Van Heeringen, 2000; Wasserman, 2001a). In particular, mood disorders (such as depression) have been implicated. A research review article noted that in the majority (98%) of completed suicides there has been a diagnosis of at least one mental disorder: mood disorders (30.2%) were followed by substance-use disorders (17.6%), schizophrenia (14.1%) and personality disorders (13.0%) (Bertolote et al., 2004). Other researchers have shown that in psychological autopsies that included all age groups, about half of the victims suffered from depression, of whom about one half had experienced a major depressive episode (Lönnqvist, 2000). This is also true for South Africans in all ethnic groups (Schlebusch, 1992a, 1995a; Schlebusch & Bosch, 2000; Schlebusch, Vawda & Bosch, 2003). Some 25 years ago, depression was considered such a major problem in South Africa that a group of experts conceived of a national treatment programme (Schlebusch, 1990b). In the twenty-first century, depression remains a common problem but, now more than ever before, improved treatment modalities bring hope for the hopeless (Lasich & Schlebusch, 1999; Schlebusch, 2005b).

As noted earlier on in this chapter, family dynamics are important considerations when assessing risk factors in suicidal behaviour. This is particularly true for dysfunctional relationships and depression (Schlebusch, 2000c). For example, a recent study reported in the press found that compared to women, men are twice as likely to feel suicidal following a divorce (*The Mercury*, 4 July 2005: 5). In my clinical practice, I have found that it is not uncommon for one partner to enter into therapy to save a relationship while the other is not willing to work at it. When the relationship eventually disintegrates the person who was reluctant to accept the need for help in the first place often then cannot cope with the resultant break-up.

I have previously summarised views on depression in a publication that dealt with the national treatment programme that I mentioned earlier (Schlebusch, 1990b). Generally there is no set point at which a sad mood is considered to have passed into a clinical depression. Rather, this is considered to have occurred when the depressed mood is observed to have persisted for too long, has become pathological and is interfering with the person's psychosocial, biovegetative and other functioning, or sometimes when the person him- or herself makes this decision. The boundaries between normal sadness and clinical depression are unclear. However, experts agree that a combination of intensity, severity and duration of the depressive symptoms are important markers when making an accurate diagnosis of the depression (Kaplan & Sadock, 1995; Lasich & Schlebusch, 1999; Schlebusch, 1990b, 2005b).

In line with other research, a South African investigation reported that the common diagnosis of mood disorders (depression) was applicable in nearly two-thirds (63.9%) of non-fatal suicidal patients. Other diagnoses reported in the same study included substance abuse, schizophrenia, and substance-induced psychosis (Schlebusch, Vawda & Bosch, 2003). In other reports on suicidal behaviour in psychiatric in-patients in acute general hospital psychiatric units, the rates were likewise high for patients with diagnoses of mood disorder and schizophrenia, although it was also found that patients with a diagnosis of alcohol-related substance-use disorder presented a high risk for suicidal behaviour (Schlebusch et al., 1986). It was established that ward milieu and staff changes might have influenced suicide rates in these patients who had actually attempted or committed suicide whilst being in-patients, but that, oddly enough, patients very seldom committed suicide when they were severely depressed. Other mood indicators of suicidal behaviour were sadness, heightened feelings of anxiety, anger, guilt and shame (Schlebusch et al., 1986).

Severely depressed people tend to have very low energy levels and their functioning is slowed down. Consequently, they often cannot reach the cognitive or physical levels required for suicide. The danger period occurs following treatment, when there is an increase in motivation levels as the depression begins to lift. South African findings are consistent with those of other researchers who have recognised that most suicide attempts occur when depressed hospitalised patients go home for weekend leave, or soon after discharge (Schlebusch et al., 1986; Sue, Sue & Sue, 2000). This suggests that there is a high risk when suicidal individuals (especially those who have been treated for psychological disorders and depression) are considered to have responded to treatment but have not recovered completely. For example, in depression the acute phase after starting treatment can last for about six to twelve weeks during which a response to treatment usually occurs (Schlebusch, 2005b). The continuation of treatment during the remission phase should last for about four to nine months to prevent relapse and to prevent recurrence and aim for recovery. Treatment should be maintained for one year or more. Obviously, the various disorders associated with suicidal behaviour respond differentially to treatment and require different periods of treatment.

Fig. 9.1 illustrates the various phases during the treatment of a depressed suicidal person as discussed above and on page 103. I have chosen depression as an example because it is so commonly associated with suicidal behaviour. The top part of Fig. 9.1 starts by depicting a non-suicidal person who develops symptoms of depression, goes into remission following treatment and eventually recovers, which is the ultimate aim of treatment. The middle part illustrates the process of the suicidal person moving from the depths of despair (when treatment starts) by showing a response to treatment (usually within six to twelve weeks). This is one of the more dangerous periods for acting on suicidal thoughts because the person is responding to treatment and has to face the reality of the situation (that is, deal with the original trigger factors for suicidal behaviour). The problem is that many therapists don't move beyond this stage by assisting the patient with problem-solving, communication and stress-management skills and how to make any necessary critical life changes to prevent a relapse and recurrence of the suicidal behaviour. The treatment phases are depicted at the bottom of Fig. 9.1. In order to prevent a relapse, the treatment should continue for at least four to nine months, and to prevent a recurrence of the depression there should be maintenance treatment for one or more years.

As found by international studies, the DPS work has shown that in South Africa depression is commonly found in general practice, with the symptoms occurring in a significant percentage of patients seen by general practitioners (Cassimjee & Pillay, 2000). This is elaborated on in Chapter ten. Depressed patients presenting at the

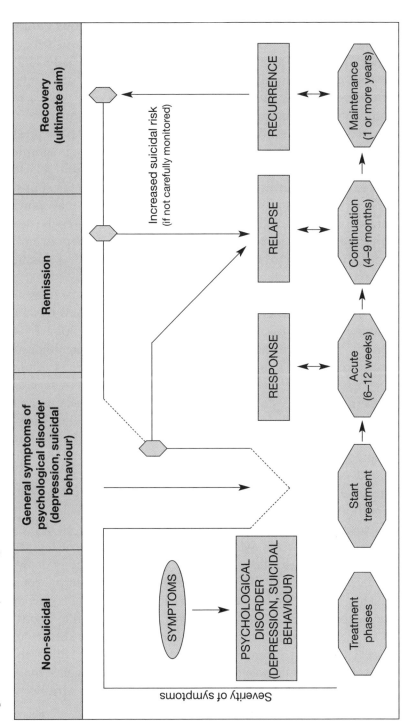

Fig. 9.1 Suicide risk following treatment

doctor's surgery often fall into a rather heterogeneous group and frequently lack the clear-cut symptoms of the various subgroups described in the professional literature (Kaplan & Sadock, 1995). For example, the patients seen in general practice are frequently unaware that they are depressed. They may present with a whole spectrum of somatic, psychological, social, occupational and other problems, but they infrequently complain directly of depression. Instead, they often describe an array of related symptoms, including anxiety, sleep disturbances, pessimism, guilt, self-doubt, appetite disturbances, weight loss or gain, lack of interest in social and/or family life, loss of libido, and so on. They may, however, present with an actual physical problem: in such cases the general practitioner should be alert to the possibility of depression and, once diagnosed, to any possible underlying medical conditions that could be associated with the depression.

Cultural and subcultural influences on prevalence rates are as yet unresolved. There is some evidence that cultural factors can modify the expression of depressive symptomatology in some groups resulting in under-diagnosis of the condition, although the exact nature of this remains unclear (Schlebusch, 1990b). For example, in some traditional beliefs in external forces such as the supernatural, ancestors or humans employing supernatural means are believed to be responsible for misfortune, and shyness, for example, could be displayed instead of more usual symptoms of depression. This could obfuscate the diagnosis of depression and could contribute to it being overlooked as a disorder requiring treatment. A sobering indication of the incidence of depression in South Africa is evidenced in a study on attitudes of black adolescents towards suicide and the prevalence of depression amongst adolescents (Mayekiso, 1995). Up to 38% of the sample was diagnosed as mildly depressed, 20% as moderately depressed and 13% as severely depressed. Only 29% of the sample could be diagnosed as being not depressed. These findings are an increasing cause for concern, especially in view of our research opinions that stress and mood disorders (which have been shown to be associated with so many other somatic and mental health problems as well as with suicidal behaviour), are one of the greatest maladies of our time and often go undetected in South African youth (Schlebusch, 2000c).

PRIOR SUICIDAL BEHAVIOUR AND SUBSTANCE ABUSE

A history of prior suicidal behaviour as well as a history of substance abuse as co-morbid factors in suicidal behaviour are causes for disquiet because of their demonstrated aetiological importance (Schlebusch, 1995a, 1998a; Schlebusch & Bosch, 2000). As emphasised earlier, my research has confirmed that easy access to method does not only include alcohol and household poisons, but also OTC substances (especially analgesics) and drugs that are available only on medical prescription, especially benzodiazepines and anti-depressants (Schlebusch, 1987, 1998a; Schlebusch, Vawda & Bosch, 2003). These substances are often methods of choice in overdose or abuse, for adults and youngsters alike, in their attempts to cope with the ravages of stress.

A serious co-morbid factor in South Africa is alcohol abuse. In this regard, figures are consistently high. In the late 1990s 45% of suicide victims had high levels of alcohol concentration in their blood, that is, a mean BAC of 0.16 g/100 ml (WHO, 1999b). In all, 15% of the deceased had a BAC of 0.2 g or more per 100 ml. Recent NIMSS figures show that alcohol was a factor in about one-third of all suicides (BACs were positive in 36.8%), and of that group 27% were at or above 0.05 g/100 ml (Donson & Van Niekerk, 2002). Some of the latest figures available generally support such findings (Matzopoulos, Cassim & Seedat, 2003).

Another astonishing fact is that in 2001 of all transport-related deaths 51.9% had elevated BACs, of whom 91% had levels in excess of 0.05 g/100 ml (Donson & Van Niekerk, 2002). In 2001 in almost 50% of South African deaths, generally due to homicide and motor vehicle accidents, BACs of 0.08 g/100 ml were present. In just over one-quarter of deaths from suicide or other 'accidents' BAC levels of 0.8 g/100 ml were present. In addition, in non-fatal injuries 61% of patients admitted to trauma units in several major South African centres had a mean BAC level of 0.12 g/100 ml. Furthermore, there is a significant relationship between BAC and injured pedestrians, and research has also shown that in some instances of violence, 74% of cases showed alcohol positive levels (Parry, 2000). Blood alcohol levels in mortality figures remain high in South Africa (Matzopoulos, Cassim & Seedat, 2003).

SOUTH AFRICA'S HISTORICAL LEGACY

It is clear that South Africa's anguished legacy of apartheid has not only severely traumatised its citizens because of human rights violations (Pillay & Schlebusch, 1997), but has left a heritage of other stress-related psychological problems with potential suicidal implications (Schlebusch & Bosch, 2002). Additional factors that combine to elevate stress levels with the potential to cause suicidal behaviour are:

- high prevalence rates of violence and trauma (McKendrick & Hoffman, 1990; Schlebusch & Bosch, 2002);
- the influences of First World forces in an internationally less isolated, post-apartheid South Africa;
- socio-economic difficulties including high unemployment levels;
- high expectations that are not always realised following political and other transformation;
- acculturation; and
- economic pressures (Schlebusch, Vawda & Bosch, 2003).

All of these factors, if not timeously addressed, combine to produce a breeding ground for potential suicidality. An analysis of increased suicides amongst Coloured males in Paarl further highlights the importance of culture in understanding suicide, especially in a post-apartheid socio-historical context rather than as a manifestation of individual psychopathology (Laubscher, 2003). Cross-cultural awareness and sensitivity are indispensible in understanding suicidal behaviour in a country such as South Africa, with its diverse cultures (Schlebusch, 1995c, 1996; Schlebusch, Wessels & Rzadkowolsky, 1990).

SUICIDAL BEHAVIOUR AND SOMATIC CO-MORBIDITY

Although the relationship between disease and suicidal behaviour has been well investigated elsewhere in the world (Lönnqvist, 2001; Stenager & Stenager, 2000), this has not been the case in South Africa in the past, where knowledge was sparse, especially with regard to chronic or potentially life-threatening diseases. For example, suicidal behaviour in patients with potentially life-threatening diseases such as some cancers and HIV/Aids (which are very prevalent conditions) has been a poorly researched area in South Africa. Recently more definitive data have been steadily gathered in this respect (Noor Mahomed, Schlebusch & Bosch, 2003; Schlebusch, 2004; Schlebusch & Noor Mahomed, 2004;

Schlebusch, Schweitzer & Bosch, 1998). I have discussed depression, suicidal behaviour and medical patients earlier in this chapter and in Chapter eight, but I specifically refer to HIV/Aids and cancer here because they are so prevalent in this country. The disruption caused by such chronic diseases can bring with it:
- fears of abandonment (real or perceived);
- social stigmatisation;
- guilt;
- role reversals;
- thwarted developmental needs;
- concerns about becoming a burden to significant others and to society;
- forced alteration and sometimes termination of relationships;
- life conflicts about productivity versus stagnation and failure to achieve, which can lead to feelings of personal impoverishment;
- withdrawal from intimacy; and
- excessive dependency or premature disengagement from society (Schlebusch, 1999b; Schlebusch & Noor Mahomed, 2004).

CANCER

One in four South Africans will develop cancer and one in two is likely to know someone who has cancer (Schlebusch, 1999b). Although considerable research has been done on cancer patients and suicidal behaviour elsewhere (Lester, 2000; Lönnqvist, 2001; Stenager & Stenager, 2000), knowledge about the prevalence of suicidal behaviour in cancer patients in South Africa is limited, but is likely to be significant. Local research on cancer patients confirms as myth that cancer patients never engage in suicidal behaviour (Noor Mohamed, Schlebusch & Bosch, 2003; Schlebush & Noor Mahomed, 2004). For example, in a sample of adult black South African women with cervical cancer (in both palliative and radical oncology treatment groups), the following factors were found:
- significant depression;
- anxiety;
- stress;
- hopelessness/helplessness;
- anxious preoccupation about their disease;

- poor current or delayed social support;
- feelings of being a burden to their significant others;
- beliefs that they would be better off dead;
- perceptions that they were stigmatised by society or that their communities suspected them of being HIV-positive; and
- suppressed anger (Noor Mohamed, Schlebusch & Bosch, 2003).

Other variables that contributed to stress included:
- the belief that cancer means a slow, unbearably painful death;
- the perception that before it kills, cancer mutilates; and
- that cancer (especially cancer of the cervix) in some black patients is seen as an unclean ('polluting') disease.

Not surprisingly, more patients in the palliative compared to the radical treatment group tended towards suicidal ideation with serious intent. Other features of the palliative group were that:
- they had significantly delayed seeking medical treatment and had used alternate treatments in the form of faith and traditional healers before coming to the hospital; and
- when they left the hosiptal for home-based care they were aware that they were going home to die, resulting in many expressing a sense of despair, hopelessness and a belief that traditional, religious and medical treatments had failed them.

Overall, most patients coped inadequately with their disease and its management. They were deemed to be a high risk group for suicidal behaviour, who needed to be timeously identified for appropriate psychological intervention. In line with other research findings (Hahn, Dunn & Helperin, 2004), local studies show that depression can be a dehabilitating condition, and that the symptoms can overlap with cancer and its oncological treatment. In a sample of cancer patients a significant percentage presented with depression.

Local findings are consistent with national and international reports that:

- cancer patients are at increased risk for suicide;
- the incidence of suicidal behaviour in cancer patients ranges from being two to ten times as frequent (or more in some cases) as for the general population;
- many cancer patients hold suicidal behaviour as an option, often to retain some sense of control;
- the frequency of passive suicidal behaviour in the form of behaviours such as 'accidental' overdosing, and the degree to which non-compliance or treatment refusal represents ISDB or a sub-intentioned decision to end life, is unknown; and
- the actual incidence of suicidal behaviour (fatal and non-fatal) in cancer sufferers is likely probably underestimated, especially because families are reluctant to report death by suicide in these circumstances or because of research limitations that skew data on actual suicidal behaviour in these patients (Noor Mahomed, Schlebusch & Bosch, 2003; Schlebusch, 1999b; Schlebusch & Noor Mahomed, 2004).

The factors implicated in suicidal behaviour in cancer patients include:
- significant depression;
- anxiety about terminal illness and death and dying issues;
- emotional stress/distress relating to the diagnosis of cancer;
- difficulty in making treatment decisions;
- undergoing oncology treatment;
- the perception of being unable to cope;
- lack of social support, which is then not available to reduce or buffer the negative impact of the disease;
- poor external control of suicidal behaviour because of a lack of appropriate social support, which can significantly reduce the risk of suicide in cancer patients;
- the nature of significant others' responses and their support for cancer patients at risk of suicidal behaviour; and
- the socio-cultural context within which cancer occurs, given that social attitudes and cultural beliefs about cancer can profoundly affect how patients perceive themselves, their disease, their future and their will to live (Noor Mahomed, Schlebusch & Bosch, 2003; Schlebusch, 1999b; Schlebusch & Noor Mahomed, 2004).

In these patients, their negative perceptions and dysfunctional cognitions have been shown to be crucial factors in creating inordinate stress. With reference to this point, in a large study on stress and cancer, I found the following major stressors, which were statistically calculated and arranged according to their importance as stressors (that is, they were subjected to rank order analysis in which maximum weighted responses were calculated):

- the diagnosis of the disease itself (100%);
- psychological complications (91%);
- physical implications including pain and suffering (78%);
- relationship problems (52%);
- concerns about the future (35%);
- financial, employment and unemployment problems (26%);
- side effects of the oncology treatment and treatment procedures (17%); and
- fear of death (4%) (Schlebusch, 1999b).

Given this last point, local research points out that it is not so much the fear of death itself that always presents as a suicide risk factor, but rather how the disease and its other sequelae are managed. If a patient is left to face the disease alone or if this is the patient's perception, it creates a sense of abandonment that is critical to the development of hopelessness and premature death by suicide.

HIV/AIDS

Sub-Saharan Africa is experiencing an HIV/Aids pandemic (Schlebusch, Schweitzer & Bosch, 1998; *South African Health Review*, 2003/2004). Estimates are that in sub-Saharan Africa about 2.3 million people have died from Aids, some 26.6 million people are infected, and the main transmission of the disease is heterosexual. More people became infected than ever before during 2003, and in southern Africa the epidemic appears out of control, with infection rates in pregnant women being very high in some areas. It has been estimated that 30% of the world's HIV-positive people can be found in southern Africa, despite the fact that less than 2% of the world's population live in this region. The region includes South Africa and, in particular, the province of KwaZulu-Natal where much research is being undertaken. Although, as for the rest of the world, accurate figures for South Africa vary, those figures that are available have pointed to the province of KwaZulu-Natal as potentially having one of the highest known incidences of HIV/Aids infection in South Africa (Lindegger & Wood, 1995). In 1995, the highest infections seem to have occurred in the 20 to 24 year age group (43.3%) and in the 25 to 29 year age group (46.6%) in KwaZulu-Natal (Lindegger & Wood, 1995). By 2002, the 25 to 29 year old age group was still the largest infected population group, with more females than males being infected (*South African Health Review*, 2003/2004). HIV/Aids is having a profound impact on households and the private sector (*South African Health Review*, 2002).

About 5.3 million people in South Africa were living with HIV/Aids at the end of 2002, and the national prevalence amongst pregnant women was about 26.5%, although it is much higher in certain areas such as KwaZulu-Natal, that is, 36.5% of patients seen in particular ante-natal clinics are HIV-positive (Schlebusch & Noor Mahomed, 2004; *South African Health Review*, 2003/2004). As a further example, findings of a study reported in 2005 that:

- 4 000 educators (teachers) had died of HIV/Aids in South Africa;
- 12.5% of educators were HIV-positive;
- 21.7% of all people living in the province of KwaZulu-Natal were HIV-positive, this being the highest prevalence in the country (Bolowana & Khan, *The Mercury*, 2005).

The same study also reported that 55% of the teachers surveyed suffered from high stress levels.

As in other chronic disease, the correlation between HIV/Aids and suicide has been under-researched in South Africa, although certain ad hoc studies have shown a high suicide risk for this group (Schlebusch & Noor Mahomed, 2004). There is a burgeoning of research outside South Africa documenting the relationship between suicidal behaviour in individuals diagnosed with HIV/Aids. This has found an increased likelihood of suicidal behaviour for these individuals (Lester, 2000). In the past, some researchers have reported a 36 times higher risk for suicidal behaviour for HIV/Aids-infected people than for the general population (Marzuk et al., 1988; Van Dyk, 2001), although with better psychological and medical interventions, the situation has now changed. Figures do, however, vary considerably. In gay and bisexual men, HIV has been linked to self-harm in deliberate attempts to become infected with HIV as a form of suicidal behaviour as well as other risk-taking sexual behaviour in those who have suffered bereavement as a result of Aids (Catalan, 2000). In one study, men with Aids were found to be seventeen times more likely to die from suicide than men of the same age from the general population (Kizer et al., 1988). Another found that nearly half of HIV-infected individuals made suicide attempts within three months of notification of seropositivity, and about two-thirds made at least one attempt within the first year after notification (Rundell, Kyle & Brown, 1992). A South African study from the eastern Cape suggests that there is a connection between the rising suicide rates in that region and the increasing prevalence of HIV/Aids, which is largest amongst blacks (Meel, 2003). The study analysed mortality statistics from 1996 to 2000 and found that:

- deaths from hanging increased from 16% to 24% (mostly males in the 20 to 30 year age group);
- deaths from poisoning increased from 4% to 28%; and
- deaths from gunshot wounds increased from 14% to 25%.

Our research (Schlebusch & Noor Mahomed, 2004) confirms other people's findings (Kelly, Raphael & Judd, 1998; Perry, Jacobsberg & Fishman, 1990) that suicidal behaviour may show different patterns through the progression of HIV/Aids. Increased risk of suicide is associated with:

- antibody testing and learning of a seropositive status (one of the greatest risks might be within the first three to six months after diagnosis of infection with HIV);
- the diagnosis of full-blown Aids; and
- in later stages of the disease, which may be characterised by pain and dementia.

A disturbing correlation has also been noted between HIV testing (that is, even before the results are known) and suicidal ideation or suicidal behaviour. Recent research has also found that fear of partner infidelity and its link with HIV/Aids has been associated with suicidal behaviour (Schlebusch & Noor Mahomed, 2004; Van Dyk, 2001). This finding is discussed in more detail later in this chapter.

Various DPS studies have pointed out that suicidal behaviour in the early stages of HIV infection in individuals who are still relatively healthy and who are not significantly incapacitated (as distinguished from the late stage when disability is severe and death from Aids seems imminent) has been described as 'pre-emptive suicide', where the person attempts to avoid the fearful prospects of life with Aids (Beckerman, 1995; Schlebusch & Noor Mahomed, 2004). Such suicidal behaviour may be stimulated by a self-labelling process (Siegel & Meyer, 1999; Thoits, 1985). This occurs when the infected persons begin to apply to themselves various frightening stereotypical images of living with Aids. Such images have the potential to disrupt a previously envisioned life course and can result in a crisis that distorts the person's self and world perceptions. In the process he or she foresees a protracted struggle to cope with the disease and experiences intense fears about future suffering and disfigurement. Relational problems might also arise that can be overwhelming, resulting in suicidal ideation or suicidal behaviour (Schlebusch & Noor Mahomed, 2004; Siegel & Meyer, 1999). Several studies have also documented that a history of psychopathology and past suicidal behaviour are closely associated with suicidal risk in HIV-infected individuals, and that a person's pre-existing psychopathology may adversely affect his or her ability to tolerate stress and so increase suicidality in HIV-diagnosed individuals (Frierson & Lippmann, 1988; Gala et al., 1992; Kelly, Raphael & Judd, 1998; O'Dowd, Biderman & McKegney, 1993; Rundell, Kyle & Brown, 1992).

Some experts have pointed to various reasons why suicidal behaviour might occur during the high-risk periods in the lives of HIV/Aids-infected individuals (Schlebusch & Noor Mahomed, 2004; Sherr, 1995). For example:
- suicidal behaviour at the time of diagnosis might be triggered by factors such as the way in which testing for HIV was carried out, a lack of social support at the time, the individual's inability to cope, and inadequate emotional resources;
- suicidal behaviour in the later phase of Aids is usually associated with deterioration of health, physical illness associated with pain, disability or disfigurement, a decrease in the quality of life, and a feeling that sufferers at least want to control the way in which they die (Pugh, 1995); and

- those whose loved ones die as a result of suicide are particularly vulnerable to committing suicide themselves, especially if they themselves are also HIV-positive or have full-blown Aids (Schlebusch & Noor Mahomed, 2004).

Furthermore, it seems that:
- anxiety, depression and suicidal ideation, which might be very high at the time of HIV testing, tend to drop later regardless of the results of the HIV tests if the person comes to terms with the facts while still fairly healthy (Pugh, 1995); and
- suicidal behaviour is often related to associated stress and uncertainty (Schlebusch & Noor Mahomed, 2004).

Consequently, the need for appropriate pre- and post-HIV test counselling cannot be sufficiently emphasised (Schlebusch & Noor Mahomed, 2004; Van Dyk, 2001).

South African hospital-based studies have found not only that there is a considerably higher risk for suicidal behaviour in HIV-positive patients compared to the general population, but emphasise that sexually transmitted diseases have always been stigmatised in society because they are widely regarded by uninformed people as being the result of sexual excess, low moral character and uncleanliness (Noor Mahomed & Karim, 2000; Schlebusch & Noor Mahomed, 2004). HIV/Aids, being no exception, carries various other unique stressors that include:
- its association with other stigmatised groups such as gays and drug users;
- the fact that persons diagnosed with HIV/Aids are often young and face major developmental task disruptions forced upon them by the disease;
- the fact that the disease is incurable, requires lifelong changes in behaviour and threatens a person's most intimate relationships;
- self-imposed withdrawal or preoccupation with physical symptoms;
- interpersonal problems ranging from blaming the partner to homicidal rage towards the person suspected of infecting him or her;

- the social stigma and fear associated with the contagious aspects of the disease, which can cause others to avoid social and physical contact with the infected person;
- the moral disapproval and negative societal attitudes;
- the fact that the entire continuum of the disease (right from exposure through infection to diagnosis) is characterised by extreme uncertainty resulting in marked psychological distress;
- the fact that the infected persons are vulnerable to feelings of guilt, self-hatred, rejection and ostracism, as well as to the commonly recognised feelings of fear, anxiety, depression and anger that accompany life-threatening diseases; and
- the fact that many patients are aware from the experience of watching others who have succumbed to Aids that the disease is associated with neurological and neuropsychiatric morbidity, and severe chronic physical disability, which sometimes results in suicidal ideation or suicidal behaviour.

Furthermore, as with other chronic or potentially life-threatening diseases (Schlebusch & Ruggieri, 1996), the socio-cultural context in which the patient is embedded and in which he or she experiences the reality of being infected with HIV/Aids plays an important role in living with the disease (Noor Mahomed & Karim, 2000; Schlebusch & Noor Mahomed, 2004). For example, in certain societies in South Africa, HIV/Aids is such a dreaded disease that infected individuals are sometimes still victimised, subtly alienated, overtly shunned or even killed when they publicly disclose their HIV/Aids status.

In some research samples, work-related stress factors, especially the fear of being dismissed from work because of HIV/Aids, have been found to be major stressors (Schlebusch & Noor Mahomed, 2004). While a considerable percentage of patients appeared to deny their diagnosis, others believed that they were in a medical crisis but failed to recognise that they were also in a psychosocial crisis resulting in high stress levels. South African researchers have also pointed out that in certain cultural groups in South Africa, HIV/Aids is conceptualised as a mystical force that diminishes resistance to diseases and also creates conditions of 'bad luck', 'misfortune', 'disagreeableness' and 'repulsiveness', resulting in a dislike of the person by others (Noor Mahomed & Karim, 2000). In these situations the affected person is socially isolated and has to speak softly and quickly, or only when necessary, and eat little, all of which are suggestive of a 'social death' experience (Noor Mahomed & Karim, 2000). These researchers emphasise the fact that their patients felt that because of the way their condition was regarded culturally, it was best to be treated by a traditional healer; it is, therefore, not surprising that a significant percentage of the suicidal HIV/Aids-infected patients in their study indicated a desire to consult such a healer. The need for cultural awareness and sensitivity in the treatment and prevention of suicidal behaviour is further discussed in Chapter ten.

Another study on the psychological considerations in the management of HIV/Aids-patients with polytrauma, revealed that patients with polytrauma may also present with symptoms of a cognitive disorder (post-concussional disorder due to head trauma), or with symptoms due to substance-related disorders (Schlebusch, Schweitzer & Bosch, 1998). Patients with HIV/Aids who are immunocompromised and subject to several disorders related to the CNS can complicate this symptom index. Many of these patients present with a constellation of cognitive, motor and behaviour changes characteristic of sub-cortical dementia (Van Gorp & Cummings, 1995). Psychomotor slowing, difficulty in concentrating, poor memory retrieval as well as problems with mood and with visuospatial skills are often initial features. The presentation is consistent with early involvement of the thalamus and basal ganglia. It has been argued that the likely involvement of subcortical and limbic structures suggests that psychological disorders might be partly attributed to a biological underpinning (Schlebusch, Schweitzer & Bosch, 1998). These complications as risk factors for suicidal behaviour require further research.

A retrospective analysis was recently conducted of the demographic and clinical data of the patients who presented at a general hospital with suicidal behaviour (suicide attempts) related to HIV/Aids and who were seen over a period of twelve months (Schlebusch & Noor Mohamed, 2004). The sample consisted of 54 patients (that is, about 10%) out of a total of 554 suicidal patients, of whom only two-thirds were actually confirmed to be HIV-positive. Their ages ranged from 25 to 45 years (the mean age was 37.5

years). They all had some level of formal education, with the average patient having at least a primary school education. Two-thirds were females and the overall ethnic distribution was Indian (22%), black (76%) and white (2%). Most were unemployed, that is, 67% of the males and 89% of the females. Only 50% of the males and 64% of the females were married, while about 30% of the males and 20% of the females were cohabiting. The rest were living alone, being either divorced or widowed. Most patients (that is, 61 of the males and 61 of the females) suffered from depression associated with partner relational problems or adjustment disorders. The reasons given by the patients for their suicide attempts were:
- partner infidelity from which arose fear of contracting HIV/Aids (all of these patients were females who were not HIV-positive);
- lack of social support;
- fear of disclosure and stigmatisation;
- a desire to end life owing to their disease;
- social problems;
- a lack of accommodation;
- unemployment; and
- substance dependence.

Although they were willing to discuss their suicide attempts, a common feature among the patients who were diagnosed with HIV/Aids was that very few volunteered information about their status, despite their medical records and referrals documenting it. They appeared to experience difficulty in openly discussing their status and the impact it had on their lives. Fears are further fuelled by patients who allege that they are sometimes refused treatment by professionals; this has given rise to press reports that HIV-related complaints will be fast-tracked by the relevant authorities (Kalideen, *The Natal Mercury*, 2005).

In clinical practice and research it has been noticed that among the non-diagnosed (well) patients who have HIV/Aids-positive partners, an increasingly common pattern of stress, depression and suicidal behaviour related to the HIV/Aids pandemic appears to be emerging. In South Africa, in the general population, infidelity of a spouse is now a commonly cited reason for suicidal behaviour.

It appears that in the past women in certain groups may have tolerated infidelity (albeit reluctantly), provided that their partners did not abandon them or threaten to separate or divorce them or stop financial support. Now, however, an increasing number of women are reflecting suicidal behaviour related to their concerns and fears specifically regarding being infected with sexually transmitted diseases, especially if they consider these potentially life-threatening, such as HIV/Aids (Schlebusch & Noor Mahomed, 2004). This also has implications for extended suicide and family murder, which is tragically illustrated by the recent newspaper report that was mentioned earlier in this chapter (Ndaba, *The Natal Mercury*, 2005).

KEY POINTS

Some of the chief factors contributing to suicidal behaviour are:
- problematic family dynamics, such as interpersonal difficulties, financial problems and problems related to schooling, as well as psychiatric disorders – especially depression;
- substance abuse (including alcohol and household poisons as well as OTC and prescription drugs);
- somatic diseases such as some cancers and HIV/Aids.

CHAPTER TEN

Management and prevention

AS DISCUSSED IN Chapter nine, it is generally recognised that suicidal behaviour is a highly complex phenomenon that cannot readily be attributed to any single cause as it involves intricate interactions between many variables (Schlebusch, 1990a; Van Heeringen, Hawton & Williams, 2000; Wasserman, 2001b). As such, we know that suicidal behaviour is a process. Stress-diathesis models (Mann et al., 1999) and stress-vulnerability models (Wasserman, 2001b) have been proposed in order to understand and explain the development and dynamics of the suicidal process. These models hold that genetic make-up as well as an acquired susceptibility can contribute to an individual's predisposition to suicidal behaviour, and also include a person's life experiences, psychopathology, and chronic illnesses as well as acute and chronic stress (that is, biological, psychosocial, cultural and environmental factors are involved).

There is extensive international literature on the management of suicidal behaviour and there are many excellent treatment and prevention guidelines (Hawton & Van Heeringen, 2000; Kosky et al., 1998; Vijayakumar, 2003; Wasserman, 2001a). Given this, I will follow the same principles espoused elsewhere in this book and focus more specifically on South African research. To start with then, not only mental health experts but also family practitioners and other primary health-care workers who usually have ongoing contact with patients can play a critical role in the prevention and management of suicidal behaviour (Cassimjee & Pillay, 2000). As long ago as 1985, I argued that South African primary health-care practitioners (especially medical doctors) should be alert to suicidal intent in their patients. This is because, as pointed out in Chapter nine, a significant preponderance of suicidal patients consult health-care workers (often with somatic symptoms and masked suicidal ideation) in the days, weeks or months preceding the suicidal act (Schlebusch, 1985a). As we move forward in the twenty-first century, little seems to have changed in South Africa in this respect (Schlebusch, 2004).

What is needed is an astute diagnosis of underlying psychopathology and its appropriate treatment (including medication and, where necessary, hospitalisation or referral for psychological/psychiatric help) by suitably trained health-care professionals. Treatment guidelines are regularly updated and made available, especially for some of the most common co-morbid conditions including depression (Lasich & Schlebusch, 1999; Schlebusch, 1990b).

In addition, research has shown that suicidal individuals often appear to:
- access only limited ways of dealing with their problems; and
- tend to slip into a cognitive rut, from which it is difficult for them to see any alternatives to their intended suicidal act (Kienhorst, De Wilde & Diekstra, 1995; Schlebusch et al., 1986).

Consequently, the central role of perception in both children (Pillay, 1995b) and adults, especially the perception of entrapment (that is, being closed in with no escape), is an important additional factor to consider in the suicidal person's feelings of hopelessness and in his or her suicidal risk profile. This has been well demonstrated by various authorities (Van Heeringen, Hawton & Williams, 2000). In another publication I have discussed extensively the role of making a perceptual shift to achieve psychological self-empowerment (Schlebusch, 2000c). Suffice it to say here, that research has shown that positive perceptions lead to positive thought patterns, emotions and self-empowering behaviour. Our work has repeatedly demonstrated that from a psychological perspective, treatment, rather than being based on an adventitious approach, can be more usefully designed around an *ad rem* organisational system (a systematic approach) that also involves structured psychotherapy, especially cognitive behaviour therapy which is often lacking when suicidal patients are treated (Schlebusch, 1990a, 1990b, 2000b, 2005a, b). I have developed a useful organisational system that is presented later in this chapter (Schlebusch, 2005b).

Follow-up psychotherapy or other treatment attendance after discharge from hospital (to assist with intervention decisions in non-fatal suicide attempts) is poor in South Africa, as is also the case internationally. Patients may keep their first out-patient appointment, but not subsequent ones. For example, a recent study at a South African general hospital found that only 43.5% of all patients kept such follow-up appointments (Pillay, Wassenaar & Kramers, 2004). The authors of this research have emphasised the importance of maximising the utilisation of initial consultations. In this regard, I have emphasised the value of structured psychotherapy, especially cognitive behaviour therapy, in which a primary goal is to increase the psychological comfort of the patient in order to reduce the need of the person to move away from unacceptable psychological pain by embracing suicidal behaviour as a solution (Lasich & Schlebusch, 1999; Schlebusch et al., 1986).

I have also found that to address the problem of management, it is essential to establish a protocol regarding the referral of suicidal patients, especially within large hospital structures. For example, the DPS research group did so in collaboration with the professor and head of the Department of Medicine at the medical school where it is based and in the affiliated relevant teaching hospitals (Schlebusch, Vawda & Bosch, 2003). I have explained elsewhere that this was done because of the significant demands that suicidal patients make on the emergency services and the Department of Medicine's clinical service load and hospital bed occupancy. Initially, all suicidal patients referred to these hospitals are seen by the trauma unit or by the emergency services. They are admitted to the relevant hospital by the Department of Medicine and are treated as a medical emergency by the staff. Once medically stabilised, these patients are referred for clinical psychological or psychiatric evaluation and treatment. It is now routine hospital policy within our clinical services delivery system that a mental health-care professional sees all patients who are admitted to hospital with suicidal behaviour once they are medically stable. This usually occurs within 24 to 48 hours of admission, and again prior to discharge. The end result of this policy is that patients and their families can be psychologically and/or psychiatrically managed more effectively. It also serves to provide a substantial data base (discussed in Chapter eleven) for research purposes aimed at seeking more effective solutions for preventing suicidal behaviour in the first place (Schlebusch, 2004).

The highly complex question of ethical and legal issues in suicidology raises a more controversial point in the management of suicidal patients in South Africa. An international group of experts on suicidology, in which I was included as the South African representative, critically examined a number of related issues such as standards of care, responsibility and failure of care, failure to diagnose appropriately, malpractice, euthanasia and assisted suicide (Leenaars, Betancourt et al., 2000; Leenaars, Cantor et al., 2000; Leenaars et al., 2001). At the same time, other international work focused on providing a framework for a better understanding of assisted suicide (especially physician-assisted suicide) and its legal and ethical implications (Snyder & Caplan, 2002). A detailed discussion of these considerations is not possible here, but what is important to note is that there are current debates in medico-legal and suicidology circles in South Africa where euthanasia (mercy killing) and assisted suicide are presently not legal (McQuoid-Mason, 1995; Sneiderman & McQuoid-Mason, 2000). In essence, assisted suicide can take several forms. These are explained in, amongst others:

- 'how to' and 'advice' publications that give step-by-step explanations on how to end a human life (Humphry, 1991);
- sites on the Internet that give detailed instructions on different ways to terminate life;
- 'death with dignity' proposals by physicians who help dying patients to end their lives (that is, physician-assisted suicides); and so on.

Some authorities even distinguish between 'rational' suicide (for example, suicide undertaken by the irreversibly handicapped or terminally ill), and 'emotional' suicide (as seen, for example, in depressed people). Other examples of assisted suicide can be found in the actions of retired pathologist, Dr J. Kevorkian (nicknamed 'Dr Death' by the media) of Detroit, Michigan (in the United States of America), who advised his patients on the use of an apparatus that he invented to self-administer a lethal combination of substances (Henry, 1991; McCarthy, *The Natal Mercury*, 1991). In South Africa, a man pulled a plastic bag over his terminally ill wife's head and subsequently told police he believed that assisted suicide was legal (*The Natal Mercury*, 1991: 4). Assisted suicide (especially physician-assisted suicide) has found support in several circles, and a number of scientific works have produced a good framework for understanding and debating the issues around assisted and rational suicide (Snyder & Caplan, 2002; Werth, 1999), as well as for transcultural issues and suicide, and euthanasia and physician-assisted suicide in the elderly (De Leo, 2001). The position in South Africa, however, is that assisted suicide remains illegal.

In addition to a variety of private and public clinical services, there are professional associations and support groups that assist with the treatment and prevention of suicidal behaviour and help those who have suffered psychologically because of such behaviour. Survivors of Loved Ones' Suicide (SOLOS), which operates in Durban, is committed to the care and support of people who have lost loved ones to suicide. The South African Depression and Anxiety Support Group is a countrywide organisation that operates a network of support groups and outreach projects and also makes resource booklets available. Lifeline is another well known countrywide organisation in South Africa that offers counselling services in this regard. In addition, the International Association for Suicide Prevention (IASP) is represented in South Africa. The IASP recommends its own suicide prevention programmes and arranges bi-annual world congresses on the management and prevention of suicide. Such groups and organisations (along with a wide network of primary health-care professionals and local hospital facilities) are valuable partners as part of prevention and treatment programmes.

PAIN MANAGEMENT AND ANALGESIC ABUSE

Despite the fact that persistent pain (which patients give as a major reason for their analgesic abuse) is one of the most frequent medical complaints, it is difficult to treat because of different aetiologies and individualised pain response. For example, a distinction can be made between acute and chronic pain, which has implications for clinical management (Lindegger, 1990). In the aftermath of trauma-related pain there may well be a psychogenic or secondary gain component for patients because of litigation, compensation, or other reasons, which might complicate effective treatment of the pain before any legal settlements have been made (Thompson, 1985b). In addition to these categories, there are two more broad groupings: nociceptive pain (resulting from tissue damage) and neurophatic pain (resulting from nerve damage). It has been well demonstrated that many patients adopt a sick role (abnormal illness behaviour) in order to avoid responsibilities such as work (Schlebusch, 1990a, 1991). To complicate things further, there is a growing acceptance that chronic pain in itself constitutes a complex illness. Along with headache, chronic lower back pain is one of the most common causes for work absenteeism (Thompson, 1985b).

One useful dimension of pain is that it serves as an early sensory warning of an incipient disease process (Thompson, 1985b). There are, however, a myriad subjective, immeasurable variables that affect pain and its perceived intensity, such as focus of attention on pain, emotional states, personality, previous experiences, and so on. Furthermore, pain can:

- serve as a symptom of and defence against psychological stress;
- be exacerbated by psychological factors;
- lead to somatic preoccupation;
- be associated with personal, social or financial secondary gain;
- provide justification for failing in interpersonal relationships (in fact, some people refer to their pain as an 'old friend');
- be affected by cultural, ethnic or religious affiliations;
- be affected by the sufferer's pain expression and family reactions to this;
- have different psychological and socio-cultural meanings;
- serve as desired punishment or atonement (the derivation of 'pain' is from the Latin *poena* and the Greek *poine*, meaning penalty or punishment);
- become a means of communication to receive attention;
- be associated with phantom limb and phantom pain phenomena; and so on (Thompson, 1985b).

It is evident that the experience of pain is not a simple stimulus-response variable. The perception of pain and reaction to it is multifactorial and involves several biopsychosocial variables

(Thompson, 1985b). It is important to note, however, that a psychological or psychiatric diagnosis for the patient who complains of pain should not preclude a concurrent medical diagnosis.

Research into the role of personality has suggested that introverted persons sometimes demonstrate a lower pain threshold than extroverted ones, and there is also evidence that individuals with high levels of neuroticism do not tolerate pain well (Bond, 1971). Personality assessments according to the Minnesota Multiphasic Personality Inventory (MMPI) have demonstrated a neurotic triad of elevated scores in chronic pain patients on the scales measuring hysteria, hypochondriasis and depression (Thompson, 1985b). This has been partly confirmed by my own findings in analgesic abusers. Evidence has shown that MMPI scores can change favourably if pain is appropriately treated (Thompson, 1985b). If introverted people with high levels of neuroticism experience pain as more severe and have a lower pain threshold, it would provide a stronger incentive for them to abuse analgesics (Murray, 1974).

Certainly some 'complaint behaviour' appears to be related to extroversion-introversion. Extroverted persons tend to communicate their symptoms more freely than introverted ones (Bond, 1971), so patients in pain who are introverted are more likely to resort to self-medication with analgesics and other substances. This particularly applies to those with hypochondriacal tendencies who withdraw from others, preferring to make their own decisions (Schlebusch & De Marigny, 1987). In fact, the hypochondriacal patient who selects pain as a 'ticket of admission' to the sick role (abnormal illness behaviour) often discourses extensively about perceived mistreatments rather than giving detailed responses to specific questions about self-medication (Thompson, 1985b). It is for this reason that it might be diagnostically more useful to discuss the substance abuser's pain, rather than probing actual consumption of analgesics or other substances directly, given the tendency of strong denial of abuse in these patients. In addition, the easy accessibility of OTC analgesics and their widespread coverage, presented in a quasi-scientific manner in advertising media, invites their abuse by such patients. The individuals' psychopathological profile, together with an inability to cope with increasing stress contributes to their escape into abuse as an acceptable method of dealing with psychological problems (Schlebusch, 1991; Schlebusch,

Lasich & Wessels, 1985). This further serves to confirm the importance of not only addressing the psychopathogenic basis of pain management and the concern about extensive commercial exploitation of OTC analgesics and other substances (Schlebusch, 1990a, 1991; Schlebusch & De Marigny, 1987), but also the importance of community education regarding the risks of these substances (Anandan & Matzke, 1981; Murray, 1981; Schlebusch, 1991; Schlebusch, Lasich & Wessels, 1985). The need for a greater awareness of self-destructive behaviour and of the associated psychopathological components involved can hardly be overstressed in treatment programmes, which should be multidisciplinary in nature.

In common with the presenting suicidal patients who overdose on analgesics, most of the psychiatric patients in my studies who abused analgesics also had a previous history of suicidal ideation or suicidal behaviour. This can be explained in part by the high prevalence of mood disorders (depression) found in these patients. However, the nature and direction of the correlation between suicidal behaviour and analgesic abuse is not always obvious, that is, whether the analgesic abuse is primarily an indirect suicidal method of choice, or whether such abuse contributes to suicidal behaviour in the first place.

An important finding in my studies quoted in Chapter eight, is that few patients were referred for or received psychiatric or psychological treatment specifically for their analgesic abuse. It appears, therefore, that analgesic abuse is a diagnosis that is either obfuscated by the patient's other psychiatric or psychological problems or that it is not entertained as warranting serious diagnostic consideration for purposes of psychological management. A few patients were diagnosed as fitting the criteria for polysubstance dependence, although analgesic abuse was not the focus of their treatment. The relatively high prevalence of mood disorders, polysubstance abuse (especially nicotine-, alcohol- and caffeine-related) and somatoform disorders in pain patients who abuse analgesics, clearly need to be addressed in a comprehensive treatment programme.

In addition, we found that alcohol abuse often featured in psychiatric patients who abuse analgesics, which further complicated the diagnostic picture (Nattrass, 1996; Schlebusch, 1991). The complications of alcohol abuse and its pharmacokinetic and pharmacodynamic interactions are well known (Goodwin, 1985). Our research showed that the alcohol abusers we studied were conditioned from an early age towards excessive analgesic use, which fits in with the importance of cultural variables at play in the aetiology and management of the analgesic abuse (Nattrass, 1996; Schlebusch, 1991). In addition, both the pain-related biomedical and psychiatric diagnosis-related reasons given by the psychiatric patients in our samples who abused analgesics are consistent with the concept that persistent pain can lead to frequent use of analgesics in patients with mental distress (Jacobsen & Hansen, 1989). This issue has been elaborated on in Chapter eight. Suffice it to say here, that because headache and pain present as prominent symptoms in many psychiatric disorders, patients are frequently referred for psychiatric consultations (especially by primary care physicians and neurologists) after extensive biomedical work-ups with negative results (Thompson, 1985a, 1985b). Such lengthy and negative searches for the aetiology of the headache or pain can be both expensive and frustrating for all concerned.

Furthermore, patients are often reassured by physicians who are not psychologically minded that there is nothing wrong, and that the pain is 'imagined' or in the 'patient's head' (Thompson, 1985a). The result is disagreement about the 'reality' of the symptomatology, which then leads to increased patient anxiety and a stressful doctor-patient relationship (Schlebusch, 1990a). This in itself can further exacerbate the headache or pain (Thompson, 1985b). Ongoing pain is stressful and it can exacerbate the index patients' failing coping mechanisms, and lead to the psychological reaction of 'pain shock' characteristic of chronic irritability, anxiety, depression, fatigue, insomnia, occupational and family distress, and eventually psychological atrophy, weakness and further disability (Thompson, 1985b). Patients who present with mood disorders are particularly prone to developing chronic pain and in severe cases it may result in delusions and metaphors of decay (cancer, rotting, death) to explain the pain (Thompson, 1985a). In many of these patients their pain leads to them seeking relief through self-medication involving a host of OTC medical preparations (such as analgesics) and non-medical preparations (such as alcohol, nicotine and others). As a result, these patients frequently develop substance-related disorders and often present with drug toxicity, over-medication or withdrawal symptoms (Thompson, 1985b). Sensitivity to pain, together with the original psychiatric disorder such as depression or anxiety, can be significantly elevated in a patient through a decreased intake of the self-medication (Thompson, 1985a), thus leading to relapse and the re-uptake of the abuse of self-medications.

From a psychological point of view, it is important to note that pain perception (which is more or less the same for most people) can be decreased by up to 40% or more in some patients by a variety of interventions (Thompson, 1985b). Other than physical therapy and analgesics, these include biofeedback, creating a positive emotional state, relaxation training, meditation, guided imagery, suggestion, hypnosis, placebo, modelling, and cognitive therapy (Lindegger, 1990; Thompson, 1985b). The value of placebo in treating medical patients has provided strong evidence of psychological components in some biomedical conditions (Schlebusch, 1990a). The clinician must be aware, though, that beneficial response to such placebo can be erroneously taken to differentiate organic from functional aetiologies in, for example, patients with chronic pain (Thompson, 1985b). A transient or positive response to placebo has been demonstrated in up to one-third of either normal people or patients who present with organic aetiology to their pain (Thompson, 1985b). Placebo has also been found to be an important consideration in my research on stress management and micronutrient supplementation (Schlebusch et al., 2000), and has been extensively explored in the context of human self-healing and the boundaries of subjectivity and objectivity (Peters, 2001).

Such scenarios are important considerations in the management of these patients. There is a body of evidence that shows the link between stress and disease and, as already noted, between suicidal behaviour and disease (Schlebusch, 1990a, 2000c). Not only can inordinate stress aggravate and maintain certain health problems, but it can also sometimes even initiate them. I have designed a programme to help patients to cope with the psychological stress associated with cancer and its treatment (Schlebusch, 1999b). This programme aims to provide the cancer sufferer with a psychological self-help programme, the primary message being that the necessary psychological changes to improve and to have a better quality of life, can be achieved. In this process psychological recovery takes place step-by-step. People with chronic disease should be identified earlier for appropriate psychological intervention. This would facilitate improved health care and better professional-patient communication. In addition, it would address and clarify the issues of palliative care and remove the patient's misperceptions of being abandoned by health-care professionals. Hospice care (in addition to home visits by hospice staff) should be provided as options to patients who need additional assistance. Support can also be given by social welfare agencies, which can assist patients' relatives with visiting them while they are in hospital. Our psychological interventions include individual crises intervention, cognitive therapy, group psychotherapy and family therapy. In this way, patients are offered not only help, but also some sense of control and psychological empowerment.

STRESS ASSOCIATED WITH CHRONIC DISEASE

The role of stress in suicidal behaviour was discussed in Chapter nine. My own and other research has shown that the ability to cope with disease-related stress is also influenced by the meaning and significance of the disease to the patient, which will determine the degree of stress invoked in the patient (Schlebusch, 1990a, 1991, 2000c). This research has analysed the stress response from a biopsychosocial point of view that considers the individual's physical, psychological and behavioural reactions, which have obvious implications for stress management. Put differently, modern understanding of stress embraces an interactive viewpoint in which stress can be construed as being in 'the eye of the beholder' and based on the individual's own perception and appraisal of the stress. Consequently, response to stress is the product of the patient-situation interaction, with individual vulnerability being dependent on many complex factors including personality, personal history, needs, wants, coping strategies and so on (Schlebusch, 2000c; Sutherland & Cooper, 1990).

Since there are wide individual differences in the ability to cope adaptively with disease-invoked stress, there is an argument for identifying patients who are likely to respond psychologically more adversely to disease. Such poor copers can be helped to control stress tolerance, although the outcome is dependent on various factors such as the type of help available, as well as individual differences in response to psychological help (Schlebusch, 1990a, 2000c).

The term 'stress' is widely used and there is little agreement on a scientifically precise definition, thus giving rise to stress research in a number of fields of study with different emphases (Schlebusch, 1990a, 2000c; Schlebusch et al., 2000). Some view stress as a 'third wave plague', and others as the current 'whipping boy' that is blamed for everything that is wrong in society today (Sutherland & Cooper, 1990). Two models that are useful for improving our understanding of stress are the physiological and psychological models (Schlebusch, 2000c; Schlebusch et al., 2000). The former involves the activation of the sympathetic-adrenal medullary (SAM) system and the pituitary-adrenocortical (PAC) axis, while the latter involves patients' perceptions of their relationship to their environment, and evaluation (cognitive appraisal) of any potential harm posed by the stimulus that triggers the stress (Schlebusch, 2000c; Schlebusch et al., 2000).

For the purposes of this discussion, stress is viewed as affecting both the SAM and PAC systems associated with an interaction of several variables, including organismic factors (that is, the genetic and constitutional make-up of the patient), as well as environmental factors that may result in frustration and conflict and so potentiate a stressful state (Schlebusch, 1990a, 2000c; Schlebusch et al., 2000). The ability to cope with stress resulting from this interaction further depends on individual coping mechanisms, including the effective use of defence mechanisms. If individuals fail to cope psychologically, they might attempt to enhance their coping skills by engaging in self-medication – as explained in the interactive model of substance abuse discussed earlier – leading to ISDB. If this fails, more direct suicidal behaviour can ensue.

The initial emphasis on the psychologically associated stressors has shifted to concern about the quality of life of such patients, disease severity, and to stress-related psychological problems associated with the advancement of medical technology (treatment) which affect the patient (Schlebusch, 2000c). Causes of stress associated with disease can, however, be attributed to many different sources, and include:

- stressors associated with the index patient and the other two important partners involved in management of the disease, namely, the family and medical staff (Schlebusch, 1991, 2000c);
- stress related to the variable system of care;
- survival and its impact on life; and
- various other relevant psychological issues, including appropriate support systems (Schlebusch, 1999a, 1999b, 2000c).

Researchers conclude that these stressors can primarily be subsumed under a twofold concept, that is:
- stress that stems from the specific characteristics of the disease itself and its treatment; and
- stress arising from living with the disease, and conflicting role expectations involving those close to the patient (Schlebusch, 1990a, 1991, 2000c).

Put differently, these sources of stress can be broadly grouped under biomedical and psychosocial categories (Schlebusch, 1991). Awareness of a patient's assessment of the importance of these sources of stress and associated psychological problems, permits appropriate psychological intervention, thereby enhancing treatment and patient adjustment. More often than not, however, the relative importance of the various stress sources and their measurement are unclear in patient management. Although many sources of stress have been described, their relative importance for the patients is, in fact, frequently inferred, and the need to recognise this point is a priority in stress management. It is against this background that the patient-perceived importance of sources of stress should be established as a baseline for treatment investigation. For example, my research findings confirmed that patient fears related to chronic disease and its treatment can be very individual (Schlebusch, 1990a, 1991, 2000c).

In my view, the fears specific to each patient can be dealt with best within a biopsychosocial framework from the perspective of behavioural medicine, that is, from the interdisciplinary interface of the behavioural and the biomedical health-care professions (Schlebusch, 1990a, 2000c). There are, moreover, many additional factors that must be considered in the treatment of these patients.

These require a multidisciplinary team approach aiming at, *inter alia*:
- structured programmes;
- physical and social rehabilitation;
- psychotherapy (which includes cognitive and other forms of behaviour modification techniques);
- planned physical activities;
- lifestyle adjustment;
- stress management;
- educational programmes;
- milieu therapy (including appropriate environmental adjustments);
- appropriate psychiatric and psychological treatment of associated psychiatric disorders; and
- the availability of a mental health specialist.

Such an approach frequently, if not always, also involves the index patient's family (Schlebusch, 1990a, 1991). Appropriate modifications can be made for individual patient histories, demographics, personality characteristics, psychopathology, coping skills, critical proportions of interaction with the environment, cultural influences, health and other belief systems, expectancy confirming and expectancy disconfirming behaviours, and so on. It is important to bear in mind that patients' individual belief systems might have to be challenged, along with their perceptions of the very meanings of their existence.

A FUNCTIONAL MODEL TO UNDERSTAND AND MANAGE ANALGESIC ABUSE

Since substance abuse features prominently as a co-morbid factor in suicidal behaviour, a functional model to understand and manage substance abuse is explained in this section (Nattrass, 1996; Schlebusch, 1991). Although based on my research on analgesic abuse, this approach may also be applicable to other forms of substance abuse (including alcohol, which features so prominently in suicidal behaviour in South Africa).

This model proposes that the abuse acts as a 'psychological tool' or psychological coping strategy in order to deal with psychological problems. According to this model, both exogenous and endogenous variables play a role in the development of analgesic abuse. The exogenous variables include (but are not exclusive to) psychologically determined and non-pharmacological components. The endogenous variables include (but are not exclusive to) physiologically determined addiction/dependence and pharmacological components. The model proposed here is therefore an integrated model which emphasises that substance use is initiated and sustained by the reasons discussed in this and previous chapters. Substance use/dependence results in abuse when the interaction between abusers and their respective situations assumes critical proportions and the individuals concerned feel that they can no longer cope psychologically. Through a process of reinforcement, this dependence eventually leads to health-risk behaviour that, in turn, is associated with self-defeating behaviour, that results in a lifestyle disease or in psychopathology such as a substance-related use disorder and potential ISDB.

This model has theoretical similarities to others, such as:
- a functional model of smoking (Warburton, 1987);
- an adaptive orientation to opiate addiction (Alexander & Hadaway, 1982);
- integrated models of self-defeating behaviours (Curtis, 1989a, b);
- the theory that the tolerance of anxiety is central to engaging in effective behaviours (Wachtel, 1987); and
- my explication of health-risk behaviours (Schlebusch, 1990a, 2000c).

According to the model proposed here and depending on the situation, substance abusers tend to adjust their substance intake in terms of the number of available commercial brands and dosage ingested in an attempt to control their psychological state (which, in turn, is associated with and/or precipitated by their underlying psychopathology). This also explains individual differences in such abuse. Should the person try to cope without the substance or with reduced intake once the abuse has started, the subsequent deprivation results in abstinence symptoms (both psychological and physiological withdrawal behaviour), which are manifested in less efficient psychological coping mechanisms.

Differences with regard to substance intake are also a function of the intensity, duration, and density (the product of intensity and duration) of the individual person-situation interaction, which, in turn, can be stress-related. The re-initiation and continuation of the abuse, like the original initiation, usually occurs when the intensity, duration, or density of the individual person-situation (psychopathology, stressors and inability to cope) assumes critical proportions. The abuse is also associated with the specific personality characteristics and psychopathology of the abuser (individual perception, appraisal and interpretation of the situation) and interaction with the cultural environment. In addition, many people abuse substances because of anticipatory needs or anticipatory anxiety (that is, before the stressful situation or critical stress levels have arisen) and whilst still coping psychologically. In such circumstances, the abuse is often in response to the person's interpretation and premature (possibly incorrect) appraisal (misperception) of the situation, which involves a 'what if' type of thinking error, as opposed to an objective assessment. If these aspects assume inordinate levels of intensity, they further reinforce abuse because of the anticipated inability to cope at some future moment when the person expects the situation to become critical (irrespective of whether it actually will or not).

The model further holds that substance abusers have learned to control (enhance or sedate) their psychological state (or mood or affect) with excessive substance intake, believing it to promote more efficient functioning. It is possible that on occasions excessive intake temporarily does promote more efficient functioning for them, which further reinforces abuse. It also assists substance abusers in avoiding the undesired sequelae of other situations where they coped inadequately, so that continued abuse is perceived as a 'legitimate' or a rational psychological coping strategy based on past 'positive' experiences and reinforcement. In this manner individuals feel that they can repeatedly gain control over their dysfunctional psychological state. This illusion is further reinforced by either denial that their substance intake constitutes abuse, or by an actual lack of knowledge of its dangers, such as the potential development of disease, substance-related disorders or other psychological problems or related cognitive disorders. This reinforcement especially applies when excessive consumption is seen as legitimate self-medicating behaviour, and can be further reinforced by family psychopathology, childhood experience and advertising media exposure.

As discussed in Chapter eight, several reasons for substance abuse have been elicited by my research. Consequently, the functional model proposed here does not require a single motive for all abusers. It requires only that a function of abuse be identified for each abuser. Studies on self-medication have shown that individuals choose substances (or classes thereof) that fulfil their individual needs (Warburton, 1987). Evidence for such self-medicating behaviour also comes from extensive research on the use of other substances such as alcohol. Abuse can be construed, therefore, as providing control of the psychological state, because it acts as an easily accessible psychological mechanism that serves as a coping strategy. Other pharmacological components might ultimately be included, specifically in relation to the well-described physiologically determined addictive and dependence-producing properties of the substance (Kaplan & Sadock, 1995).

Understanding how abuse develops then, includes a delineation of:

- the history of reinforcement of the abuse;
- the psychological variables and intra- and interpersonal processes by which objective reinforcement stimuli occur; and
- the psychodynamic and psychopathological representations of self and others composing the implicit and/or explicit personal reality, by which the substance abusers organise their psychological coping skills.

According to this model, substance-abuse behaviour and related affective components, such as beliefs, perceptions, interpretations and appraisals of stressors, develop through reinforcement by actual experiences, culture and the situation (environmental circumstances).

Against this background, the model further proposes that individuals generally have expectations (beliefs held consciously or unconsciously) about behavioural outcomes, which they incorporate into their own social and self theories (Curtis, 1989a, b). If the efforts that individuals put into expected outcomes do not result in these or similar outcomes, they might act to change (modify) their specific expectations and engage in expectancy-disconfirming behaviours (or discrepancy-production behaviours) by further reinforcement of their psychopathology associated with their substance abuse. For example, such people might increasingly focus on symptoms of psychiatric disorders such as somatoform disorders (especially hypochondriasis and somatoform pain disorders), which, in turn, result in greater levels of self-medication. Although substance abusers now risk obtaining poorer outcomes (for their biopsychosocial health) because of their changed risk-taking behaviour (which is now more psycho-pathological and is therefore more self-defeating and self-destructive), they may actually obtain (albeit dysfunctionally so) self-perceived better outcomes in the form of psychological coping. Therefore, by taking risks (such as engaging in health-risk behaviour by excessive self-medication) substance abusers may obtain outcomes closer to their desired ones (but which were not the original expected ones). For them this constitutes psychological coping behaviour (again, albeit dysfunctional), achieved by self-medication and enhanced levels of substance abuse. Underlying this sequence of behavioural events is the theory that anxiety tolerance is a key element for an individual to be able to engage in effective behaviour, something which the substance abuser ultimately lacks (Wachtel, 1987).

The entire process described here serves to reinforce further the potential for self-destructive (health-risk) behaviour. If the intensity of individuals' experience of non-contingent reinforcement behaviour (psychological symptomatology, pain, stress, anxiety and/or depression, etc.) is marked, they will fear to discontinue such behaviour (which leads to punishment in the form of reduced coping abilities). In such circumstances they will persist, by continued abuse, to engage in behavioural outcomes to control their adverse psychological state – even if this means further risk-taking as in ISDB as part of an unrecognised suicidal process. This behaviour is sustained because of a fear that the efforts for the desired outcome (as distinct from the expected outcome) may have to be abandoned if the individual reduces his or her abusive substance intake. If the discrepancy between the desired outcome and the expected outcome increases unduly, it becomes aversive (intensifying fears of increased psychological anguish, physical suffering and lack of coping). It is evident that although expectancy-disconfirming behaviours (psychopathology) themselves can be unpleasant, they can be adopted to achieve coping as explained in this model. The unavoidable result is that the very fear of engaging in expectancy-disconfirming behaviours reinforces the abuser's engagement in expectancy-confirming behaviours to avoid adverse outcomes, thus setting in motion a 'catch-22' cycle.

This is akin to the concept of the 'self-fulfilling prophecy' or 'living up to the label' behaviour (expectancy-confirmation processes), where the 'fear of success' is associated with self-defeating behaviours and the 'choice to suffer' (Curtis, 1989a), even if it is part of a pattern of self-destructive behaviour (Schlebusch, 1990a, 1991). The substance abuser's erroneous belief causes him or her to persist in a self-destructive cycle and his or her health-risk behaviour is, therefore, perpetuated (Schlebusch, 1990a, 1991). Although he or she might acknowledge that behaviours leading to alternative (health-promoting) outcomes do exist, the person has difficulty in engaging in them for several reasons, including a lack of knowledge thereof and how to carry out such behaviour. Such self-defeating psychological coping, in which denial plays a significant role, is to some extent also rooted in employing faulty ego defence mechanisms (Schlebusch, 1990a). In the same way then, that the model proposed here does not require only a single motive for abuse, it also does not require that the expectations and motives of abusers are always conscious ones.

Similarly, my research on the concept of health-risk behaviour showed that serious physical and mental health problems can be predisposed, initiated, sustained or exacerbated by the substance abusers' ISDB. Such health-risk behaviour can lead to 'lifestyle diseases' or 'diseases of choice'. In fact, studies show that dealing with the prevailing high stress levels and destructive lifestyle diseases has been identified as a high priority for South Africa, and that the abuse of alcohol and medicinal substances is of particular concern (Nattrass, 1996; Schlebusch, 1990a, 1991, 2000c, 2004; Suffla, Van Niekerk & Duncan, 2004). Furthermore, according to my research, between 30% and 80% of medical out-patients have psychological complaints severe enough to require specialised attention, 50% of respondents to public surveys have at least one psychological symptom or complaint, and between 60% and 90% of patients who consult general practitioners have some sort of psychological problem (Schlebusch, 1989).

Of great importance for the present model are the individual patient's belief systems within a cultural context, a biopsychosocial understanding of substance abuse and the need for behaviour change in patient management (Schlebusch, 1990a). This includes the behavioural concept of relapse, which involves exploring three stages:

- the patient's motivation and commitment to behaviour change;
- the process of initial behaviour change; and
- the process of behaviour change maintenance.

To understand this better it is necessary to make a distinction between lapse (a behavioural process involving slips or mistakes), and relapse (which is the eventual behavioural result of the process of lapse). The Health Belief Model (HBM) is important here (Schlebusch, 1990a). The HBM is rooted in value expectancy theories which hold that individual health beliefs (and decisions) are based on an analysis of cost-benefit alternatives, and therefore have major implications for health care (Feuerstein, Labbe & Kuczmierczyk, 1986; Schlebusch, 1990a). In the case of the substance abuser, it means weighing up the psychological cost of reduced substance intake (leading to ineffective psychological control), compared to the benefits of continued high-level substance intake (leading to a feeling of effective psychological coping or control) against the risk of health-risk behaviour. Put differently, the person is prepared to take the risk of abuse in order to achieve the desired outcome of psychological control (coping) based on a belief system that the reward is worth the risk or that the health risk is minimal.

As I have stressed earlier, it is important in the treatment of such problems to realise that such behaviour is a misperception and also involves a denial of reality (Schlebusch, 2000c). Whether this belief system is erroneous or not is frequently irrelevant for the abuser – it achieves the desired outcome as a psychological coping strategy. The current model accordingly emphasises the role of health beliefs to explain abuse. Furthermore, these health beliefs are based on previous experiences, including exposure to cultural influences and the meaning of substance use in a given culture (Room, 1989).

Relapse is associated with 'craving', a term commonly used to describe the urge to use a substance repeatedly (Jaffe, 1989). Such a definition of the term 'craving' is inadequate as it does not imply any specific biological or psychological mechanisms (Jaffe, 1989). Reasons for this view of its inadequacy include the arguments that:

- although adverse withdrawal syndromes can generate the urge to use a particular substance repeatedly, craving is also reported in patients in whom classical symptoms of substance-dependence are minimal; and
- robust substance-seeking behaviour has been reported when physical dependence has not developed (Jaffe, 1989).

Consequently, research on substance abuse suggests differences between a biological basis for craving and withdrawal-induced craving (Jaffe, 1989). It has been emphasised that changes induced in the nervous system by the repeated use of dependence-producing substances are not limited only to tolerance and physical dependence (withdrawal syndromes). They also involve memory traces that link the reinforcing effects of substances to psychological states and environmental stimuli. When the overt symptoms of withdrawal have abated, these states can have a 'priming' effect that can cause an increased craving for the substance of dependence, when a substance that produces a positive reinforcement is ingested (Jaffe, 1989; Nattrass, 1996; Schlebusch, 1991). As a result, approaches to treatment and relapse-prevention programmes should incorporate techniques to teach former substance abusers how to avoid situations that can evoke craving and how to cope with craving when such situations cannot be avoided.

The psychological basis of substance dependence has been considered from various other viewpoints. A review of three main approaches that have considerable bearing on the model proposed here, looked at substance dependence as a problem of motivation from the point of view of decision theory, drive theory and behaviourism, all three of which offer some help in understanding the problem (West, 1989). According to decision theory, abusers work out the costs and benefits of their behaviour (including the function provided by the abuse and withdrawal symptoms because of abstinence). Such consideration is seen by theorists as tying in with cognitive theories about how relevant beliefs and feelings are generated. By contrast, drive theory asserts that powerful forces energise and direct the behaviour in substance abusers. These forces may result from the abuse tapping into existing drive mechanisms, creating disturbances in them, or from the acquisition of new drives that may operate at physiological, psychological or social levels. The behaviourist approach focuses chiefly on directly observable contingencies between behaviour and environmental events. Authorities have pointed out that all three approaches have something to offer (West, 1989). These thories have obvious implications for the management of suicidal behaviour, ISDB and substance abuse. They also have relevance given the wide variety of complaints with a notable psychological component frequently mentioned by substance abusers, and their significant denial of such abuse. This also applies to a minority of persons who appear to have a genuine lack of knowledge of the fact that they are abusing substances such as analgesics because of an actual underestimation of the amounts they ingest (Murray, 1981; Schlebusch, 1991). One study estimated that some patients consume three to four times the actual amounts of analgesics that they admit to taking (Murray, 1973).

In summary, the long-term outlook for management improves if patients admit to accurate quantities of substances abused, accept their dependence on them as actual and accept that this behaviour has been hazardous to their health (Schlebusch, 1991). In terms of this, authorities have long pointed out that the following are helpful:

- taking blood to establish substance levels;
- getting information from the patient's family or pharmacist;
- calling on the assistance of a mental health specialist (especially when other psychiatric disorders are prominent);
- establishing the initial reasons for abuse;
- monitoring the patient in hospital when he or she is off the offending substances;

- doing regular follow-up; and
- using a supportive approach (Gault & Wilson, 1978; Schlebusch, 1991).

My research findings have also provided support for the shared concern about the extensive commercial exploitation of OTC medications, as well as for the importance of community education regarding the risks of excessive intake. Any comprehensive treatment programme should take into account the need for greater patient and public awareness of drugs causing toxicity or other problems. This not only implies health promotion and preventative health care, but also efforts at the primary health-care level and active treatment of the abuser (or potential abuser) before such a person develops a medical or psychiatric disorder that will become a focus of treatment and perhaps precipitate a suicidal crisis (Schlebusch, 1990a, 1991). The proposed functional model also has practical clinical value for the management of treatment non-adherence (non-compliant) behaviour, which is known to be problematic in many psychiatric and medical patients (Schlebusch, 1990a).

SOMATIC CO-MORBIDITY: HIV/AIDS
The role of physical disease has received little attention in research on suicidal behaviour in South Africa. This is despite the fact that international research has shown that in many cases somatic disease can be associated with an increased risk for suicidal behaviour (Lönnqvist, 2001; Stenager & Stenager, 2000). In a 1998 study on psychological considerations in the management of the HIV-infected patient with polytrauma, I and members of my DPS research group discuss the multidisciplinary management of the HIV/Aids-infected patient with polytrauma (Schlebusch, Schweitzer & Bosch, 1998). We subsequently extended this work to include HIV/Aids patients who present with suicidal behaviour in hospitals (Schlebusch & Noor Mahomed, 2004). The following summary is provided here to assist in dealing with potential suicidal behaviour in these patients. As soon as a patient's general condition allows, a mental health expert (usually a clinical psychologist with neuropsychological expertise) can function in a unique consultative role in several ways.

1. Initially the task may be to provide objective and systematic assessment of the patient's psychological and neurocognitive status in order to assist in making a differential diagnosis. Psychopathology, notably depressive and anxiety states, often becomes evident at this early stage. These patients might also have both psychological and neurological difficulties that are secondary to their primary medical conditions. Any psychological sequelae that could be associated with other physical problems have to be teased out. In addition, many consequences of HIV/Aids infection can contribute to behavioural reactions that can mimic cognitive changes seen in anoxia (a deficient supply of oxygen) resulting from head injury, chest injury, or Adult Respiratory Distress Syndrome (ARDS). Differential diagnosis is important for both management and prognosis since it is known that HIV does enter the CNS and that neuropsychological complications as well as both dementia and delirious states can arise from CNS infection, as also CNS neoplasms, CNS abnormalities caused by systemic disorders and endocrinopathies as well as adverse CNS responses to drugs (Kaplan & Sadock, 1995).
2. It is important to evaluate the impact of disease processes on behaviour (that is, perform an assessment of deficits that are causally related to the brain trauma or disease process at issue). Clinically, neuropsychiatric complications occur in at least 50% of HIV-infected patients and neuropsychological symptoms may be the first signs of the disease in about 10% to 30% of cases (Lezak, 1995; Schlebusch & Noor Mahomed, 2004). Damage to the brain can occur as a direct result of the HIV infection involving brain cells, or indirectly, because of mass lesions (from tumour or other infection) or infectious processes, which result from a deteriorating immune system (Lezak, 1995). Where patients have sustained head trauma (as is often the case in South Africa as a result of road accidents and other causes) the often subtle neuropsychological sequelae of mild head injury – headaches, dizziness, concentration and memory problems, fatigue, irritability, anxiety and depression – may easily be misattributed to causes other than the brain injury. Furthermore, the presence of any pre-existing condition (such as prior substance abuse, psychiatric illness and CNS damage from head injury or HIV infection) can influence the impact of the injury

and serve to exacerbate the damage due to the injury itself. In such cases, a comprehensive clinical and neuropsychological investigation can provide a firm foundation from which to render valid opinions.
3. A clinical and neuropsychological assessment can provide essential information around the issues of the influence of the patient's personality structure on disease, on behaviour in the hospital, on the expected extent of and time for prognosis and recovery, and on the patient's neurocognitive ability to:
   - give informed consent as well as to understand explanations and instructions (that is, comprehension);
   - comply with medication/treatment regimes (that is, compliance);
   - perform activities of daily living and live independently; and
   - benefit from specific interventions, learning or training experiences (that is, rehabilitation potential).
4. It is necessary to facilitate a medical climate that is patient-orientated and psychologically minded, that is, to take cognisance of the effect of the hospital environment on the patient's reactions and to help assess and meet the needs of the staff as mental health facilitators by providing practical suggestions for management.
5. The need to minimise stress in the Intensive Care Unit (ICU) is another important aspect that must be addressed by the mental health expert (Schlebusch, 1990a; Schlebusch, Schweitzer & Bosch, 1998). It is severely stressful to be placed in a situation where the lights are on 24 hours a day and where there is constant activity. Patients have often undergone a tracheotomy and/or are intubated. They are thus unable to talk and communication between patients and members of the medical and nursing staff is only possible through writing. This is a slow and frustrating experience that is very stressful for these patients. The 24-hour continuous monitoring and the physical care provided by the medical and nursing staff in the ICU can deprive patients of their normal sleep rhythms. Patients' awareness of the environment is at times lost or impaired and may result in confusion, agitation, and even hallucinations. The patient's presence in the ICU is also likely to be very stressful for his or her family. Major stressors centre around the intensity of

contact (or lack of physical touch) with patients, and their dependency on the staff. Furthermore, the optimism of the staff and especially the psychological climate of a unit are important factors in patient adjustment, as is the availability of a good psychological service. Conversely, a patient's response can affect the psychological climate of a unit and its staff: if the patient does well the impact on the unit can be psychologically positive, and if he or she does poorly it can be psychologically negative for both staff and patient.

Dependence on the technological procedure and on the unit's staff is a crucial problem for patients. In order for the staff to keep reality-orientated restrictions in focus, an awareness is needed of the patient's utilisation of denial with its adaptive and maladaptive features. Various additional factors experienced by the staff as stress sources include: the organisation of the unit, team member ties, staff-patient interdependence, actual working conditions, tensions within the team, a patient's physical deterioration and a patient's death. Staff-patient interaction is further complicated when patients are reproachful, hostile and/or aggressive. However, it is important in a psychotherapeutic programme to allow patients some independence and expression of aggression as a strategy to decrease the need to develop an extremely defensive structure. By the same token, setting up staff discussion groups can help to alleviate stresses experienced by the unit staff. Several other important issues in this regard merit consideration:

- *ICU psychosis*: The term 'ICU psychosis' is a popular diagnosis. It is often applied to patients exhibiting abnormal behaviour in a critical care setting, despite the fact that the occurrence of acute psychosis in the critical care setting is rare. The implication is that the environment in critical care settings is capable of inducing psychosis, the rationale being sensory deprivation, monotony and/or excessive stimulation. As noted, the ICU environment can have profound psychological effects on patients. However, the use of 'ICU psychosis' as a diagnosis, implies that the aetiology of a disturbed mental state such as delirium is unknown, and it is frequently used as a convenient 'diagnostic catch-all'. There

are implicit risks in this, because such a diagnosis tends to discourage an astute differential diagnosis, with obvious treatment implications.
- *Fear and anxiety*: The patient's life could be endangered for a period of time and the family might suffer anguish. The sight of a person with intravenous lines, catheters and intercostal drains, together with a confusing array of electronic and mechanical equipment, could add to the uncertainty and anguish of both patients and their families. Admission to the ICU setting is invariably associated with life-threatening conditions, and even when the fear of death has ceased to be a stressor, a patient may fear being maimed for life. Subsequent stress may be expressed in many guises, for example, verbosity, outbursts of anger, paranoia and silent withdrawal.
- *Denial and the threat to sign out*: Denial allows the acute patient a 'way out' by avoiding panic and minimising (or excluding) the threatening implications of his or her condition(s). If the patient feels psychologically out of control and panic sets in, there may be the urge to flee, expressed in the threat to sign out (the flight component of the 'fight-or-flight' response). The issue of a patient who refuses hospital treatment can seriously complicate patient management (Schlebusch, 1990a).
- *Mood disorders and feelings of hopelessness*: Careful investigation of the ICU patient might reveal feelings of hopelessness and depression that need to be considered.
- *Cardiac arrest*: As one of the ultimate complications, cardiac arrest can leave psychological scars on both patient and staff. The survivor almost invariably demonstrates some increase in apprehension or anxiety, even though it may not be verbalised as such.
- *The difficult patient*: This refers to a patient with a personality disorder. Some of the most troublesome patients are those with narcissistic and borderline personalities. The mental health expert's help is invaluable here.
6. There is a need to address both premorbid psychological disorders and the onset of new ones that may complicate diagnosis and the patient's response to treatment. In addition, it

is important to consider any iatrogenic (treatment-induced) phenomena. The treatment can be both psychological and pharmacological and the patient should be informed of the neuropsychological findings as well as be taught appropriate coping measures – bearing in mind that his or her safety is a priority.
7. Given the discussion in Chapter nine on HIV/Aids and suicidal behaviour, and in view of our experience, the biological, psychological, and social variables in these patients should be holistically considered from a multidisciplinary point of view (Schlebusch & Cassidy, 1995). This is especially so in view of the potential psychological and neuropsychological complications in these patients that could increase their risk for suicidal behaviour (Grant & Atkinson, 1995).
8. Pre- and post-test counsellors must emphasise the aforementioned information to HIV/Aids-infected patients. It is imperative that mental health professionals and others involved in the care of HIV/Aids-infected individuals be able to identify and minimise the risk of suicide attempts experienced during periods of crisis. These periods are immediately after the notification of the disease and up to a year following notification, as well as during the onset of Aids symptoms. In addition, the lack of recognition by Western-trained professionals of the cultural beliefs of patients that affect the patient's perception of diagnosis, treatment and prognosis, warrants attention. Patients are unlikely to pursue and comply with medical treatment if a more holistic approach, including culturally relevant practices, is not included in the comprehensive biopsychosociocultural management of HIV/Aids-infected suicidal patients, and others similarly diagnosed with a life-threatening illness (Schlebusch, 1991).

Understanding the suicide risk in these HIV/Aids patients (and indeed in other medical conditions) not only assists in identifying risk profiles, but facilitates the planning of better informed and more effective psychological intervention.

There are several other purposes in studying those patients at risk for suicide. Identifying patients with high vulnerability is not exclusively intended as a means to ascertain the suicidal risk, but also helps to discover ways in which coping behaviour is impaired, so that preventative psychosocial interventions can be initiated for suicidal patients in need (Noor Mahomed, Schlebusch & Bosch, 2003; Schlebusch & Noor Mahomed, 2004). By writing about this, I hope to create awareness of the problem and thereby raise the profile for the need for intervention strategies.

In South Africa, there are many voluntary programmes that try to combat the HIV/Aids pandemic and offer assistance to the people who are infected or affected. A key issue is the development of strategies to deal with children orphaned by Aids (including institutional care, community-based care, strengthening of family capacity, government protection for the most vulnerable children, creating a supportive environment for the children affected, dealing with issues of discrimination and poor nutrition, and so on). There are particularly vulnerable and disadvantaged communities that are in extreme need in this regard. Key components for suicide prevention strategies for this group include:
- strengthening and supporting community-based responses;
- creating national awareness of the problem; and
- improving access to mental health services.

The aim should not only be to transplant knowledge on suicide prevention that could be appropriate to HIV/Aids into Africa from the Western world, but to create uniquely African strategies. Experience gained in this regard could have significant implications for dealing with suicide within the broader context, and could also assist in examining the link between other life-threatening diseases and suicidal behaviour.

PREVENTION OF SUICIDAL BEHAVIOUR IN SOUTH AFRICA
Nearly two decades ago I argued that because of the magnitude of the problems associated with suicidal behaviour in South Africa and the social consequences, national, provincial and local health services ought to share responsibility for the development of prevention programmes (Schlebusch, 1988a). When programmes such as these are developed, there are important considerations concerning educational and training facilities. There is an urgent need to disseminate information about the clues to suicidal

behaviour, the prevention of which is ultimately the concern of everyone. Some of the primary aims of such programmes should be:
- eliminating myths surrounding suicidal behaviour;
- making it possible for suicidal patients to seek help;
- facilitating early recognition of suicidal risk and high-risk patients;
- securing the co-operation of suicidal patients and providing them with support;
- alerting other professional groups, including educators, the police, the legal profession, the clergy and so on, to become involved in the prevention of suicidal behaviour; and
- making provision for informing the families of high-risk patients.

I have also stressed that it is often erroneously assumed that all mental health specialists and medically qualified professionals are adequately trained in the management and prevention of suicidal behaviour. Rather, specialised, appropriate training in dealing with it is necessary. This training should be extended to medical and nursing undergraduates, since patients are frequently admitted to general hospital wards following an unsuccessful suicidal act, as well as to other disciplines.

Usually suicidal behaviour can be assessed by taking a careful history and by examining the mental status of a patient. This should be augmented by a psychodynamic exploration of the focal motives underlying the suicidal behaviour, an examination of existing social support systems, and by raising alertness to the patient's lethality and potential self-destructiveness. This exploration should not be omitted as it has the additional value of demonstrating to a patient a willingness to listen to some of his or her most forceful fears and desires. This, in turn, tends to reassure and add supportive depth and validity to the assessment. As there are many factors that should be considered in the assessment of a suicidal patient, international authorities recommend a semi-structured assessment procedure (Bongar, 1991; Hawton & Van Heeringen, 2000).

Prevention and education are two solutions to the problems that undermine sound mental and physical health. Despite some accomplishments in these key areas, the prevention of suicidal behaviour remains an important public health responsibility in South Africa, and effective measures to decrease its prevalence and incidence depend on early identification and appropriate treatment of at-risk populations. This implies shifting the focus of health care away from a biomedical, technology-based approach. In order to prevent a fatal outcome, implementing prevention strategies implies accessibility to professional emergency services at all times. These include psychiatric and psychological follow-up services. There are not enough mental health specialists to cope with the magnitude of problems associated with suicidal behaviour and its social, economic and other consequences, which have a spiralling effect throughout the community. National, provincial, local, and primary health-care services ought to share the responsibility for the development of prevention programmes. When developing such programmes, consideration must also be given to the provision of educational facilities to train personnel and to disseminate information generally about suicidal behaviour and its prevention. To this we may add a few linchpins:

- the need for continued scientific research;
- the need to set priorities;
- finding solutions to the ethical and practical dilemmas of poverty and crime;
- attention to civil rights, employment, housing, environmental protection; and
- encouraging active participation by the public in their own health care.

With the exception of the suicide prevention programme of the South African Police Services, there is no national suicide prevention programme in place at present. There is an obvious, urgent need for such a programme as research on suicide prevention in South Africa has languished as a relatively minor endeavour.

These issues are not readily taken into account when explaining the high prevalence of suicidal behaviours in this country. In Chapter eleven, I briefly discuss the DPS group's research track on stress and suicidal behaviour that is attempting to address this caveat.

We need to recognise that implementing prediction, prevention, management, and their corollaries (that is, health education, promotion and prevention of health-risk behaviour) is incumbent on several groups of people and cuts across the entire spectrum of society. For too long we have focused on a health-care system that is almost exclusively science- and technology-based for treating the patient who presents with suicidal behaviour. The socio-economic costs of such a system are, however, rapidly becoming insupportable. Although health-care scientists need to continue with their research, increased concern with prevention of health-risk behaviour and promotion of healthful lifestyles must be given priority as this has been shown to have a decidedly positive impact on health-care costs. In essence, that means a shift to a health behaviour-based approach rather than a morbidity-based health-care approach. Such an approach must involve not only health-care workers but also health-care consumers as active participants in the process.

In the media we are confronted almost daily with gloomy reports of suicidal behaviour and high stress levels in our society. Unfortunately, the publicity given to self-destructive lifestyles has done little to win the war against such conduct. By contrast, many other diseases have been conquered by fairly mundane measures such as providing improved education, nutrition, sanitation and socio-economic conditions. In many instances, such a basic approach could also work to bring down stress and associated suicidal behaviour. Prevention rather than cure is the best hope for combating the sharp rise in suicidal behaviour.

A primary role of any programme aimed at the prevention of suicidal behaviour is to avoid a fatal outcome. This implies accessibility for the index patient to professional emergency services at all times. In some areas, help is available from lay organisations to individuals who may not regard their suicidal behaviour as serious enough to require professional help, or to those who refuse to seek help. Clearly, such lay services should also be in a position to utilise professional services whenever the situation demands. Since a percentage of patients who present with suicidal behaviour suffer from mental disorders and because suicidal risk increases in patients with a history of suicidal behaviour, psychiatric/psychological follow-up is necessary for many patients seen in emergency services or by lay organisations, as well as for all potentially high-risk patients who are identified.

The WHO has emphasised that intervention as well as prevention are highly effective in reducing suicide rates (WHO, 1999b). I have pointed out that in South Africa some of these interventions (for example, the early and effective diagnosis and treatment of individuals with stress-related problems, depression or other psychopathology who are at a particular high risk for suicidal behaviour), are cost-effective and could be integrated into primary health-care programmes (Schlebusch, 2004). In working towards developing a national suicide prevention programme in South Africa, this is one of the primary thrusts of the current research of the DPS, as discussed in Chapter eleven. However, such a programme cannot be developed without the support and assistance of all interested parties in the community and the government. I have stressed the relevance for South Africa of the following WHO recommendations that:
- the problem of prevention concerns society as a whole;
- solutions should be sought with full participation of non-governmental organisations;
- a national task force on suicide prevention should be established;
- policies on the availability of pesticides should be reviewed;
- training of health-care workers should be tailored to specific local conditions;
- assistance should be given to suicide support groups; and
- media co-operation should be enlisted (Schlebusch, 2004; WHO, 1999b).

In addition, as a member of the WHO International Network for Suicide Prevention, I recommend the resource booklets by the WHO containing guidelines on the prevention of suicide. These guidelines target:
- survivor groups: the importance of self-help support groups, surviving a suicide, impact of a suicide, sources of help for the bereaved, how to initiate a self-help support group for survivors of suicide, developing the operational framework for the group, identifying and gaining access to resources to support the group, gauging success, potential risk factors for

the group, survivor support in developing countries and rural areas, and survivor support through 'involvement therapy' in other activities (WHO, 2000a);
- general physicians: the burden of suicide, suicide and mental disorders, suicide and physical disorders, suicide and socio-demographic factors, how to identify patients at high risk of suicidal behaviour, the management of suicidal patients, referral to specialist care and a summary of steps in suicide prevention (WHO, 2000b);
- the media: the impact of media reporting on suicide, sources of reliable information, how to report on suicide in general, how to report on a specific suicide, providing information on help available, and a summary of what to do and what not to do (WHO, 2000c);
- primary health-care workers: why it is necessary to focus on primary health-care staff, suicide and mental disorders, physical illness and suicide, suicide-sociodemographic and environmental factors, the state of mind of suicidal persons, how to reach out to the suicidal person, suicide – fiction and fact, how to identify a suicidal person, how to assess the risk of suicide, how to manage a suicidal person, and things to do and not to do (WHO, 2000d);
- prison officials: general suicide facts, inmates as a high-risk group, suicide prevention in correctional settings, the development of suicide profiles, intake screening, post-intake observation, management following screening, if a suicide attempt occurs, and a summary of best practices (WHO, 2000e); and
- teachers and other school staff: suicide is an underestimated problem, protective factors, risk factors and risk situations, how to identify students in distress and at possible risk of suicide, and how suicidal students should be managed at school (WHO, 2000f).

Suicidal behaviour results not only in much psychological anguish, but invariably leads to a spate of hospital admissions and attendant expensive procedures that escalate already high health-care costs and result in more stress for those affected. This does not take into account costs incurred because of post-hospital treatment and the treatment of the devastated family members or loved ones. Apart from the enormous cost in human suffering, the spiralling health-care bill in South Africa necessitates that health-care planners and government cannot continue to ignore the financial implications, loss of skills and psychological suffering in this regard. In addition, it needs to be recognised that implementing prediction, prevention, management and their corollaries (that is, health education, health promotion and the prevention of health-risk behaviour) is incumbent on various groups of people across society because of the diverse disciplines and differing approaches involved. In short, preventing suicidal behaviour is everyone's responsibility. As I have previously argued:

> For too long we have focused on a health-care system that is almost exclusively science and technology based with a consequent essential aim of treating the patient who presents with suicidal behaviour. Although health-care scientists need to continue with their scientific research, increased concern with prevention of health-risk behaviour and promotion of healthful lifestyles must now be given top priority. In essence, that means a shift to a health-behaviour-based approach rather than a morbidity-based health-care approach. This obviously includes a healthy dose of both patient and health-care workers' education. Clearly, the linchpin in this effort is no longer just the health-care worker; it has to involve health-care consumers as active participants in the process.
>
> Most people are not aware of how widely pervasive suicidal behaviour in South Africa has become. The truth of the matter is that it has reached almost epidemic proportions. One of the main problems in this regard is that there is a prevalent attitude surrounding suicide which construes it as being a matter of social taboo. Therefore, suicidal behaviour is sometimes seen as a shameful act and the person who might be considering it may, accordingly, not be encouraged to, or want to, discuss his or her thoughts and emotions openly with a professional (or even a friend or family member). The consequences of this are that many people who feel depressed, alone and hopeless (the keys to suicidal

behaviour) imagine themselves to be even more alone and more isolated. Frequently family members and health-care workers would then miss an opportunity to help prevent the ensuing tragedy. The said social stigma often also makes recovery for those who survive suicidal behaviour a problem (Schlebusch, 1995a: 1–2, 2004).

PREVENTION AND THE YOUTH
South African researchers have emphasised that preventing suicidal behaviour should start early in life (Schlebusch, 2004). Studies have demonstrated the importance of the school, university, college and family as first levels of intervention and prevention, as these are obvious targets for identifying and preventing suicidal behaviour in all age groups, but especially amongst children and adolescents. Several of the studies quoted in this overview revealed that suicidal patients often use firearms or ingest medical substances (available over the counter or on prescription) and household poisons. These trends suggest that the availability of firearms and these substances influences the nature of the suicidal act, yet availability does not always appear to be seriously considered. A decade and a half ago I argued strongly that there is a prima facie case for considering the availability of substances as a major cause of concern in suicide prevention (Schlebusch, 1987).

Suitable school programmes, educating children and adolescents particularly, but also adults, should be a priority in any suicide prevention programme. Of course, the findings mentioned in this chapter suggest several avenues of prevention, but particularly that of continuing education with regard to the dangers associated with access to lethal weapons, OTC substances, medicine storage and issuing of medical prescriptions to vulnerable patients. In this regard, local as well as other research has emphasised that reducing the availability of lethal equipment and substances is one approach to prevention, but that this needs to be combined with knowledge about who is potentially the most vulnerable (Schlebusch, 2004; Williams & Pollock, 1993).

Others have observed that to achieve even a modest chance of success in preventing suicidal behaviour, programmes should be directed at an individual level as well as at the family, school, workplace, and on a larger scale at organisations and the community (Pillay, 1995a, b). The reduced numbers of teacher-counsellors in schools, as part of the rationalisation process in South African education, is lamented in Pillay's noteworthy study. This points out that even where there are counsellors, the number of guidance periods is limited as counsellors are expected to teach mainstream subjects as well. This situation is believed to have had a negative impact on the mental health of school-going children, especially those at risk for suicidal behaviour. There should also be liaison between the various clinical services and the education department in order to prevent adolescent suicidal behaviour. In another study on the prevalence of suicidal behaviour amongst secondary schoolchildren in South Africa, it was recommended that:

- screening services should be established in schools;
- referral for appropriate professional help should be implemented for at-risk learners;
- recognition of suicide risk factors and mental health information should be incorporated in educational programmes;
- education of parents should be a priority, and school personnel should receive in-service training;
- suicide prevention awareness should be promoted amongst policy-makers, community leaders, health-care personnel and the general public; and
- research preventative programmes should be encouraged (Madu & Matla, 2003).

Closer co-operation between educators and health-care providers could effect more successful prevention of suicidal behaviour in young people. Teachers should be alerted to the fact that when determining suicide risk factors in these learners, family background and history should be assessed in conjunction with other factors such as relationships outside the family, relationships with siblings, changes in living conditions and potential psychopathology such as depression and stress.

Suicidal behaviour remains one of the many psychological problems of childhood and adolescence requiring intersectoral collaboration between the education and health departments. From the large number of schoolteacher referrals of children with suicidal behaviour, it is evident that closer co-operation between educators and health-care providers is in children's best interests. In this regard, a proposal on child and adolescent mental health policy for South Africans recommended a multi-level system with the first tier incorporating schools as one of the many service sites at district level (Dawes et al., 1997).

Those at risk for suicidal behaviour need an empathetic ear in moments of crisis. This applies to all potential victims, but especially to the young, not only because of the high incidence of suicidal behaviour and/or ideation in school-going children and university students, but because all young people need help in developing crisis-resolution techniques (Flisher et al., 1992; Mayekiso & Mkize, 1995; Mayekiso & Ngcaba, 2000; Noor Mahomed, Selmer & Bosch, 2000; Pillay, 1995a, b). To this end, a school-based prevention programme provided encouraging results. The programme was found to:
- increase schoolteachers' understanding of the problem;
- improve schoolteachers' attitudes and helpfulness to schoolchildren; and
- decrease schoolchildren's inclinations towards viewing suicidal behaviour as an option (Wassenaar et al., 1993).

A time-series analysis of hospital records of attendances and admissions for the catchment area where the study was done showed a 58% reduction in young people who presented with suicidal behaviour during the six-month period following the programme. Others have also expressed the view that adolescents as a group, rather than just symptomatic suicidal individuals, could particularly benefit from supportive intervention within the school context (Mayekiso & Mkize, 1995). In addition, attempts to address the problem of young people's suicidal behaviour should also reflect their attitudes and perceptions towards such behaviour.

It is essential to take note of this when designing suicide prevention programmes because several studies presented at the four southern African conferences on suicidology to date showed that adolescents and children as a group need help (or training) in dealing with life stresses and conflict resolution. This implies a shift in prevention, in the sense that there should not just be a focus on those with suicidal thoughts and suicidal behaviour, but that, along with adults, school-going children and university/college students should also be taught stress management and conflict resolution skills. Such programmes have been published (Schlebusch, 2000c). Frequently young people seem to resort to suicidal behaviour as a means to cope with stress. However, suicide in all age groups, especially also the elderly, needs to be considered.

CULTURAL AND TRADITIONAL ROLE EXPECTATIONS
The DPS research studies have shown that traditional social role expectations are changing in many patients. This seems significant among black South Africans, especially women. In this regard, the DPS workgroup also emphasised the importance of undertaking more cross-cultural research within the ambit of suicidal behaviour (Schlebusch, 1995c). Researchers need to examine more carefully the influential role of traditional health beliefs in shaping responses to health messages, subsequent role expectations and changes in health behaviour as part of suicide prevention programmes (Schlebusch & Ruggieri, 1996). These issues, in part, also tie in with the predicted shift from traditional cultural identification to more Western lifestyles, as this likely will intensify the impact on at-risk individuals, with subsequent significant implications for suicide prevention programmes. To prevent suicidal behaviour we need to examine its aetiology and co-morbid factors. Strategies should include life or social skills components, education programmes for adults and the youth on the various risks associated with suicide, including alcohol consumption, and more specifically for high-risk individuals and their families. Finally, it has been emphasised that an effective local system for monitoring trends and the variables associated with suicidal behaviour is essential for the prevention of suicidal behaviour (Bertolote, 2001).

Ultimately, the prevention of suicidal behaviour is all about awareness: knowing about and paying attention to the warning signs, and taking active steps to treat them in the early stages. Watch for the signs. Questions to ask can include:
- Is there evidence of expressed suicidal ideation?
- Is there evidence of suicidal threats or a suicide plan?
- Is there a history of prior suicidal behaviour (attempts or parasuicide)?

- Is there a history of prior 'acting out' behaviour?
- Is there a history of an inhibited personality (for example, feeling lonely, being withdrawn) or dysfunctional thoughts or assumptions, problem-solving deficits, cognitive rigidity and/or deficits, dichotomous thinking or other cognitive distortions that may have been present in suicidal thinking, or of viewing suicide as a 'desirable solution' to any specific problem?
- Is there evidence of acute or chronic perturbation (distress) or of a constriction in seeing alternatives to a self-perceived intolerable situation or to any stress that might be present?
- Is there evidence of psychopathology (including a depressive mood and/or other related symptoms), or a history of previous treatment with any psychotropic (psychiatric) medication for depression or other psychological disorder, or for suicidality?
- Is there a history of treatment for depression or for any other psychological problems, or for suicidality?

THE VALUE OF THE PSYCHOLOGICAL AUTOPSY: A SOUTH AFRICAN ADAPTATION

A psychological autopsy is concerned with a retrospective approach to suicide. That is, it involves taking a backward glance to recover relevant information about a person who is already dead. This goal is accomplished by various procedures, including through interviews with significant others in an attempt to reconstruct the role that the deceased played in eventuating his or her own demise, and (if possible) an *in loco* inspection of the site where it occurred. The suicidologist is primarily interested in interview data from anyone who knew the deceased as well as any other relevant information. The psychological autopsy is a well-known technique used by experts in suicidology in a variety of settings where suicide occurs (Harward & Jacoby, 2000; Hawton et al., 1998; Hawton & Van Heeringen, 2000; Lönnqvist, 2000, 2001; Shneidman, 1981, 1985; Wasserman, 2001c). It has also been used in South Africa.

The original use of the psychological autopsy grew out of the joint efforts in the 1950s of the Los Angeles County Chief Medical Examiner/Coroner, and the staff of the Los Angeles Suicide Prevention Centre in California (Shneidman, 1981). It was an attempt to bring the skills of the suicidologist to bear on the problems of equivocal deaths, because it was noted that in about 10% of coroners' cases, even where the cause of death was clear, the mode of death was questionable or equivocal. In such cases this equivocation usually lies between the modes of accident, murder and suicide and also relates to intent and motivation. A primary purpose of the psychological autopsy includes reconstructing the suicidal process up to the time of the suicidal act, including reviewing the treatment process, if any. At the same time, the retrospective analysis and review of the suicidal death provides an opportunity to deal with the sometimes-powerful emotional reactions of others involved. In order to provide a better understanding of the events that occurred, this approach can be used in clinical settings, in hospital departments and in various other settings where suicides happen. I have utilised it where a suicide occurred in a busy academic department at a medical school, to assist the staff in dealing with their feelings about losing a colleague, as well as for medico-legal purposes. Based on available research, a brief summary is provided here on how this technique was adapted for local use in two other cases that had major medico-legal implications. In all these cases, the circumstances of death were well documented in the various medical and legal reports I perused. As these are lengthy, I shall not repeat them here, save to note that allegedly in each case there were no eye-witnesses, and that the individuals allegedly committed suicide.

In essence, when interviews are conducted with persons who knew the deceased and an attempt is made to reconstruct the lifestyle of the deceased, there is a significant focus on the deceased's lifestyle just prior to the death and on obtaining information about any prodromal clues to possible suicide (that is, in particular, some 48 hours preceding the death, but also in the months and years before the tragic event). Careful note is taken of any overt or covert communications related to the death, which would illuminate the deceased's role (if any) in his or her own demise and possible reasons for it. A scientific extrapolation of the deceased's intention and behaviour over the hours, days and months preceding the death is then made, using all the information obtained.

In line with the nature of the psychological autopsy, all the techniques described above were used to arrive post-morbidly at a

psychological opinion. I used various clinical, psychological and other instruments as aids to provide the guidelines and structure for my assessment in each instance. I decided that, given the very nature of the psychological autopsy, I had to conduct the investigation as if examining the deceased when alive but based on the data I had posthumously gleaned, as well as on an acceptable definition of suicide. In particular, I considered three risk factors that correlate highly with suicide:
- primary indications of suicidal intent;
- previous suicide attempts or ideation (including thoughts and feelings of hopelessness);
- any related antecedent circumstances such as psychopathology (especially depression and substance abuse) lifestyle changes, financial and legal problems, disease, substance abuse, etc.

I also took into account research which shows that certain biological factors (often associated with psychopathology) can be associated with suicide.

In each of the cases that I studied I learned that the mental state of the deceased did not fluctuate before death. All were psychologically stable and there was no hidden depression or other related psychopathology. There was also no reported or disguised talk of death (or suicidal ideation), no prior suicide attempt or suicidal behaviour, no disposing of belongings, no suicide note. In addition, the deceased were described as 'positive' persons who mixed happily with their family and friends and the staff at the businesses where they worked. They made friends easily and socialised readily. According to everyone I interviewed, they both had an extremely effective psychosocial support system, no reported financial or legal problems of note, and no mental or physical health problems.

Generally suicide ideators not only actually think about suicide but they may have a pre-formulated plan. This was not shown to be the case.

My view (also based on my inspection of the sites where the alleged suicides occurred) concurred with the opinions expressed by the various people who I interviewed, that is, during the periods that the witnesses knew the victims, the deceased were not predisposed to suicide at any time prior to their deaths. Rather, their actions and behaviour reflected the opposite.

Consequently, my findings were consistent with the balance of probabilities favouring the following facts:
- The deceased did not have the intention to commit suicide.
- There was no reasonable possibility that their deaths were associated with depression and/or other psychopathological symptoms or disorders.
- They were mentally fully competent to appreciate and understand their actions and behaviour.
- They had no history of expressing suicidal intent or of having being treated for it or for depression or for any other psychological disorders.
- They had no problems that could be associated with suicide and, in fact, had everything to live for, and looked forward to an exciting and meaningful future.
- The profiles that emerged were not consistent with those of individuals who had committed suicide.
- There was no reported evidence of cognitive deficits that would have impeded their thinking processes or behaviour. Depression or other psychopathology are often associated with cognitive dysfunctioning, and can complicate the clinical presentation if a cognitive disorder is present. There was no evidence of this in the deceased. They were described as very intelligent persons who could engage in good conversation in a social situation. Collectively, therefore, there were no cognitive, intellectual or related problems.
- They were able to comprehend and understand their actions and those of others, and had a realistic appreciation of their own strengths and limitations.

In both instances I concluded from the psychological autopsies that suicide was not committed. In the one case, it was subsequently proved that the patient had been murdered and the situation then set up to look like suicide (a so-called fake suicide). In the second case, the patient had suffered a cardiac arrest, but because traces of different anti-depressants were detected in his system, suicide was incorrectly suspected. Such findings have various medico-legal implications (including insurance payouts) as well as important psychological effects on the family.

Discussion of the psychological autopsy

The guiding principles of my assessments were determined by what would constitute the weight of probabilities favouring suicide or not, and why? Based on the literature, certain important psychological considerations were taken into account in this regard (Hawton & Van Heeringen, 2000; Shneidman, 1985). These included the following:

1. Communication of suicidal behaviour or clues thereto can be direct or indirect.
2. The presence of direct prodromal clues to suicide (that is, in the preceding 48 hours) or any earlier ones, that are (a) verbal, (b) written or (c) behavioural, is established.
3. The clearest example of (a) direct verbal communication is a statement such as, 'I am going to commit suicide' or an expression of suicidal ideation. (b) Direct written communication usually involves a suicide note or communicating suicidal ideation. (c) Behavioural communication of the intention to commit suicide includes, for example, a 'practice run' in the form of either a suicide attempt (a fortuitous survival of a suicide with high intent), or a parasuicide (a cry for help with low suicidal intent).
4. Usually a minority of the clues to suicide are direct verbal or behavioural clues; most of the clues that precede a suicidal act are indirect or covert. In human communication, words frequently tell only part of the story; the main 'message' often has to be decoded.
5. Likewise, even many clearer indirect pre-suicidal communications have to be deduced or decoded, along with statements that reflect the victim's private decision to kill him- or herself.
6. Examples of indirect verbal communications would generally be any statement that mirrors the individual's intention to stop his or her self-perceived intolerable, psychologically painful existence (unendurable psychological anguish), expressed in, for example, 'I don't know how much longer I can cope!'
7. Generally examples of indirect behavioural communications of high intent are comparable to such actions as a person:
   - putting his or her affairs into order;
   - making a will under certain peculiar and special circumstances;

- giving away prized possessions; or
- making arrangements for beloved pets to be taken care of.

8. Ideally these communications are to be established from information that is obtained from the person him- or herself. If the person is deceased, the communications are obtained on the basis of data obtained from significant others, and from the data derived from a psychological autopsy.
9. When this is done, in essence, the potential for suicide can be evaluated in terms of five essential clusters/questions:
    - *Who and what were they?* This includes information about the persons' developmental, social, sexual and occupational history, and especially focuses on any prior suicidal behaviour and/or intent.
    - *What had recently happened in their lives?*
    - *What or whom did they have in their lives?* This includes any personal resources, psychosocial support systems and people they could really count on.
    - *What were their plans and future expectations?* What had they been thinking about doing? What alternatives had they considered? How specific and firm had these plans become? What future was there to look forward to?
    - *How did they function psychologically?* This includes emotional content and cognitive schemata (how and what they thought and wanted, and the presence or not of relevant psychological or psychiatric problems).
10. Questions about character and personality are then also explored. They have to do with the individual's pervasive and habitual modes of behaviour, wherein a number of symptoms can be rated and divided into:
    - physical symptoms: include specific areas such as any diseases or recent surgery;
    - psychosocial symptoms: include potent feelings of despondency or hopelessness and/or helplessness; depression or other psychiatric/psychological disorders; withdrawal behaviour; loss of interest; as well as feelings of: chaos, agitation, tension, anxiety, guilt, shame, embarrassment, rage, anger, hostility, revenge, poor impulse control, poor judgement, frustrated dependency, high stress levels and others; and

- suicidal symptoms: primarily rated according to any previous noticeable onset of any specific symptoms related to suicidal behaviour, ideations or intent.

The biopsychosocial model, which is rooted in systems theory, is useful here.

11. Examples of additional stressors to explore could include:
    - the recent loss of a loved one;
    - divorce or separation;
    - the recent loss of a job, money, prestige or status;
    - recent accidents;
    - recent threats of prosecution or criminal involvement;
    - recent exposure to 'endings' in life in the person's environment;
    - recent successes or recent promotions and the inability to cope with them;
    - increased responsibility;
    - failure or fear of failure; and so on.

12. Inquiries in these areas are intended to answer such questions as:
    - What's new?
    - Why is the person suicidal now?
    - What has happened?

13. Stress, or a crisis for an individual, often relates to the fact that the person has run out of interpersonal resources and that other individuals in their lives on whom they had counted for emotional support are now either gone or can no longer be counted upon. The intensity of such feelings is heavily dependent on the person's perception and appraisal of the stress (Schlebusch, 2000c).

14. If the suicidal crisis is the typically dyadic (two-person) crisis, then the reaction of the 'significant other' is crucial in the assessment. For example, a suicidogenic or rejecting family unit can be fatal. Conversely, a genuinely concerned and helpful family unit can be a lifesaver.

15. A rule of thumb approach is that the more specific the person's suicidal plan is, the higher the intent. For example, if a person provides a particular date or ties any possible suicidal behaviour to a specific event, or talks about or considers a definite plan, a higher potential rating is considered.

16. Practically all suicidal behaviours stem from the person's self-perceived sense of isolation and from his or her feelings of some intolerable emotional pain and unbearable psychological anguish.
17. Understanding what 'intolerable' means to the suicidal person is important as it differs from person to person, especially if the individual's experiences combined feelings of hopelessness and helplessness. The concept of 'intolerable' would be affected by his or her perception and appraisal of his or her situation as well as by any psychological disorder or other variable that could affect the individual's perception and thoughts (cognitions).
18. Additional clues as to suicidal intent can be obtained from being empathetic to the existential meaning or view of the suicidal individual. We have to bear in mind that although engaging in suicidal behaviour is usually an 'all-or-nothing behaviour', a process is still involved that encompasses contemplating it, as part of a complicated internal debate with significant existential dimensions that include questions about the meaning of life.
19. It is further possible to delineate at least two different kinds of questions to which the psychological autopsy can be addressed:
    - Why did the individual do it? In this the mode of death is clear, but the reasons for the individual's choosing a self-imposed death remain puzzling. In this sense, a psychological autopsy is no less than a reconstruction of the motivations, philosophy, psychodynamics and existential crises of an individual and, in a way, involves the practice of the science of personology.
    - How did the individual die? This refers to the method and actual death.
20. The mode must be distinguished from the cause of death. It is often possible to tell accurately the cause of death. However, in the case of equivocal death, the expert in suicidal behaviour is placed in the position where he or she must determine the mode of death. This arises primarily where mode relates to the victim's intention and motivation to kill him- or herself.
21. Intention and motivation (including reasons) are psychological in nature.
22. Assessment of intention includes taking into account special features in which the deceased played a direct, conscious role in effecting his or her own demise.

23. Death from a deliberate action must be distinguished from an unintentioned (accidental) death in which the deceased played no intentional role in effecting his or her own demise and where death is due entirely to a situation from without and not from any internal psychological one.
24. According to some authorities (as already discussed in Chapter eight), an unintentional death can be distinguished from a sub-intentioned death in which the deceased played a partial, covert, latent, unconscious role in hastening his or her own demise, as manifested by imprudence, lifestyle, misuse of alcohol and drugs, disregard of life-prolonging medical regimens, and so on.
25. Sub-intentional and other indirect methods are ways in which individuals can participate in hastening their own demise – leaving the decision 'to fate' as it were.
26. The more isolated and abandoned and the more hopeless and helpless that individuals feel, the more suicidal they become. It has often been argued that the single best criterion for combating suicidality is good communication between suicidal individuals and their significant others.
27. As discussed in the Introduction, my own research and that of others has confirmed the importance of an adequate classification, definition and good communication with regard to suicidal behaviour.
28. Likewise, my own research and that of others has confirmed the link between feelings of hopelessness and suicide. Hopelessness has been found to be a better indicator of the intensity of a person's current suicidal ideation than depression (or other psychological disorders) is itself. Hopelessness is conceptualised as negative expectancies of the future and forms the link between depression or other psychological disorders and suicidal ideation on actual suicidal behaviour.
29. Because depression is such a prominent co-morbid factor in suicidal behaviour, I use it as an example here. The processing of information in depression is usually negatively biased in that the suicidal person views the self, the world and the future in terms of defeat and/or deprivation. This is classically referred

to as the triad of depression and can lead to a perception of hopelessness and helplessness.
30. Helplessness can be construed as a perception that the problem causing the psychological anguish is insoluble (for example, 'There is nothing I can do about my problems').
31. Depression and hopelessness as well as helplessness are components for assessing a person's potential for suicide risk and suicidal intent.
32. Dysfunctional assumptions and cognitions (frequently present in depression) play a key role in suicidal intent and ideation, as does dichotomous thinking. This includes dysfunctional cognitive schemata such as the exaggeration of a person's problems, minimising his or her resources or problem-solving skills, and predicting the worst for the future. The depressed person typically engages in various cognitive distortions (thinking errors). A classic example of a rigid form of dichotomous thinking is the 'all-or-nothing thinker'.
33. Another classic cognitive deficit related to the 'all-or-nothing' cognitive distortion ultimately views suicidal behaviour as a 'desirable solution'. Suicidal behaviour then becomes an escape from perceived problems as both a 'desirable' and an 'ultimate' solution (indeed, the 'perfect' solution).
34. Many of the authorities in this sector agree that there is no magic formula in arriving at an answer as to whether the act of self-cessation is suicide or not, or what the motivation and subtle psychodynamics were. The process is essentially a clinical operation in which the suicidologist weighs up the variables and nuances and gives an overall rating that best conveys the impression of the intent of the person who allegedly engaged in suicidal behaviour.
35. Any other issues relevant to the psychological autopsy (including variables related to the maintenance, enhancement and dignity associated with the deceased's quality of life), are taken into account. What should be borne in mind is the fact that depression is eminently treatable in most cases, and that suicidal behaviour is eminently preventable, provided that early diagnosis and the appropriate steps for therapeutic intervention are effected (Lasich & Schlebusch, 1999).

PREVENTION

The information contained in this section is based on my own clinical experience and on other research quoted in this book.

General considerations

It is important to emphasise that there should not be an inevitable suicidal destiny. Although suicidal impulses/behaviour may be perceived as impossible to eliminate, they are usually more or less transient. Once the suicidal crisis is over, the person can be made to realise that there are new opportunities; the essence is that people have an infinite capacity to find new pathways that are more fulfilling and less stressful.

Suicidal behaviour can be prevented. There are various ways in which this may be achieved, such as:
- providing the opportunity to confide in someone who understands;
- making it possible to obtain support in handling stressful situations;
- putting the person in touch with someone who can provide further help;
- making an accurate diagnosis and providing an appropriate treatment strategy of psychological disorders if they are present; and
- preventing access to methods of suicidal behaviour.

Emphasise that help is always available. It is important to realise that knowledge of suicidal problems and how they are associated with co-morbid and related factors is constantly accumulating and being distributed.

In addition, the WHO (amongst others) recommends several basic steps for the prevention of suicidal behaviour. These include:
- the treatment of mental disorders;
- gun possession control;
- detoxification of domestic gas;
- control of toxic substance availability; and
- toning down reports in the media.

Bodies such as the IASP and others have called on government health organisations, non-governmental health and welfare groups and volunteer organisations as well as the general public to share

the responsibility for the prevention of suicide, and also to work towards:
- the allocation of sufficient funds and human resources for research and suicide prevention strategies;
- the establishment of appropriate government agencies to provide leadership co-ordination and resources to prevent suicide;
- the establishment of national and local networks of support and partnership for suicide prevention; and
- the provision of resources to groups who may have special requirements.

To this may be added the need to:
- keep suicide prevention near the top of the health agenda;
- ensure international co-operation and access to the latest information about suicide prevention;
- encourage and promote research into the efficacy and feasibility of suicide prevention programmes; and
- ensure that adequate care is available to those affected by suicide.

Basic issues around psychobiology and the prevention of suicidal behaviour

The current neurochemical theories of biological correlates of suicidal behaviour principally involve the *serotonergic system*. The association between serotonin disturbance and suicidal behaviour is clearly evident. This has opened up the possibility for a search for other biological variables that may also be related to suicidal behaviour. Such variables include catecholamines, cortisol and other hormones as well as several neuropeptides. Furthermore, monoamines have neuromodulating effects on the endocrine axes, such as the hypothalamus-pituitary-adrenal (HPA) axis, and a dysfunction may be reflected through abnormal secretion of steroids as an effect of stressors.

A significant amount of research on stress and the HPA axis has demonstrated the importance of its link to an understanding of the relationship between the *psychobiology* of suicidal behaviour, and *stress* and *mood* as an important scientific and public health issue.

The introduction of *preventative* programmes on suicidal behaviour should, therefore, include a careful evaluation of the expected *psychological* as well as the *physical* effects of these on suicidal behaviour. Suicidal persons tend to use dysfunctional coping strategies in stressful situations or when they are socialising. Individual and family psychological interventions are, therefore, extremely important as well. Recent advances in brain imaging in humans are likely to lead to a new era where biological research will be utilised for suicide prevention.

Suicide survivor programmes
In South Africa in the past, suicide prevention efforts focused almost entirely on the suicidal person. A comparatively new initiative in the field of suicidology is the development of programmes to help families following their bereavement after a suicide. Research has shown that survivor help assists those individuals through their intensely painful experience of loss, and also reduces prejudice, facilitates research, helps with investigations into the effectiveness of prevention programmes, and encourages studies on overcoming cultural hurdles, restrictions and associated biases.

An organisational system for managing and preventing suicidal behaviour
One of the major sources of concern in managing a patient who presents with suicidal behaviour is the absence of a meaningful conceptual framework. Such a framework is presented here (Fig. 10.1) in a step-by-step conceptualisation of psychological intervention from a combined dynamic and systems analysis approach, developed as a viable guide in the management of suicidal behaviour based on current available data and my previous research (Schlebusch, 1985c, 2000b). It is flexible enough for modification to meet both particular patient needs and therapist orientation as the situation requires, since the heterogeneity of problems associated with suicidal behaviour demands the availability of a wide range of treatment options.

The approach is presented in the form of a summary flow chart, broadly divided into seven closely related stages of management, namely:
- assessment of the patient;
- recognition of significant life events;
- special problems;
- specific problem-orientated treatment;
- additional components of treatment;

- prevention and control; and
- reduction of psychological pain and addressing risk factors.

Each stage is further detailed in the text in a separate extension of the relevant box of the summary flow chart. The aim is to learn how to identify suicidal behaviour as well as how to manage and prevent it. The questions explored are given as examples and may be extrapolated when and where necessary.

Fig. 10.1 Summary flow chart of the management and prevention of suicidal behaviour

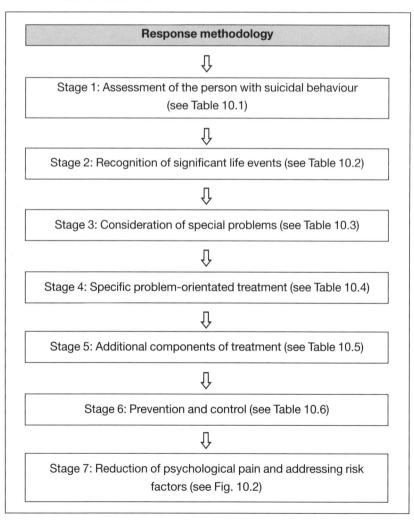

Table 10.1 Assessment of the person with suicidal behaviour

Questions to ask	Explore/Clarify
What were/are the person's focal motives?	Reasons given, circumstances, expected consequences, dynamic explanations
Is it possible to understand the event?	Detailed sequential account of previous 48 hours, whether patient was alone, precautions taken to prevent discovery
How serious was the suicidal behaviour?	Suicide note, planned, self-harm, method (knowledge of lethality), suicidal intent, risk of repetition, use of drugs or alcohol, was patient alone?
What was the impact on the environment?	Response of family/friends, acting out, communication of unresolved needs, manipulative act
What is the person's self-destructive capacity?	Immediate/continuing risk, access to method, previous suicidal behaviour, previous psychological treatment
Is there a mental disorder present?	Mental status, symptoms, diagnosis
How does the person see the future?	Hopelessness, value of trying, use of hopelessness scales
What are the person's resources?	Capabilities to resolve motives, internal and external resources, collateral from relatives
What treatment is appropriate?	Accepting help, competence to refuse, arrangements, outline patient care, referral

Table 10.2 Recognition of significant life events

Events to consider	Explore/Clarify
Health	Physical/mental disorder, stress, bereavement, impending loss, excessive use of alcohol/drugs
Moves	Housing, emigration, social isolation, loss of support systems
Legal	Offences, court proceedings, prison, lawsuits, recent alteration of will
Family	Marital problems, separation, sexual problems/adjustment, relationships
Children	Relationships with, problems with, children leaving home
Financial matters	Debts, large loans, bankruptcy, recent extra insurance, financial provision for family
Employment	Demotion, promotion, argument with employer, retirement, unemployment
Education	Studying for examinations, failing examinations, study problems
Other changes	Social relationships, any expected changes that might create problems

Table 10.3 Consideration of special problems

Person	Consider	Therapist response
Who refuses hospital treatment	Mental disorder, rapport, defence mechanisms, serious intent	Alert family, explore patient perceptions of treatment
Claiming rational suicidality	Decision-making skills, age, attitude to death, social support	Consider hidden mental disorder, quality of life
With repetitive suicidality	Pathological need, reinforcement, dynamics of self-harm, manipulation	Long-term therapy, contract or accessibility, open-door policy
With high risk	Mental disorder, prodromal symptoms, suicidality in hospital	Improve in-patient care, suicidesitter/ preceptorship
Who survives suicide pact	Possible legal problems, mental disorder (especially where two closely related persons share the same delusions), repeated act	In-patient care
With delayed complications	Risk of late complications especially in overdoses, method	Refer to nursing and medical back-up team
Who is very young/ adolescent	Distorted information, problems with authority figures/verbalisation/ communication of needs	Encourage trust, involve parents, specific techniques
Who is seductive	Professional relationship, manipulative behaviour, transference/counter transference	Redefine relationship, work through transference/counter transference, consult senior colleague
Who acts out	Personality and/or impulse/control/conduct disorders, difficulty in communicating needs	Encourage discussion of feelings, narcissistic collusion, pressure-cooker model

Table 10.3 Consideration of special problems (continued)

Person	Consider	Therapist response
With sub-intentional suicidal behaviour	Denial, precipitated accidents, unconscious wish to die, lifestyle	Explore possible underlying causes, for example, hopelessness, depression

Table 10.4 Specific problem-orientated treatment

Decide based on results of assessment package	• Whom to see (spouse, parents, other patients) • Where to treat (in-patient, out-patient) • Frequency/duration of sessions (determined by patient's needs) • Which problem areas have been identified/defined? • The settings in which identified problems occur • Other performance discrepancies • Role of other team members (including general practitioner)
Negotiate a therapeutic contact	• Agree on unambiguous operational therapeutic alliance • Modalities of treatment, including medication • Work on defined problem areas, establishment of motivation
Establish goals	• Choose between alternatives (Must I leave her/him?), specifics (How can I improve the relationship?) • Choose appropriate goals attainable in a relatively short period • Clarify successful methods to attain chosen goals
Begin initial therapy	• Agree on what patient has to do before next session • Monitor/review progress in detail • Specify performance discrepancies

Table 10.4 Specific problem-orientated treatment (continued)

Continue therapy	• Develop the relationship as focus of treatment (convey trust, understanding, interest, concern) • Facilitate communication (to resolve conflicts and express needs) • Emphasise alternative techniques to suicidality for expressing emotions • Be receptive to non-verbal communication (notes, withdrawal, acting out) • Modify attitudes by using, *inter alia*, confrontation and/or interpretation • Provide information (for example, on side effects of medication, correct misinformed beliefs)
Continue therapy	• Give guidance on issues such as where to get help, family planning clinic, and so on • Work towards decreased alienation from dominant value demands • Emphasise self-responsibility (reduce impulsive behaviour) • Explore direction of aggression (for example, self-harm and/or to harm others) • Enlist community resources/ patients/family/friends • Set limits to unreasonable demands on therapeutic relationship • Emphasise availability of help (open-door policy)

Table 10.5 Additional components of treatment

| Telephone intervention | - Engage patient in realistic talk of death to reinstate control
- Reduce anxiety through problem clarification
- Narrow down/open negative statements, reinterpret events
- Provide hope, use caller's name, reinforce availability of help |
|---|---|
| Mental disorder | - Consider in-patient psychiatric care, psychotropics, etc.
- Review inappropriately prescribed medication prior to suicidal behaviour
- Co-ordinate suicide prevention for patients at risk
- Carefully plan programme for subsequent care
- Consider psychological autopsy if suicidal behaviour occurs on in-patient unit, or when necessary |
| Psychotherapy | - Consider in-patient or out-patient basis, depending on need
- Consider greater involvement of therapist from usual crisis intervention
- Avoid pitfalls (for example, counter transference)
- Consider the fact that behaviour therapy can be very effective (cognitive restructuring, assertiveness training)
- A main aim is to move towards a problem-solving approach
- Designate a primary therapist; ventilation of emotions is important
- Insight psychotherapy is generally inappropriate in the early phase of distress or in adolescents and children
- Group psychotherapy can be helpful |

Table 10.5 Additional components of treatment (continued)

Family therapy	• Where there is a family crisis • With child and adolescent suicidal behaviour • Conjoint treatment of couples where necessary
Hospital admission	• Patients in acute state of distress who temporarily cannot cope • Crisis admission to relieve pressure on family or patient • History of maladaptive coping mechanisms may need repeated crisis admissions
Impact of treatment	• Determine response decrement (decreasing maladaptive behaviour) • Determine response increment (increasing adaptive behaviour) • Determine response acquisition (learning new behaviour) • Determine effects on personal problem-solving skills • Transfer of learning from therapeutic to extra-therapeutic situations
Training of staff	• Training in assessment of patients • Supervision (detailed daily discussion of new patients, regular review, other discussions)
Emergency settings	• Objective schema for grading suicidal behaviour • Flexible treatment approach • Review limitations of clinical and demographic risk factors

Table 10.6 Prevention and control

Primary prevention	• Immediate availability of emergency access help • Identification/management of at-risk patients, prediction scales • Improved control of substances/methods used • Education of public/health-care provider • Improvement of social and material circumstances of those at risk • Alertness to communication of suicidal intent/suicidal behaviour • Develop prevention in the hospital (hospital populations are at higher risk) • Early treatment of contributory mental disorders • Psychopharmacological prevention, including dangers of prescription • Resolve administrative/professional resistances, funding, management, attitudes • Prediction within a long-term time frame (high-risk group)
Secondary prevention	• Reduction of possible further suicidal behaviours (effective treatment) • Alleviation of stressors preceding suicidal behaviours • Serious consideration of trivial suicidal acts – they are not harmless • Prediction within a short-term time frame (individual patient)
Tertiary prevention	• Acute sensitivity to sibling/family response after suicidal behaviour • Behavioural sensitivity to response of friends (particularly with children and adolescents)

Remember that it is not so much that the suicidal person wants to die, but more that he or she wants to end his or her psychological pain. The person might try using alternative methods to achieve this, including the abuse of substances, high-risk behaviours or anything that will dull the psychological anguish that he or she is suffering from. Ultimately, when nothing works, the person slips into a cognitive rut from which the only alternative perceived is to end his or her life. As a result, a primary aim of therapeutic intervention is to reduce the suicidal person's psychological pain, thereby enabling him or her to reconsider his or her suicidal behaviour and lower his or her intent to die. This implies that simply removing the method without addressing the psychological pain of the precipitator of the suicidal act is not enough.

This process is illustrated in Fig. 10.2.

Fig. 10.2 Reduction of the psychological pain and addressing risk factors

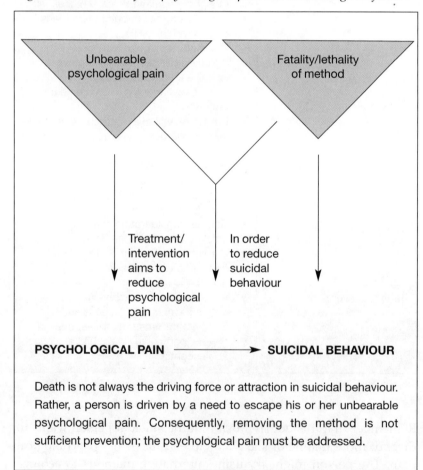

ETHICS AND SUICIDE PREVENTION

As discussed previously, ethical and legal issues in the field of suicidology are complex, multitudinous and vary worldwide. Although some universal principles regarding standards of care have been outlined, no single standard of care applies globally. Standards of community practice and the resources available tend to define standards of care. A basic conceptual struggle between promoting individual freedom and autonomy versus protecting people from self-harm or self-injury underlies the ethical (and legal) aspects of suicide and the clinical management of suicidal persons. The assessment and treatment of suicidal patients generally involves a clinical judgement. Unfortunately, however, conflicting ethical principles and ambiguities, the threat of litigation as well as restrictions imposed by the legal system often compromise clinical judgement.

In discussing these issues from both an international and a South African perspective, one of the members of the DPS group offered some additional ethical guidelines in managing and preventing suicidal behaviour (Bosch, 2000). Bosch makes the point that the terminology used globally in referring to topics of death and dying is both diverse and wide-ranging. In general, the definitions and literal meanings of the terms do not appear to be disputed. Rather, the disagreement seems essentially to involve the moral significance of the words. These specific moral or ethical disagreements are mostly with respect to particular acts, namely, euthanasia and withholding or withdrawing life-saving treatment or life-support systems. The dispute is around whether or not withholding or withdrawing life-saving treatment or support systems (which involve acts allowing natural death to occur) is fundamentally distinct from euthanasia (which involves acts that are the cause of death) or assisted suicide (which involves acts that help an individual to die).

Bosch goes on to emphasise that suicidal behaviour represents a central clinical and ethical dilemma in clinical practice that is dramatic and demanding for patients, their families and healthcare professionals. With sustained rate of increases in the young and under-reported rates in the adult and geriatric populations, suicide constitutes a serious public and mental health problem. In reviewing the ethics of suicide, two questions predominate:

- Does the patient have the moral right to commit suicide?; and
- What is the moral obligation of the clinician, and others, to intervene to prevent the suicide?

The prevailing traditional approach to suicide, which is often called the scientific or determinist view, holds that factors beyond the individual's control cause suicidal behaviour. As a consequence, the patient's decision to commit suicide is not seen as rational or autonomous. The patient is not responsible and is therefore not faced with a moral decision. By contrast, society is seen to have a moral obligation to intervene and save the patient; it is permitted, even mandated, to prevent suicide.

KEY POINTS

- Biological, psychosocial, cultural and environmental factors can all be involved in suicidal behaviour.
- Accurate diagnosis and appropriate treatment of the risk factors involved in suicidal behaviour include:
    - a biopsychosocial approach, which is important to understanding the contributing factors to suicidal behaviour;
    - the involvement of governmental and non-governmental organisations and the community at large; and
    - an organisational system with a clear conceptual framework, which is a useful tool for understanding, managing and/or preventing suicidal behaviour.
- There is no national South African suicide prevention programme in place at present, an unfortunate situation that urgently needs to be remedied.

CHAPTER ELEVEN

The Durban Parasuicide Study (DPS)

THE RESEARCH-BASED INTERVENTION and prevention model to deal with suicidal behaviour in South Africa that is presented here and in Chapter ten is based, in part, on previous work that I have published (Schlebusch, 1992a, 2004). Members of my research group from the Department of Behavioural Medicine at the Nelson R. Mandela School of Medicine, University of KwaZulu-Natal, Durban, South Africa, and its affiliated teaching hospitals and community clinics have had an active interest in service delivery to victims of suicidal behaviour. This includes research on the management and prevention of suicidal behaviour in South Africa stretching over the past 25 years. As mentioned earlier, these activities have been grouped into an ongoing programme known as the Durban Parasuicide Study (DPS), which is a multicentre, research-based intervention programme involved in studying suicidal behaviour in South Africa. A brief review of some major themes from the research findings over this period are presented here, against the backdrop of the rapid socio-political, economic and other changes that have occurred in South Africa, especially since the advent of a democratic system of government in 1994. Some of these changes have impacted on the population at risk for suicidal behaviour during the period under review. Certain crucial issues for health-service delivery and policy development on suicidal behaviour into the next decade and beyond, are also discussed in this chapter. By contextualising research on suicidal behaviour and the various research themes that have been undertaken by the DPS, conclusions have been reached and proposals for future research on suicidal behaviour are outlined. The work and ideas summarised here are based on an adaptation and update of earlier findings as well as on more recent contributions (Du Preez & Schlebusch, 1992; Schlebusch, 2004).

ORIGINS, DESIGN AND AIMS OF THE DPS

The DPS originated two years after my appointment (in 1976) as the first full-time clinical psychologist to a university-affiliated general teaching hospital (Addington Hospital in Durban, KwaZulu-Natal) as opposed to a psychiatric hospital, because of the significant numbers of suicidal patients who were being referred to the hospital's psychological services at the time (Schlebusch, 1978a). Much of the early work done by members of the DPS grew out of the establishment of formal consultation-liaison clinical psychology services, which were later extended to other principal general teaching hospitals and clinics in the province of KwaZulu-Natal (Schlebusch, 1983). The 'consultation' aspect of these services refers to the health services rendered to patients and families, whilst the 'liaison' component refers to the assessment and management of services offered to referring physicians and medical departments throughout the hospitals. This development occurred as a corollary to the development of acute psychiatric units in general hospitals in the metropolitan area that the service covered (Schlebusch, 1990a).

The impetus for the original service at Addington Hospital came from a growing awareness by both the casualty/trauma units and the medical/surgical units of the various hospitals that only medical stabilisation was being provided to those patients who were admitted because of some form of suicidal behaviour. A referral protocol was soon established, which allowed all patients admitted for medical treatment of suicidal behaviour to be comprehensively assessed by a clinical psychologist.

The initial work undertaken by the DPS culminated in various early conference presentations (Schlebusch, 1978a), and the first publications on suicidal behaviour (Minnaar, 1978; Minaar, Schlebusch & Levin, 1980; Schlebusch, 1978b, 1985a, b, c, 1986; Schlebusch & Minnaar, 1980). The original attempt to draw together the work of the DPS and of other researchers on suicidal behaviour in southern Africa was realised in the convening of the First Southern African Conference on Suicidology (Schlebusch, 1988a). Two years later saw the publication of an academic text that, *inter alia*, reflected contributions by members of the DPS to the field of medical psychology as related to suicidal and health-risk behaviour and medical problems in South Africa (Schlebusch, 1990a). At this point in the research programme it was possible to comment on suicidal behaviour in South Africa from a wide variety of medical and psychological contexts, and to include training in the prediction, management and prevention of suicidal behaviour. The three subsequent Southern African Conferences on Suicidology provided a platform for further consolidation of the research on suicidology in the southern African region (Schlebusch, 1992a, 1995a; Schlebusch & Bosch, 2000).

Fig. 11.1 A summary of essential features of the DPS

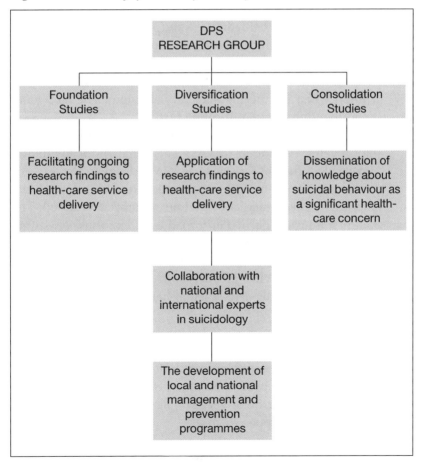

PROBLEM AREAS

As a result of the experience of the DPS research group over the past 25 years, a number of problem areas have been identified. These are probably applicable across the nation and include the following issues.

- Identifying suicidal behaviour can be difficult: (a) because it is frequently masked by the patient and/or family; and (b) because of the unhelpful method of note-taking by the attending health practioners. For example, although it should be a simple matter for emergency staff in a particular hospital to which a patient is admitted to enter a note that states 'intentional overdose', it is apparent that with many patients who present in emergency rooms, suicidal behaviour or ideation is obscured by entry notes about 'patient intoxication', or 'belligerence' and/or other 'non-suicidal' behaviours. Risk factors and assessment were discussed in Chapters nine and ten, along with management issues. Clearly the principles outlined there require careful consideration when identifying suicidal behaviour. The DPS team seeks to refine this identification further.
- It is necessary to identify suicidal behaviour that involves motor vehicle accidents (MVAs). This behaviour is frequently recorded in patients' records as 'MVA-drunken driving', or 'non-suicidal intentions', while questions about potential sub-intentioned suicidal behaviour are not entertained. The fact that injuries (particularly road traffic injuries) constitute a serious public health problem in South Africa has been repeatedly emphasised in this book (Suffla, Van Niekerk & Duncan, 2004). What is uncertain, is how many of these injuries can be linked to suicidal behaviour in both drivers and pedestrians.
- Any enquiry into suicidal behaviour should include data about previous suicidal behaviour in a patient. Enquiries need to be broad in scope and include questions such as:
    - Have you ever tried to harm yourself in any way before?
    - Have you ever done very reckless things without caring what might happen to you?
    - Have you ever accidentally or otherwise taken more medication than you should have?

- This type of enquiry is also useful for identifying sub-intentioned suicidal behaviour, and for identifying previous suicidal behaviour that did not require medical attention. Given this, a comprehensive method for the assessment of suicidal behaviour has been developed, which was discussed in Chapter ten (Schlebusch, 2000b).
- Data collection and storage can occasionally be problematic. This is because teaching hospitals and associated medical academic departments have a large component of rotating and temporary personnel. Individual styles of conducting interviews and recording data can become a problem when longitudinal or historical data are sought. Experience has shown that training in standardised interview formats and careful supervision of staff-in-training are essential for the compilation of accurate data about suicidal behaviour, and that the use of a structured assessment is invaluable, as discussed in Chapters nine and ten (Schlebusch, 2000b).
- There are problems relating to terminology and definitions of suicidal behaviour when varied terminology is used (for example, parasuicide, attempted suicide, sub-lethal suicide, sub-intentioned suicide, failed suicide, suicide gestures, etc.). Some of these terms are mutually exclusive whilst others clearly overlap. A clarification of the different variants of suicidal behaviour is discussed in the Introduction to this book to assist with the use of a common nomenclature in suicidal behaviour (Schlebusch, 1992b, 2000b).
- Problems are further compounded by individual suicidal patients' knowledge or lack of knowledge of the lethality of the particular method chosen and/or accessibility to such method(s).
- Most data and statistics to date have been based on samples drawn from academic hospitals and/or mortuary settings. With a few exceptions that involve community studies, data on patients receiving treatment from private practitioners, private facilities and occupational health services are often missing, as are the data on non-fatal suicide attempts based on community surveys because they are not systematically reported or recorded. It is generally agreed in both the local and international literature that prevalence data in suicidal

- behaviour are sadly under-reported and frequently lack generalisability to the population at large. This is particularly true for South Africa.
- A general overview of the literature of suicidal behaviour research in South Africa reveals various methodological problems and diversity of research designs, sampling procedures and methods of analyses. There is frequently a heavy preponderance of retrospective data and descriptive style research and a significant paucity of replicated, or potentially replicable, well-controlled, prospective studies or research that focuses on prevention and management. In short, this reveals that too many researchers are still locked in the phase of merely 'describing the problem', or 'counting heads'. There is an urgent need to move beyond this to a research level of managing and/or 'preventing the problem' as part of a more effective strategy. This is, in fact, one of the underlying contemporary aims of the DPS group and one of my primary aims.
- An appropriate national prevention programme is lacking in South Africa. This places major obstacles in the way of obtaining reliable and useful national data (WHO, 1999b).

A CONCEPTUAL MODEL FOR THE FUTURE AND A NATIONAL SUICIDE PREVENTION PROGRAMME

The motivation for developing a conceptual model to deal with suicidal behaviour in South Africa springs from the early work undertaken by the DPS group (Du Preez & Schlebusch, 1992). There are also compelling present-day considerations, especially the persistently high prevalence rates of both fatal and non-fatal suicidal behaviours in South Africa (Schlebusch, 2004).

Tremendous changes associated with socio-political and socio-economic factors, increased violence, and other related issues have been witnessed in South Africa over the last decade (Suffla, Van Niekerk & Duncan, 2004). These have elevated stress levels in South Africans and I have argued strongly for the need for teaching appropriate stress-management skills (Schlebusch, 2000c; Schlebusch & Bosch, 2002). The changes in South Africa have impacted on the catchment population served by suicide researchers in the country. An example of positive change that has occurred in South

Africa is evidenced in that the DPS research group has seen both the birth and the decline of racially segregated health services. Segregated services lead to replication and to inequality. Now that South Africa is a respected democracy, there is little doubt that the country is on the threshold of a new era in health-service management and provision, with a major drive towards primary health care and preventative strategies. Nevertheless, the call remains for the urgent development of relevant and contextualised services for the present and future. In this process, cost-effectiveness will be an essential factor in determining the nature and practices of health-service delivery in the future. In addition, these services will need to take cognisance of the significant increase of violence in South Africa that includes suicidal behaviour (WHO, 1999b) and trauma-producing behaviours (Schlebusch & Bosch, 2002) with associated potential suicidal risk factors (Schlebusch, 2004).

Given these concerns regarding suicidal behaviour in South Africa, it becomes imperative on a national basis to:

- expand the existing data base and to develop programmes for gathering more reliable statistics;
- identify current demographic and epidemiological trends;
- evaluate the existing services in the light of these trends;
- identify groups or areas of special concern that require the development of more proactive, relevant service strategies;
- develop more refined criteria for describing what constitutes suicidal behaviour;
- differentiate between various forms of suicidal behaviours;
- highlight the role of substance taking and health-risk behaviour (including alcohol consumption and driving behaviour, given the carnage on South African roads) in the context of suicidal behaviour (Donson & Van Niekerk, 2002; Hooper-Box, *The Sunday Tribune*, 2003; Matzopoulos, 2002; Matzopoulos, Cassim & Seedat, 2003; Suffla, Van Niekerk & Duncan, 2004);
- refine existing models of guidelines for the management of health-risk behaviour (Schlebusch, 1990a);
- promote educational guidelines for use in primary health settings, for both patients and health practitioners, regarding non-compliance (non-adherence behaviour), medicine-taking behaviour, control of medicines in the home including

storage and disposal of medicines as well as poisons (Schlebusch, 1990a);
- develop guidelines for the communication between health-care professionals and patients, as well as for the cost-effectiveness of existing and future services (Schlebusch, 1990a);
- utilise an appropriate model for contextualising research programmes on suicidal behaviour, such as the bio-psychosocial model (based on systems theory), which can be utilised as a base point because of its robustness and its demonstrated usefulness in a variety of health-care contexts (Schlebusch, 1990a);
- focus on cognate dimensions associated with the different applicable variables related to people who display suicidal behaviour, the methods used in suicidal behaviour, and the context in which suicidal behaviour occurs;
- look at future needs;
- reflect on where the DPS and other suicidal behaviour research groups in South Africa now feature in relation to national and international suicide research activities and needs; and
- examine the role of somatic co-morbidity, especially in terms of HIV/Aids, in suicidal behaviour (Schlebusch, 2004; Schlebusch & Noor Mahomed, 2004).

The research work of the DPS is ongoing. It has facilitated the gathering of detailed data on:
- suicidal patient demographic and biological characteristics;
- methods employed in suicidal behaviour;
- the psychiatric and psychological diagnostics of patients who display suicidal behaviour; and
- the psychiatric/psychological treatment of these patients.

The DPS hopes to extend its research activities into a national and international programme by inviting participation from other groups that are researching suicidal behaviour. This has partly been achieved as new data obtained from the DPS are currently being incorporated into a database being gathered for an international WHO suicide research prevention programme. With regard to broadening the work of the DPS, I would like to invite wider research collaboration from South African and other researchers on suicidal behaviour as part of future DPS research endeavours. There are currently a number of research projects on the go under the auspices of the DPS. These include the link between suicidal behaviour and potentially life-threatening diseases; cross-cultural issues and suicidal behaviour; crimes of passion (murder-suicide) and suicidal behaviour; the effective use of existing health-care and educational structures to prevent suicidal behaviour; as well as the role of stress in suicidal behaviour.

KEY POINTS

- The DPS was established in 1978 and has since been involved in research into the prevention and management of suicidal behaviour in South Africa.
- In its pursuit of a research-based model for use in the prevention and management of suicidal behaviour in South Africa, the DPS has highlighted various problems concerning the identification of suicidal behaviour, especially in relation to the collection and interpretation of data, as well as the need for a conceptual model for future use.

Conclusion

THANKS TO THE expertise of many researchers there have been significant developments in our understanding of the phenomenon of suicidal behaviour in South Africa. Nevertheless, much remains to be done including, in particular, the pressing need to address the problem of suicidal behaviour on a collective national basis. Suicidal behaviour should and could be prevented and is an increasingly critical issue facing official health services and structures, health-care professionals, other professionals, employers, administrators, various organisations and the public in general.

The prediction, prevention and treatment of such tragic suffering and loss of life require a comprehensive understanding of the underlying aetiology and risk factors. Given the evident persistence of such behaviour in South African society, it is clear that the struggle against it is far from being won. This is especially the case because, as I have pointed out in this book, most research data point to the fact that suicidal behaviour is generally underestimated.

A significant percentage of young people are now indulging in suicidal behaviour and, as a result, family problems have become a focus of attention. The number of extended suicides and murder-suicides committed in South Africa has also caused attention to be directed to family dynamics. Poor problem-solving skills and an inability to communicate effectively can give rise to such intense frustration that suicidal behaviour could result.

The role of depression is almost ubiquitous, while substance abuse and the effects of trauma are also cited as causes of suicidal behaviour. In addition, the HIV/Aids pandemic is now becoming enormously significant as a co-morbid factor. Aetiological and co-morbid factors are varied, but the data presented in this book suggest that violence, socio-economic difficulties, family conflict, as well as inter-personal and educational pressures seem to be major contributors to the high stress levels and suicidal behaviour in South Africa.

I have emphasised before that most people feel that suicidal behaviour constitutes a tragedy that should be prevented. For example, in Chapter one we saw the agony that such an event can bring to a family. The question is, how do we prevent such a tragedy from occuring when our understanding of the underlying causes, prediction, management and prevention is still imperfect? Effective preventative measures and efforts to decrease the incidence of suicidal behaviour depend significantly on early identification and appropriate treatment of populations at high risk. Chapter six provided a sample of the many different types of suicidal behaviour that are reported in the press. Future research could look at a more critical analysis of such press reports in South Africa in order to assist with preventative efforts.

Organisational systems need to be developed to facilitate both improved understanding and more effective management of suicidal behaviour. In this regard, Chapter ten provides details of how to conduct a psychological autopsy, as well as an example of a clearly developed conceptual framework in the form of a flow chart and its corresponding extensions. Furthermore, hospital and other records are often ambiguous and there is an evident need for a standardised format to be used to record data on suicidal behaviour. Guidelines have been developed by the DPS group for the development of a conceptual model that it sees as crucial for future practice when dealing with suicidal behaviour.

South Africa has a diverse population with a wide variety of perceptions of suicidal behaviour. More research is required on cultural factors that might affect the incidence of suicidal behaviour, especially within the various African cultures in our country. In order to educate people about suicidal behaviour and to prevent it from occurring, we need community involvement, the help of schools and universities, professional help from non-governmental initiatives and organisations as well as direct governmental intervention at the highest level. In short, as I have repeatedly emphasised, every person in our society has some role to play, some responsibility to assume, in combating suicidal behaviour.

Select references

Alfrey, A.C. and Chan, L. (1992). Chronic renal failure: Manifestations and pathogenesis. In R.W. Schrier, ed. *Renal and Electrolyte Disorders*, 539–79. Boston: Little, Brown.

Allers, E. (2003). Drug overuse, misuse, abuse and addiction: Co-morbid to psychiatric disorders. *Serenity* 1(2): 1.

Alexander, B.K. and Hadaway, P.F. (1982). Opiate addiction: The case for an adaptive orientation. *Psychological Bulletin* 92: 367–81.

Anandan, J.V. and Matzke, G.R. (1981). Nephropathy as a hazard of analgesic abuse. *American Journal of Hospital Pharmacy* 38: 1 536–9.

Barron, C. (2005). *Collected South African Obituaries*. Johannesburg: Penguin.

Beckerman, N.L. (1995). Suicide in relation to AIDS. *Death Studies* 19: 223–34.

Beckett, S.W. (1994). *The Story of Painting*. London: Kindersley.

Bertolote, J.M. (2001). Suicide in the world: An epidemiological overview 1959–2000. In D. Wasserman, ed. *Suicide: An Unnecessary Death*, 3–10. London: Martin Dunitz.

Bertolote, J.M., Fleischmann, A., De Leo, D. and Wasserman, D. (2004). Psychiatric diagnoses and suicide: Revisiting the evidence. *Crisis* 25: 147–55.

Bille-Brahe, U. (2000). Sociology and suicidal behaviour. In K. Hawton and K. van Heeringen, eds. *The International Handbook of Suicide and Attempted Suicide*, 193–207. Chichester: Wiley.

Bond, M.R. (1971). The relation of pain to the Eysenck Personality Inventory, Cronell Medical Index and Whitely Index of Hypochondriasis. *British Journal of Psychiatry* 119: 671–8.

Bongar, B. (1991). *The Suicidal Patient: Clinical and Legal Standards of Care*. Washington: American Psychological Association.

Bosch, B.A. (2000). Workshop on ethics and suicide. In L. Schlebusch and B.A. Bosch, eds. *Suicidal Behaviour 4: Proceedings of the Fourth Southern African Conference on Suicidology*, 216–47. Durban: Department of Medically Applied Psychology, Faculty of Medicine, University of Natal.

Bosch, B.A., McGill, V.R. and Noor Mahomed, S.B. (1995). Current trends in suicidal behaviour at a general hospital. In L. Schlebusch, ed. *Suicidal Behaviour 3: Proceedings of the Third Southern African Conference on Suicidology*, 71–94. Durban: Department of Medically Applied Psychology, Faculty of Medicine, University of Natal.

Bosch, B.A. and Schlebusch, L. (1991). Neuropsychological deficits associated with uraemic encephalopathy. *South African Medical Journal* 79: 560–2.

Bradshaw, D., Masiteng, K. and Nannan, N. (2000). Health status and determinants. In *South African Health Review*, 89–124. Durban: Health Systems Trust.

Breetzke, K.A. (1988). Suicide in Cape Town: Is the challenge being met effectively? *South African Medical Journal* 73: 19–23.

Brink, G. (1992). Suicide in the South African defence force. In L. Schlebusch, ed. *Suicidal Behaviour 2: Proceedings of the Second Southern African Conference on Suicidology*, 187–94. Durban: Department of Medically Applied Psychology, Faculty of Medicine, University of Natal.

Burkart, J.M., Hamilton, R.W. and Buckalew, V.M. (1989). Prevention of renal failure. In J.F. Maher, ed. *Replacement of Renal Function by Dialysis: A Textbook of Dialysis*, 1 119–32. 3rd ed. Dordrecht: Kluwer Academic Publishers.

Burrows, S., Vaez, M., Butchart, A. and Laflamme, L. (2003). The share of suicide in injury deaths in the South African context: Sociodemographic distribution. *Public Health* 117: 3–10.

Cantor, C.H. (2000). Suicide in the western world. In K. Hawton and K. van Heeringen, eds. *The International Handbook of Suicide and Attempted Suicide*, 9–28. Chichester: Wiley.

Cassimjee, M.H. and Pillay, B.J. (2000). Suicidal behaviour in family practice: A pilot study. In L. Schlebusch and B.A. Bosch, eds. *Suicidal Behaviour 4: Proceedings of the Fourth Southern African Conference on Suicidology*, 49–55. Durban: Department of Medically Applied Psychology, Faculty of Medicine, University of Natal.

Catalan, J. (2000). Sexuality, reproductive cycle and suicidal behaviour. In K. Hawton and K. van Heeringen, eds. *The International Handbook of Suicide and Attempted Suicide*, 293–307. Chichester: Wiley.

Chambers Dictionary of Quotations. (2005). Edinburgh: Chambers Harrap Publishers.

Cheng, A.T.A. and Lee, C.S. (2000). Suicide in Asia and the Far East. In K. Hawton and K. van Heeringen, eds. *The International Handbook of Suicide and Attempted Suicide*, 29–48. Chichester: Wiley.

Collings, S.J. (1992). Suicidal thoughts and behaviours in men who were sexually molested as children: A study of a nonclinical sample. In L. Schlebusch, ed. *Suicidal Behaviour 2: Proceedings of the Second Southern African Conference on Suicidology*, 182–6. Durban: Department of Medically Applied Psychology, Faculty of Medicine, University of Natal.

Collomb, H. and Zwingelstein, J. (1968). Depressive states in an African community (Dakar). In T. Lambo, ed. *First Pan-African Conference Report*. Nigeria: Abeokuta.

Colt, G.H. (1991). *The Enigma of Suicide*. New York: Simon and Schuster.

Current Practice (January 1988). Headache: A day-to-day guide for the busy general practitioner. *Medical Chronicle*: 7–8.

Curtis, R.C. (1989a). Preface. In R.C. Curtis, ed. *Self-defeating Behaviors: Experimental Research, Clinical Impressions, and Practical Implications*, ix–xi. New York: Plenum.

———. (1989b). Integration: Conditions under which self-defeating and self-enhancing behaviors develop. In R.C. Curtis, ed. *Self-defeating Behaviors: Experimental Research, Clinical Impressions, and Practical Implications*, 343–61. New York: Plenum.

Davenport, A. and Finn, R. (1988). Paracetamol (acetaminophen) poisoning resulting in acute renal failure without hepatic coma. *Nephron* 50: 55–6.

Dawes, A., Robertson, B., Duncan, N., Ensink, K., Jackson, A., Reynolds, P., Pillay, A. and Richter, L. (1997). Child and adolescent mental health policy. In D. Foster, M. Freeman and Y. Pillay, eds. *Mental Health Policy Issues for South Africa*, 193–215. Cape Town: MASA Multimedia.

De Leo, D., ed. (2001). *Suicide and Euthanasia in Older Adults: A Transcultural Journey*. Seattle: Hogrefe and Huber.

Deonarain, M. and Pillay, B.J. (2000). A study of parasuicide behaviour at the Chris Hani Baragwanath Hospital. In L. Schlebusch and B.A. Bosch, eds. *Suicidal Behaviour 4: Proceedings of the Fourth Southern African Conference on Suicidology*, 112–27. Durban: Department of Medically Applied Psychology, Faculty of Medicine, University of Natal.

Dingfelder, S.F. (2004). Fatal friendships. *Monitor on Psychology* 35: 20–1.

Dixon, A.S., Smith, M.J.H., Martin, B.K. and Wood, P.H.N. (1963). *The Salicylates: An International Symposium*. Boston: Little, Brown.

Dolce, R. (1992). *Suicide*. New York: Chelsea House.

Donson, H. and Van Niekerk, A. (2002). Suicide. In R. Matzopoulos, ed. *A Profile of Fatal Injuries in South Africa: Third Annual Report of the National Injury Mortality Surveillance System*, 31–4. Tygerberg: Medical Research Council-UNISA Crime, Violence and Injury Lead Programme.

Du Plessis, W.F and Schlebusch, L. (1992). Suicidal behaviour and parental loss: A comparative study. In L. Schlebusch, ed. *Suicidal Behaviour 2: Proceedings of the Second Southern African Conference on Suicidology*, 86–98. Durban: Department of Medically Applied Psychology, Faculty of Medicine, University of Natal.

Du Preez, M.R. and Schlebusch, L. (1992). An outline of a multistudy research protocol on suicidal behaviour. In L. Schlebusch, ed. *Suicidal Behaviour 2: Proceedings of the Second Southern African Conference on Suicidology*, 99–106. Durban: Department of Medically Applied Psychology, Faculty of Medicine, University of Natal.

Durkheim, E. (1897). *Le Suicide*. Paris: Alcan.

Faber, G.L. (1990). A cost-effective, equitable and durable health care delivery system for South Africa: Recommendations by the Pharmaceutical Manufacturers' Association of South Africa. Paper presented to the Faculty of Medicine, University of Natal, Durban.

Farberow, N.L., ed. (1980). *The Many Faces of Suicide: Indirect Self-Destructive Behavior*. New York: McGraw-Hill.

Felthous, A.R. and Hempel, A. (1995). Combined homicide-suicides: A review. *Journal of the Forensic Sciences* 40: 846–57.

Feuerstein, M., Labbe, E.E. and Kuczmierczyk, A.R. (1986). *Health Psychology: A Psychobiological Perspective*. New York: Plenum.

Flisher, A.J. and Parry, C.D.H. (1994). Suicide in South Africa: An analysis of nationally registered mortality data for 1984–1986. *Acta Psychiatrica Scandenavica* 90: 348–53.

Flisher, A.J., Ziervogel, C.F., Chalton, D.O. and Robertson, B.A. (1992). Suicidal ideation and behaviour of Cape Peninsula high school students. In L. Schlebusch, ed. *Suicidal Behaviour 2: Proceedings of the Second Southern African Conference on Suicidology*, 107. Durban: Department of Medically Applied Psychology, Faculty of Medicine, University of Natal.

Frierson, R.L. and Lippmann, S.B. (1988). Suicide and AIDS. *Psychosomatics* 29: 226–9.

Fritsche, G., Nitsch, C., Pietrowsky, R. and Diener, H.C. (2000). Psychological descriptors of excessive use of analgesic medication. *Schmerz* 7: 217–25.

Furman, K.I. (1987). Preventive aspects of analgesic nephropathy. *Membrane* 9: 6–7.

Furman, K.I., Galasko, G.T.F., Meyers, A.M. and Rabkin, R. (1976). Post-transplantation analgesic dependence in patients who formerly suffered from analgesic nephropathy. *Clinical Nephrology* 5: 54–6.

Gala, C., Pergami, A., Catalan, J., Riccio, M., Durbano, F., Musicco, M., Baldeweg, T. and Invernizzi, G. (1992). Risk of deliberate self-harm and factors associated with suicidal behaviour among asymptomatic individuals with human immunodeficiency virus infection. *Acta Psychiatrica Scandenavica* 86: 70–5.

Gangat, A.E. (1988). Suicide in South Africa: A general overview and research findings. In L. Schlebusch, ed. *Suicidal Behaviour: Proceedings of the First Southern African Conference on Suicidology*, 18–28. Durban: Department of Medically Applied Psychology, Faculty of Medicine, University of Natal.

Gault, M.H., Rudwal, T.C., Engles, W.D. and Dossetor, J.B. (1968). Syndrome associated with the abuse of analgesics. *Annals of Internal Medicine* 68: 906–25.

Gault, M.H. and Wilson, D.R. (1978). Analgesic nephropathy in Canada: Clinical syndrome, management, and outcome. *Kidney International* 13: 58–63.

German, G.A. (1982). Aspects of clinical psychiatry in sub-Saharan Africa. *British Journal of Psychiatry* 121: 461–79.

Goodwin, D.W. (1985). Alcoholism and alcoholic psychoses. In H.I. Kaplan and B.J. Sadock, eds. *Comprehensive Textbook of Psychiatry*, 1 016–26. 4th ed. Baltimore: Williams and Wilkens.

Grant, I. and Atkinson, J.H. (1995). Psychiatric aspects of acquired immune deficiency syndrome. In H.I. Kaplan and B.J. Sadock, eds. *Comprehensive Textbook of Psychiatry*, 1 644–69. 4th ed. Baltimore: Williams and Wilkens.

Graser, R.R. (1992). *A Study of Selected Cases of Family Murder in South Africa*. Pretoria: Human Sciences Research Council.

Greden, J.F. (1985). Caffeine and tobacco dependence. In H.I. Kaplan and B.J. Sadock, eds. *Comprehensive Textbook of Psychiatry*, 1 026–33. 4th ed. Baltimore: Williams and Wilkens.

Hahn, C.A., Dunn, R. and Halperin, E.C. (2004). Routine screening for depression in radiation oncology patients. *American Journal for Clinical Oncology* 27: 497–99.

Harwood, D. and Jacoby, R. (2000). Suicidal behaviour among the elderly. In K. Hawton and K. van Heeringen, eds. *The International Handbook of Suicide and Attempted Suicide*, 275–91. Chichester: Wiley.

Hawton, K., Appelby, L., Platt, S., Foster, T., Cooper, J., Malmberg, A. and Simkin, S. (1998). The psychological autopsy approach to studying suicide: A review of methodological issues. *Journal of Affective Disorders* 50: 271–8.

Hawton, K. and Van Heeringen, K., eds. (2000). *The International Handbook of Suicide and Attempted Suicide.* Chichester: Wiley.

Henrich, W.L. (1988). Southwestern Internal Medicine Conference: Analgesic nephropathy. *American Journal of Medical Sciences* 295: 561-8.

Henry, W.A. (1991). Do-it-yourself death lessons. *Time* 19 August: 45.

Heuer, N.A.C. (1988). The inside and outside of suicide: Subjective and objective perspectives from pastoral analysis. In L. Schlebusch, ed. *Suicidal Behaviour: Proceedings of the First Southern African Conference on Suicidology,* 69-86. Durban: Department of Medically Applied Psychology, Faculty of Medicine, University of Natal.

Hinkin, C.H., Van Gorp, W.G. and Satz, P. (1995). Neuropsychological and neuropsychiatric aspects of HIV infection in adults. In H.I. Kaplan and B.J. Sadock, eds. *Comprehensive Textbook of Psychiatry,* 1 669-80. 4th ed. Baltimore: Williams and Wilkens.

Humphry, D. (1991). *Final Exit.* Eugene, OR: Hemlock Society.

Jacobsen, B.K. and Hansen, V. (1989). Mental problems and frequent use of analgesics. *Lancet* i: 27.

Jacobsson, L. (1985). Suicide and attempted suicide in a general hospital in western Ethiopia. *Acta Psychiatrica Scandenavica* 71: 596-600.

Jaffe, J.H. (1989). Addictions: What does biology have to tell? *International Review of Psychiatry* 1: 51-61.

Jeffreys, D. (2004). *Aspirin: The Remarkable Story of a Wonder Drug.* London: Bloomsbury.

Juang, K.D., Wand, S.J., Fuh, J.L., Lu, S.R. and Su, T.P. (2000). Co-morbidity of depressive and anxiety disorders in chronic daily headache and its subtypes. *Headache* 10: 818-23.

Kaplan, H.I. and Sadock, B.J., eds. (1995). *Comprehensive Textbook of Psychiatry.* 6th ed. Baltimore: Williams and Wilkins.

Keller, F. and Schwarz, A. (1983). Analgesic dilemma in chronic hemodialysis patients. *New England Journal of Medicine* 309: 50-1.

Kelly, B., Raphael, B. and Judd, F. (1998). Suicidal ideation, suicide attempts and HIV intention. *Psychosomatics* 39: 405-15.

Kerkhoff, J.F.M. (2000). Attempted suicide: Patterns and trends. In K. Hawton and K. van Heeringen, eds. *The International Handbook of Suicide and Attempted Suicide,* 49-64. Chichester: Wiley.

Kienhorst, I.W.M., De Wilde, E.J. and Diekstra, R.F.W. (1995). Suicidal behaviour in adolescents. *Archives of Suicide Research* 1: 185-209.

Killduff, M. and Javers, R. (1978). *The Suicide Cult: The Inside Story of the People's Temple Sect and the Massacre in Guyana.* New York: Bantam.

Kincaid-Smith, P. (1978). Analgesic nephropathy. *Kidney International* 13: 1–4.

Kingsley, D.P.E., Goldberg, B., Abrahams, C., Meyers, A.J., Furman, K.I. and Cohen, I. (1972). Analgesic nephropathy. *British Medical Journal* 4: 656–9.

Kizer, K.W., Green, M., Perkins, C.L., Doebbert, G. and Hughes, M.J. (1988). Aids and suicide in California. *Journal of the American Medical Association* 260: 1 881.

Knapp, M. and Avioli, L.V. (1982). Analgesic nephropathy. *Archives of Internal Medicine* 142: 1 197–9.

Kosky, R.J., Eshkevari, H.S., Goldney, R.D. and Hassan, R., eds. (1998). *Suicide Prevention: The Global Context*. New York: Plenum.

Kreitman, N., ed. (1977). *Parasuicide*. London: Wiley.

Kunkel, R.S. (1990). Tension-type (muscle contraction) headache: Evaluation and treatment. *Modern Medicine of South Africa* January: 25–34.

Lader, M. (1983). *Introduction to Psychopharmacology*. Kalamazoo: The Upjohn Company.

Lasich, A.J. and Schlebusch, L. (1999). Depressive disorders. *Disease Review*, 623–8. Pretoria: MIMS.

Laubscher, L.R. (2003). Suicide in a South African town: A cultural psychological investigation. *South African Journal of Psychology* 33: 133–43.

Leenaars, A., Betancourt, M., Cantor, C., Connolly, J., EchoHawk, M., Gailiene, D., Zhoa Xiong He, Kokorina, N., Lopatin, A., Lester, D., Rodriguez, M., Schlebusch, L., Yoshitomo Takahashi and Vijayakumar, L. (2000). Ethical and legal issues. In K. Hawton and K. van Heeringen, eds. *The International Handbook of Suicide and Attempted Suicide*, 421–35. Chichester: Wiley.

Leenaars, A., Cantor, C., Connolly, J., EchoHawk, M., Gailiene, D., Zhao Xiong He, Kokorina, N., Lester, D., Lopatin, A., Rodriguez, M., Schlebusch, L., Yoshitomo Takahashi, Vijayakumar, L. and Wenchstern, S. (2000). Controlling the environment to prevent suicide: International perspectives. *Canadian Journal of Psychiatry* 45: 639–44.

Leenaars, A., Connolly, J., Cantor, C., EchoHawk, M., Zhao Xiong He, Lester, D., Lopatin, A., Rodriguez, M., Schlebusch, L., Yoshitomo Takahashi, Vijayakumar, L. (2001). Suicide, assisted suicide and euthanasia: International perspectives. *Irish Journal of Psychological Medicine* 18, 1: 33–7.

Leenaars, A., Connolly, J., Gailiene, D., Goldney, R., Nambi, S., Schlebusch, L., Bosch, B.A. and Srinivasaraghavan, J. (2003). Ethical and legal issues: A workshop. In L. Vijayakumar, ed. *Suicide Prevention: Meeting the Challenge Together*, 85–110. Chennai: Orient Longman.

Lerer, L.B. (1992). The violent death of a woman: Victim or self-destruction. Towards an understanding of the role of alcohol in female homicide and suicide. In L. Schlebusch, ed. *Suicidal Behaviour 2: Proceedings of the Second Southern African Conference on Suicidology*, 108–16. Durban: Department of Medically Applied Psychology, Faculty of Medicine, University of Natal.

Lerer, L., Knobel, G. and Matzopoulos, R. (1995). The epidemiology of suicide in a South African city: From mortality surveillance to injury control. In L. Schlebusch, ed. *Suicidal Behaviour 3: Proceedings of the Third Southern African Conference on Suicidology*, 54–63. Durban: Department of Medically Applied Psychology, Faculty of Medicine, University of Natal.

Lester, D. (2000). *Why People Kill Themselves: A 2000 Summary of Research on Suicide*. 4th ed. Springfield, Ill: Charles C. Thomas.

Lester, D., Wood, P., Williams, C. and Haines, J. (2004). Motives for suicide: A study of Australian suicide notes. *Crisis* 25: 33–4.

Levin, A. (1988). The costs of suicide. In L. Schlebusch, ed. *Suicidal Behaviour: Proceedings of the First Southern African Conference on Suicidology*, 6–17. Durban: Department of Medically Applied Psychology, Faculty of Medicine, University of Natal.

———. (1992). Suicide patterns and trends in South Africa's population groups. In L. Schlebusch, ed. *Suicidal Behaviour 2: Proceedings of the Second Southern African Conference on Suicidology*, 5–22. Durban: Department of Medically Applied Psychology, Faculty of Medicine, University of Natal.

Lezak, M.D. (1995). *Neuropsychological Assessment*. 3rd ed. New York: Oxford University Press.

Lindegger, G.C. (1990). Applications of clinical health psychology to chronic pain. In L. Schlebusch, ed. *Clinical Health Psychology: A Behavioural Medicine Perspective*, 128–35. Halfway House: Southern Book Publishers.

Lindegger, G.C. and Wood, G. (1995). The AIDS crisis: Review of psychological issues and implications, with special reference to the South African situation. *South African Journal of Psychology* 25: 1–11.

Lönnqvist, J.K. (2000). Psychiatric aspects of suicidal behaviour: Depression. In K. Hawton and K. van Heeringen, eds. *The International Handbook of Suicide and Attempted Suicide*, 107–20. Chichester: Wiley.

———. (2001). Physical illness and suicide. In D. Wasserman, ed. *Suicide: An Unnecessary Death*, 93–8. London: Martin Dunitz.

Maaga, M.M. (1998). *Hearing the Voices of Jonestown.* New York: Syracuse University Press.

Madu, S.N. and Matla, M.P. (2003). The prevalence of suicidal behaviours amongst secondary school adolescents in the Limpopo Province, South Africa. *South African Journal of Psychology* 133: 126–32.

Mann, J.J., Waternaux, C., Haas, G. and Molone, K. (1999). Toward a clinical model of suicidal behaviour in psychiatric patients. *American Journal of Psychiatry* 156: 181–9.

Marazziti, D., Toni, C., Pedri, S., Bonuccelli, U., Pavese, N., Lucetti, C., Nuti, A., Muratorio, A. and Cassano, G.B. (1999). Prevalence of headache syndromes in panic disorder. *International Clinical Psychopharmacology* 4: 247–51.

Marusie, A. (2004). Towards a new definition of suicidality: Are we prone to Fregoli's Illusion? *Crisis* 25: 145–6.

Maruta, T., Swanson, D. and Finlayson, R. (1979). Drug abuse and dependency in patients with chronic pain. *Mayo Clinic Proceedings* 54: 241–4.

Marzuk, P.M., Tiemey, H., Tardiff, K., Gross, E.M., Morgan, E.B., Hsu, M.A. and Mann, J.J. (1988). Increased suicide risk of suicide in persons with AIDS. *Journal of the American Medical Association* 259: 1 333–7.

Matzopoulos, R., ed.(2002). *A Profile of Fatal Injuries in South Africa: Third Annual Report of the National Injury Mortality Surveillance System.* Tygerberg: Medical Research Council-UNISA Crime, Violence and Injury Lead Programme.

———. (2004). *A Profile of Fatal Injuries in South Africa: Fifth Annual Report of the National Injury Mortality Surveillance System.* Tygerberg: Medical Research Council-UNISA Crime, Violence and Injury Lead Programme.

Matzopoulos, R., Cassim, M. and Seedat, M. (2003). *A Profile of Fatal Injuries in South Africa: Fourth Annual Report of the National Injury Mortality Surveillance System.* Tygerberg: Medical Research Council-UNISA Crime, Violence and Injury Lead Programme.

Matzopoulos, R., Norman, R. and Bradshaw, D., eds. (2004). The burden of injury in South Africa: Fatal injury trends and international comparisons. In S. Suffla, A. van Niekerk and D. Duncan, eds. *Crime, Violence and Injury Prevention in South Africa: Developments and Challenges,* 9–21. Tygerberg: Medical Research Council – UNISA, Crime, Violence and Injury Lead Programme.

Mayekiso, T.V. (1995). Attitudes of black adolescents towards suicide. In L. Schlebusch, ed. *Suicidal Behaviour 3: Proceedings of the Third Southern African Conference on Suicidology,* 46–53. Durban: Department of Medically Applied Psychology, Faculty of Medicine, University of Natal.

Mayekiso, T.V. and Mkize, D.L. (1995). The relationship between self-punitive wishes and family background. In L. Schlebusch, ed. *Suicidal Behaviour 3: Proceedings of the Third Southern African Conference on Suicidology*, 95–103. Durban: Department of Medically Applied Psychology, Faculty of Medicine, University of Natal.

Mayekiso, T.V. and Ngcaba, R.L. (2000). Suicidal thoughts and behaviour among first-year medical students at the University of Transkei. In L. Schlebusch and B.A. Bosch, eds. *Suicidal Behaviour 4: Proceedings of the Fourth Southern African Conference on Suicidology*, 34–7. Durban: Department of Medically Applied Psychology, Faculty of Medicine, University of Natal.

McKendrick, B. and Hoffman, W., eds. (1990). *People and Violence in South Africa*. Cape Town: Oxford University Press.

McQuoid-Mason, D.J. (1995). Recent developments concerning euthanasia in South Africa. *Law and Medicine* 1: 7–23.

Meel, B.L. (2003). Suicide in HIV/AIDS in Transkei, South Africa. *Anil Aggrawal's Internet Journal of Forensic Medicine and Toxicology* 4(1): 1–9.

Meer, F. (1976). *Race and Suicide in South Africa*. London: Routledge and Kegan Paul.

Menninger, K.A. (1938). *Man Against Himself*. New York: Harcourt Brace.

Mhlongo, T. and Peltzer, K. (1999). Para-suicide among youth in a general hospital in South Africa. *Curationis* 22: 72–6.

MIMS Medical Specialities. (1991, 2004). Pretoria: *MIMS* 31: 10–20.

Minnaar, G.K. (1978). Facets of attempted suicide: The results of a survey. In L. Schlebusch, ed. *The Vulnerable: Understanding and Preventing Suicide*, O1–O9. Durban: Lifeline, Natal Coastal Region.

Minnaar, G.K., Schlebusch, L. and Levin, A. (1980). A current study of parasuicide in Durban. *South African Medical Journal* 57: 204–7.

Mkize, D.L. (1992). Suicide rate in Umtata: 1971–1990. In L. Schlebusch, ed. *Suicidal Behaviour 2: Proceedings of the Second Southern African Conference on Suicidology*, 9–22. Durban: Department of Medically Applied Psychology, Faculty of Medicine, University of Natal.

Murray, R.M. (1973). The origins of analgesic nephropathy. *British Journal of Psychiatry* 16: 99–106.

———. (1974). Personality factors in analgesic nephropathy. *Psychological Medicine* 4: 69–73.

Murray, T.G. (1981). Analgesic use and kidney disease. *Archives of Internal Medicine* 141: 423–4.

Nattrass, C.M. (1995). Alcohol abuse and suicidal behavior. In L. Schlebusch, ed. *Suicidal Behaviour 3: Proceedings of the Third Southern African Conference on Suicidology*, 39–45. Durban: Department of Medically Applied Psychology, Faculty of Medicine, University of Natal.

———. (1996). Psychological features of self-medication leading to abuse or dependence in the use of alcohol and over-the-counter analgesics and/or benzodiazepines. Ph.D. thesis, University of Natal, Durban.

Nock, M.K. and Marzuk, P.M. (2000). Suicide and violence. In K. Hawton and K. van Heeringen, eds. *The International Handbook of Suicide and Attempted Suicide*, 437–56. Chichester: Wiley.

Noor Mahomed, S.B. and Karim, E. (2000). Suicidal ideation and suicide attempts in patients with HIV presenting at a general hospital. In L. Schlebusch and B.A. Bosch, eds. *Suicidal Behaviour 4: Proceedings of the Fourth Southern African Conference on Suicidology*, 38–48. Durban: Department of Medically Applied Psychology, Faculty of Medicine, University of Natal.

Noor Mahomed, S.B., Schlebusch, L. and Bosch, B.A. (2003). Suicidal behaviour in patients diagnosed with cancer of the cervix. *Crisis* 24: 168–72.

Noor Mahomed, S.B., Selmer, C.A. and Bosch, B.A. (2000). Psychological profiles of children presenting with suicidal behaviour, with a specific focus on psychopathology. In L. Schlebusch and B.A. Bosch, eds. *Suicidal Behaviour 4: Proceedings of the Fourth Southern African Conference on Suicidology*, 56–70. Durban: Department of Medically Applied Psychology, Faculty of Medicine, University of Natal.

O'Carrol, P.W., Berman, A.L., Maris, R., Moscicki, E., Tanney, B. and Silverman, F. (1998). Beyond the Tower of Babel: A nomenclature for suicidology. In R.J. Kosky et al., eds. *Suicide Prevention: The Global Context*, 23–39. New York: Plenum.

O'Dowd, M.A., Biderman, D.J. and McKegney, F.P. (1993). Incidence of suicidality in AIDS and HIV-positive patients attending a psychiatry outpatient program. *Psychosomatics* 34: 33–40.

Oosthuizen, G.C. (1988). Suicide and religions. In L. Schlebusch, ed. *Suicidal Behaviour: Proceedings of the First Southern African Conference on Suicidology*, 61–8. Durban: Department of Medically Applied Psychology, Faculty of Medicine, University of Natal.

Orley, J. (1970). *Culture and Mental Illness*. Nairobi: East African Publishing House.

Osborne, S. (2001). Murder-suicide in South Africa: A newspaper surveillance of press reports (1997–2001). Honours dissertation, University of Natal, Pietermaritzburg.

Parry, C. (2000). Alcohol and other drug use. In *South African Health Review*, 441–54. Durban: Health Systems Trust.

Parsoo, I., Seedat, Y.K., Naicker, S. and Kallmeyer, J.C. (1983). An interracial study of continuous ambulatory peritoneal dialysis (CAPD) in Natal. *South African Medical Journal* 63: 403–5.

Pelser, D.J.W. and Oberholzer, D.J. (1987). Attempted suicide (parasuicide), Medunsa/Ga-Rankuwa Hospital, South Africa. *Psychotherapia* 14: 22–4.

Peltzer, K. and Cherian, V.I. (1998). Attitudes towards suicide among South African secondary school pupils. *Psychological Reports* 83: 1 259–65.

Perry, S., Jacobsberg, L. and Fishman, B. (1990). Suicidal ideation and HIV testing. *JAMA* 263: 679–82.

Peters, D., ed. (2001). *Understanding the Placebo Effect in Complementary Medicine: Theory, Practice and Research*. Edinburgh: Churchill Livingstone.

Phillips, D.P. and Carstensen, L.L. (1988). The effect of suicide stories on various demographic groups, 1968–1985. In R. Maris, ed. *Understanding and Preventing Suicide*, 100–14. New York: The Guilford Press.

Pienaar, J. (2003). Coping, stress and suicide ideation in the South African Police Service. Ph.D. thesis, Potchefstroom University.

Pieterse, J.J. (1993). 'n Psigologiese outopsie van polisieselfmoord. MA Thesis, University of Pretoria.

Pillay, A.L. (1988). Methods of self-destructive behaviour in adolescents and young adults. *Psychological Reports* 63: 552–4.

Pillay, A.L. and Wassenaar, D.R. (1997a). Family dynamics, hopelessness and psychiatric disturbance in parasuicidal adolescents. *Australian and New Zealand Journal of Psychiatry* 31: 227–31.

———. (1997b). Recent stressors and family satisfaction in suicidal adolescents in South Africa. *Journal of Adolescence* 20: 155–62.

Pillay, A.L., Wassenaar, D.R. and Kramers, A.L. (2004). Attendance at psychological consultants following non-fatal suicidal behaviour: An ethical dilemma. *South African Journal of Psychology* 34: 350–63.

Pillay, B.J. (1995a). A study of suicidal behaviour at a secondary school. In L. Schlebusch, ed. *Suicidal Behaviour 3: Proceedings of the Third Southern African Conference on Suicidology*, 9–18. Durban: Department of Medically Applied Psychology, Faculty of Medicine, University of Natal.

———. (1995b). Children's perceptions of suicide: A study at a primary school. In L. Schlebusch, ed. *Suicidal Behaviour 3: Proceedings of the Third Southern African Conference on Suicidology*, 162–71. Durban: Department of Medically Applied Psychology, Faculty of Medicine, University of Natal.

Pillay, B.J. and Schlebusch, L. (1997). Psychological intervention to assist victims and others exposed to human rights violations in South Africa. *International Psychologist* 37: 94.

Pirkis, J. and Burgess, P. (1998). Suicide and recency of health care contacts: A systematic review. *British Journal of Psychiatry* 11: 983–6.

Pretorius, H.W. and Roos, J.L. (1995). Chronic and acute stressors in non-fatal suicide behaviour. In L. Schlebusch, ed. *Suicidal Behaviour 3: Proceedings of the Third Southern African Conference on Suicidology*, 64–70. Durban: Department of Medically Applied Psychology, Faculty of Medicine, University of Natal.

Prince, R. (1968). The changing picture of depressive syndromes in South Africa: Is it a fact or diagnostic fashion? *Canadian Journal of African Studies* 1: 177–92.

Prinsloo, M. (2002a). Participating facilities and data representivity. In R. Matzopoulos, ed. *A Profile of Fatal Injuries in South Africa: Third Annual Report of the National Injury Mortality Surveillance System*, 5. Tygerberg: Medical Research Council-UNISA Crime, Injury and Violence Lead Programme.

———. (2002b). Manner of non-natural death. In R. Matzopoulos, ed. *A Profile of Fatal Injuries in South Africa: Third Annual Report of the National Injury Mortality Surveillance System*, 7–14. Tygerberg: Medical Research Council-UNISA Crime, Injury and Violence Lead Programme.

Pugh, K. (1995). Suicide in patients with HIV infection and AIDS. In L. Sherr, ed. *Grief and AIDS*, 45–58. Chichester: Wiley.

Radat, F., Irachabel, S., Swendsen, J. and Henry, P. (2002). Analgesic abuse and psychiatric co-morbidity in headache patients. *Encephale* 1: 466–71.

Radat, F., Sakh, D., Lutz, G., El Amrani, M. and Bousser, M.G. (1999). Psychiatric co-morbidity is related to headache induced by chronic substances use in migraineurs. *Headache* 7: 477–80.

Room, R. (1989). Drugs, consciousness and self-control: Popular and medical conceptions. *International Review of Psychiatry* 1: 63–70.

Roos, J.L., Beyers, D. and Visser, M.J. (1992). Family murder: Psychiatric and psychological causes. *Geneeskunde* 34: 25–30.

Rossouw, L. (2000). Die samestelling van 'n dinamiese profiel vir SAPD – Personeel met 'n hoë risiko vir selfmoord. MA Thesis, University of Pretoria.

Rundell, J.R., Kyle, K.M. and Brown, G.R. (1992). Risk factors for suicide attempts: Human immunodeficiency virus screening program. *Psychosomatics* 33: 24–7.

Sakinofsky, I. (2000). Repetition of suicidal behaviour. In K. Hawton and K. van Heeringen, eds. *The International Handbook of Suicide and Attempted Suicide*, 385–404. Chichester: Wiley.

Schlebusch, L., ed. (1978a). *The Vulnerable: Understanding and Preventing Suicide*. Durban: Lifeline, Natal Coastal Region.

———. (1978b). Mental disorder and attempted suicide. In L. Schlebusch, ed. *The Vulnerable: Understanding and Preventing Suicide*, N1–N7. Durban: Lifeline, Natal Coastal Region.

———. (1982). Cognitive changes associated with the uraemic syndrome in patients with end-stage renal disease. In S.G. Tollman and A.D. Watts, eds. *Neuropsychology 1: Proceedings of the First South African Neuropsychology Conference*, 111–20. Durban: Department of Psychology, University of Natal.

———. (1983). Consultation-liaison: Clinical psychology in modern general hospital practice. *South African Medical Journal* 64: 781–6.

———. (1985a). Self-destructive behaviour in adolescents. *South African Medical Journal* 68: 792–5.

———. (1985b). Short-term precipitants of parasuicide in adolescents. *South African Medical Journal* 70: 165–7.

———. (1985c). Current management of parasuicide. *South African Prescriber*, supplement in *Stress: The Modern Scourge* 1: 25–9.

———. (1985d). Difficulties in treating South African renal patients in a multiethnic society. *Contemporary Dialysis and Nephrology* 6(5): 39–40.

———. (1986). Comments on medical psychology and the aetiology of adolescent parasuicides. *Psychiatric Insight* 3: 3–6.

———., (1987). Drug accessibility and the overdose epidemic. *South African Medical Journal* 71: 746–7.

———., ed. (1988a). *Suicidal Behaviour: Proceedings of the First Southern African Conference on Suicidology*. Durban: Department of Medically Applied Psychology, Faculty of Medicine, University of Natal.

———. (1988b). Family murder. *Psychiatric Insight* 5(3): 5–7.

———. (1989). *Mind-Body Synthesis: The Interactive Health Care Equation*. Pietermaritzburg: University of Natal Press.

———., ed. (1990a). *Clinical Health Psychology: A Behavioural Medicine Perspective.* Halfway House: Southern Book Publishers.

———., ed. (1990b). *A Basic Guide to the Diagnosis and Treatment of Depression. [National Depression Colloquia Programme.]* Johannesburg: Ciba-Ceigy.

———. (1990c). Applications of clinical health in psychology to psychiatry. In L. Schlebusch, ed. *Clinical Health Psychology: A Behavioural Medicine Perspective,* 200–66. Halfway House: Southern Book Publishers.

———. (1991). The psychopathogenesis of analgesic nephropathy. M Med Sc (Psychiat.) thesis, University of Natal, Durban.

———., ed. (1992a). *Suicidal Behaviour 2: Proceedings of the Second Southern African Conference on Suicidology.* Durban: Department of Medically Applied Psychology, Faculty of Medicine, University of Natal.

———. (1992b). The classification of suicidal behaviour, the abuse of analgesics and indirect self-destructive behaviour. In L. Schlebusch, ed. *Suicidal Behaviour 2: Proceedings of the Second Southern African Conference on Suicidology,* 23–35. Durban: Department of Medically Applied Psychology, Faculty of Medicine, University of Natal.

———., ed. (1995a). *Suicidal Behaviour 3: Proceedings of the Third Southern African Conference on Suicidology.* Durban: Department of Medically Applied Psychology, Faculty of Medicine, University of Natal.

———. (1995b). Stress, analgesic abuse and suicidal behaviour. In L. Schlebusch, ed. *Suicidal Behaviour 3: Proceedings of the Third Southern African Conference on Suicidology,* 19–38. Durban: Department of Medically Applied Psychology, Faculty of Medicine, University of Natal.

———. (1995c). A cross-cultural comparison of suicidal behaviour. In L. Schlebusch, ed. *Suicidal Behaviour 3: Proceedings of the Third Southern African Conference on Suicidology,* 104–19. Durban: Department of Medically Applied Psychology, Faculty of Medicine, University of Natal.

———. (1996). Health psychology in South Africa: An introduction. *South African Journal of Psychology* 26: 1–3.

———. (1998a). Recent advances in stress research and implications for health and well-being. In L. Schlebusch, ed. *South Africa Beyond Transition – Psychological Well-Being: Proceedings of the Third Annual Congress of the Psychological Society of South Africa,* 265–83. Pretoria: Psychological Society of South Africa.

———. (1998b). *Proverbial Stress Busters*. Cape Town: Human and Rousseau.

———. (1999a). Suicidal behaviour in South Africa as we enter the new millennium. Paper presented at the second Congress of the International Association for Suicide Prevention. Abstract published in *Programme and Book of Abstracts*, 143 and *Congress News*, 4.

———. (1999b). *Psychological Recovery from Cancer*. Cape Town: Maskew Miller Longman.

———. (2000a). An overview of suicidal behaviour in South Africa at the dawn of the new millenuim. In L. Schlebusch and B.A. Bosch, eds. *Suicidal Behaviour 4: Proceedings of the Fourth Southern African Conference on Suicidology*, 3–11. Durban: Department of Medically Applied Psychology, Faculty of Medicine, University of Natal.

———. (2000b). Workshop on stress and the management of the suicidal patient. In L. Schlebusch and B.A. Bosch, eds. *Suicidal Behaviour 4: Proceedings of the Fourth Southern African Conference on Suicidology*, 191–215. Durban: Department of Medically Applied Psychology, Faculty of Medicine, University of Natal.

———. (2000c). *Mind Shift: Stress Management and Your Health*. Pietermaritzburg: University of Natal Press.

———. (2003). An overview of research on suicidal behaviour in South Africa. Paper presented at the XXII World Congress of the International Association for Suicide Prevention (IASP), 10–14 September 2003, Stockholm. Abstract published in *Book of Abstracts*, 104: 4.

———. (2004). Current perspectives on suicidal behaviour in South Africa. In S. Suffla, A. van Niekerk and D. Duncan, eds. *Crime, Violence and Injury Prevention in South Africa: Developments and Challenges*, 9–21. Tygerberg: Medical Research Council-UNISA Crime, Violence and Injury Lead Programme.

———. (2005a). Suicidal behaviour within an international context. *Serenity* 3(2): 4–5, 9.

———. (2005b). Depression and suicidal behaviour. *South African Family Practice* 47: 61–3.

Schlebusch, L. and Bosch, B.A., eds. (2000). *Suicidal Behaviour 4: Proceedings of the Fourth Southern African Conference on Suicidology*. Durban: Department of Medically Applied Psychology, Faculty of Medicine, University of Natal.

———. (2002). The emotional injuries of indirect trauma. In C.E. Scout, ed. *The Psychology of Terrorism: Clinical Aspects and Responses* 2, 133–41. Westport, Connecticut: Preager.

Schlebusch, L., Bosch, B.A., Polglase, G., Kleinschmidt, K., Pillay B.J. and Cassimjee, M.H. (2000). A double-blind, placebo-controlled, double-centre study of the effects of an oral multivitamin combination containing calcium and magnesium on stress. *South African Medical Journal* 90: 1 216–23.

Schlebusch, L. and Cassidy, M.J. (1995). Stress, social support and biosychosocial dynamics in HIV/AIDS. *South African Journal of Psychology* 25: 27–30.

Schlebusch, L. and De Marigny, J.F. (1987). Analgesic nephropathy and psychological adjustment to dialysis. *Peritoneal Dialysis Bulletin* 7: 206.

Schlebusch, L., Lasich, A.J. and Wessels, W.H. (1985). Psychological problems, analgesic nephropathy and substance use disorder. *South African Medical Journal* 68: 912.

Schlebusch, L., Luiz, H.A., Bosch, B.A. and Levin, A. (1986). On suicide in South African general hospital psychiatric inpatient unit. *South African Journal of Psychology* 16: 15–20.

Schlebusch, L. and Minnaar, G.K. (1980). The management of parasuicide in adolescents. *South African Medical Journal* 57: 81–4.

Schlebusch, L. and Noor Mahomed, S.B. (2004). Suicidal behaviour in cancer and HIV/AIDS patients in South Africa. Paper presented at the tenth European Symposium on Suicide and Suicidal Behaviour, Copenhagen, 23–28 August. Abstract published in *Book of Abstracts*, 84.

Schlebusch, L. and Ruggieri, G. (1996). Health beliefs of a sample of black patients attending a specialised medical facility. *South African Journal of Psychology* 26: 35–8.

Schlebusch, L., Schweitzer, G. and Bosch, B.A. (1998). Psychological considerations in the management of the HIV-infected patient with polytrauma: A case presentation. In L. Schlebusch, ed. *South Africa Beyond Transition: Psychological Well-Being*, 260–83. Pretoria: Psychological Society of South Africa.

Schlebusch, L., Vawda, N. and Bosch, B.A. (2003). A brief review of research on suicidal behaviour in black South Africans. *Crisis* 24: 24–8.

Schlebusch, L., Wessels, W.H. and Rzadkowolsky, A. (1990). Cross-cultural indicators of help-seeking behaviour in aggressive general hospital patients. *South African Journal of Psychology* 20: 223–34.

Schmidtke, A. and Schaller, S. (2000). The role of mass media in suicide prevention. In K. Hawton and K. van Heeringen, eds. *The International Handbook of Suicide and Attempted Suicide*, 675–97. Chichester: Wiley.

Schmidtke, A., Schaller, S. and Wasserman, D. (2001). Suicide clusters and media coverage of suicide. In D. Wasserman, ed. *Suicide: An Unnecessary Death*, 265–8. London: Martin Dunitz.

Seedat, Y.K. (1990). Perspectives on dialysis and transplantation in South Africa. *South African Medical Journal* 77: 549–50.

Seedat, Y.K. and MacSearraigh, E.T.M. (1984). The abuse of analgesics leading to nephropathy in South Africa. *South African Medical Journal* 66: 751.

Seedat, Y.K., Naicker, S., Rawat, R. and Parsoo, I. (1984). Racial differences in the causes of end-stage renal failure in Natal. *South African Medical Journal* 65: 956–8.

Segasothy, M., Suleiman, A.B., Puvaneswary, M. and Rohana, A. (1988). Paracetamol: A cause for analgesic nephropathy and end-stage renal disease. *Nephron* 50: 50–4.

Sherr, L. (1995). The experience of grief: psychological aspects of grief in AIDS and HIV infection. In L. Sherr, ed. *Grief and AIDS*, 1–27. Chichester: Wiley.

Shneidmann, E.S. (1981). The psychological autopsy. *Suicide and Life-Threatening Behavior* 11: 325–40.

———. (1985). *Definition of Suicide*. New York: Wiley.

———. (2001). *Comprehending Suicide: Landmarks in 20th Century Suicidology*. Washington: American Psychological Association.

Siegel, K. and Meyer, I.H. (1999). Hope and resiliance in suicide ideation and behaviour of gay and bisexual men following notification of HIV infection. *AIDS Education and Prevention* 11: 53–64.

Smith, M.J.H. and Smith, P.K. (1966). *The Salicylates*. New York: Interscience Publishers.

Sneiderman, B. and McQuoid-Mason, D. (2000). Decision-making at the end of life: The termination of life-prolonging treatment, euthanasia (mercy killing), and assisted suicide in Canada and South Africa. *The Comparative and International Law Journal of Southern Africa* 33: 193–209.

Snyder, L. and Caplan, A.L. (2002). *Assisted Suicide: Finding Common Ground*. Indiana: Indiana University Press.

South African Dialysis and Transplantation Registry (SADTR). (1987). *Combined Report on Maintenance Dialysis and Transplantation in the Republic of South Africa*. Cape Town: South African Dialysis and Transplantation Registry.

———. (1988). *Combined Report on Maintenance Dialysis and Transplantation in the Republic of South Africa*. Cape Town: South African Dialysis and Transplantation Registry.

———. (1990). *Combined Report on Maintenance Dialysis and Transplantation in the Republic of South Africa*. Cape Town: South African Dialysis and Transplantation Registry.

South African Health Review. (2000). Edited by A. Ntuli, N. Crisp, E. Clark and P. Barron. Durban: Health Systems Trust.

———. (2002). Edited by P. Ijumba, A. Ntuli and P. Barron. Durban: Health Systems Trust.

———. (2003/2004). Edited by P. Ijumba, C. Day and A. Ntuli. Durban: Health Systems Trust.

Spuhler, O. and Zollinger, H.U. (1953). Die chronische-interstitielle nephritis. *Zeitschrift für Klinische Medizin* 151: 1.

Steger, J.C. and Fordyce, W.E. (1982). Behavioral health care in the management of chronic pain. In T. Millon, C. Green and R. Meagher, eds. *Handbook of Clinical Health Psychology*, 467–97. New York: Plenum.

Stenager, E.N. and Stenager, E. (2000). Physical illness and suicidal behaviour. In K. Hawton and K. van Heeringen, eds. *The International Handbook of Suicide and Attempted Suicide*, 405–20. Chichester: Wiley.

Stengel, E. (1983). *Suicide and Attempted Suicide*. Harmondsworth: Penguin.

Sue, D., Sue, D.W. and Sue, S. (2000). *Understanding Abnormal Behaviour: HIV/AIDS Care and Counselling*. Boston: Houghton Mifflin.

Suffla, S., Van Niekerk, A. and Duncan, N., eds. (2004). *Crime, Violence and Injury Prevention in South Africa: Developments and Challenges*. Tygerberg: Medical Research Council-UNISA Crime, Violence and Injury Lead Programme.

Sukhai, A. and Van Niekerk, A. (2002). Transport-related deaths. In R. Matzopoulos, ed. *A Profile of Fatal Injuries in South Africa: Third Annual Report of the National Injury Mortality Surveillance System*, 23–6. Tygerberg: Medical Research Council-UNISA Crime, Violence and Injury Lead Programme.

Sutherland, V.J. and Cooper, C.L. (1990). *Understanding Stress: A Psychological Perspective for Health Professionals*. London: Chapman and Hall.

Thoits, P. (1985). Self-labelling process in mental illness: The role of emotional defiance. *American Journal of Sociology* 91: 221–48.

Thompson, T.L. (1985a). Headache. In H.I. Kaplan and B.J. Sadock, eds. *Comprehensive Textbook of Psychiatry*, 1 203–5. 4th ed. Baltimore: Williams and Wilkens.

———. (1985b). Chronic pain. In H.I. Kaplan and B.J. Sadock, eds. *Comprehensive Textbook of Psychiatry*, 1 212–15. 4th ed. Baltimore: Williams and Wilkens.

Townsend, K.L. (2003). A pilot investigation into the phenomenon of murder-suicide in Durban, KwaZulu-Natal. MA thesis, University of Natal, Pietermaritzburg.

Van Dyk, A. (2001). *HIV/AIDS: Care and Counselling, a Multidisciplinary Approach*. Cape Town: Pearson Education.

Van Gelder, A.L. (1990). Analgesic nephropathy. *Continuing Medical Education* 8: 609–12.

Van Gorp, W.G. and Cummings, J.L. (1995). Neuropsychiatric aspects. In H.I. Kaplan and B.J. Sadock, eds. *Comprehensive Textbook of Psychiatry*, 235–41. 4th ed. Baltimore: Williams and Wilkens.

Van Heeringen, K., Hawton, K. and Williams, J.M.G. (2000). Pathways to suicide: An integrative approach. In K. Hawton and K. van Heeringen, eds. *The International Handbook of Suicide and Attempted Suicide*, 223–34. Chichester: Wiley.

Van Niekerk, A., Suffla, S. and Seedat, M. (2004). Crime, violence and injury prevention in South Africa: Trends, emerging issues and opportunities. In S. Suffla, A. van Niekerk and D. Duncan, eds. *Crime, Violence and Injury Prevention in South Africa: Developments and Challenges*, 1–8. Tygerberg: Medical Research Council-UNISA Crime, Violence and Injury Lead Programme.

Vawda, N. (2005). Suicidal behaviour among black South African children and adolescents. In S. Malhotra, ed. *Mental Disorders in Children and Adolescents: Need and Strategies for Intervention*, 94–100. Delhi: CBS Publishers and Distributors.

Vijayakumar, L. (2003). *Suicide Prevention: Meeting the Challenge Together*. Chennai: Orient Longman.

Wachtel, P.L. (1987). *Action and Insight*. New York: Gilford Publications.

Walton, H. (1951). Attempted suicide in Cape Town. *South African Medical Journal* 24: 933–5.

Warburton, D.M. (1987). The functions of smoking. In W.R. Martin et al., eds. *Tobacco Smoking and Nicotine: A Neurobiological Approach*, 51–61. New York: Plenum.

Wassenaar, D.R. and Naidoo, P. (1995). Suicide rates amongst Indians and Whites in Pietermaritzburg: A comparison with South African suicide data. In L. Schlebusch, ed. *Suicidal Behaviour 3: Proceedings of the Third Southern African Conference on Suicidology*, 172–86. Durban: Department of Medically Applied Psychology, Faculty of Medicine, University of Natal.

Wassenaar, D.R., Pillay, A.L., Burns, K.D. and Davies, M. (1993). Evaluation of suicide prevention in schools. In D. Lester, ed. *Suicide '93*, 71–4. Denver: American Association of Suicidology.

Wassenaar, D.R., Pillay, A.L., Descoins, S., Goltman, M. and Naidoo, P. (2000). Patterns of suicide in Pietermaritzburg 1982–1996: Race, gender and seasonality. In L. Schlebusch and B.A. Bosch, eds. *Suicidal Behaviour 4: Proceedings of the Fourth Southern African Conference on Suicidology*, 97–111. Durban: Department of Medically Applied Psychology, Faculty of Medicine, University of Natal.

Wasserman, D., ed. (2001a). *Suicide: An Unnecessary Death*. London: Martin Dunitz.

———. (2001b). In a stress vulnerability model and the development of the suicidal process. In D. Wasserman, ed. *Suicide: An Unnecessary Death*, 13–27. London: Martin Dunitz.

———. (2001c). The work environment for health-care staff. In D. Wasserman, ed. *Suicide: An Unnecessary Death*, 237–42. London: Martin Dunitz.

Wells, C.E. (1985). Organic syndromes: Dementia. In H.I. Kaplan and B.J. Sadock, eds. *Comprehensive Textbook of Psychiatry*, 851–70. 4th ed. Baltimore: Williams and Wilkens.

Wenger, J.W. and Einstein, S. (1970). The use and misuse of aspirin: A contemporary problem. *International Journal of the Addictions* 5: 757–75.

Werth, J.L., ed. (1999). *Contemporary Perspectives on Rational Suicide*. Philadelphia: Brunner/Mazel.

West, R. (1989). The psychological basis of addiction. *International Review of Psychiatry* 1: 71–80.

Williams, J.M.G. and Pollock, L.R. (1993). Factors mediating suicidal behaviour. *Journal of Mental Health* 2: 3–26.

———. (2000). The psychology of suicidal behaviour. In K. Hawton and K. van Heeringen, eds. *The International Handbook of Suicide and Attempted Suicide*, 79–93. Chichester: Wiley.

Wood, F. and Goldston, D. (2000). Learning disabilities: A hidden source of suicidal thought and behaviour. In L. Schlebusch and B.A. Bosch, eds. *Suicidal Behaviour 4: Proceedings of the Fourth Southern African Conference on Suicidology*, 79–96. Durban: Department of Medically Applied Psychology, Faculty of Medicine, University of Natal.

World Health Organisation (WHO). (1999a). *Figures and Facts about Suicide*. Geneva: Department of Mental Health, WHO.

———. (1999b). *Report on a Workshop on Suicide: Prevention for Countries in the African Region*. Geneva: Department of Mental Health, WHO.

———. (2000a). *Preventing Suicide: How to Start a Survivors Group*. Geneva: Department of Mental Health, WHO.

———. (2000b). *Preventing Suicide: A Resource for General Physicians*. Geneva: Department of Mental Health, WHO.

———. (2000c). *Preventing Suicide: A Resource for Media Professionals.* Geneva: Department of Mental Health, WHO.

———. (2000d). *Preventing Suicide: A Resource for Primary Health Care Workers.* Geneva: Department of Mental Health, WHO.

———. (2000e). *Preventing Suicide: A Resource for Prison Officers.* Geneva: Department of Mental Health, WHO.

———. (2000f). *Preventing Suicide: A Resource for Teachers and Other School Staff.* Geneva: Department of Mental Health, WHO.

Wyngaard, G., Matzopoulos, R. and Van Niekerk, A. (2002). The national injury mortality surveillance system. In R. Matzopoulos, ed. *A Profile of Fatal Injuries in South Africa: Third Annual Report of the National Injury Mortality Surveillance System,* 1–3. Tygerberg: Medical Research Council-UNISA Crime, Violence and Injury Lead Programme.

NEWSPAPER AND MAGAZINE ARTICLES

Ajam, K. Violent death toll behind gun amnesty. *The Independent on Saturday,* 26 March 2005: 3.

Bolowana, A. and Khan, F. Poll shows high HIV prevalence in teachers. *The Mercury,* 1 April 2005: 3.

Booyens, H. Suicide by cell phone. *You Magazine,* 20 May 2004: 158–9.

Broughton, T. Mother of two gets 15 years for corruption. *The Mercury,* 1 July 2005: 5.

Carvin, G. Woman (67) sets herself alight. *The Mercury,* 29 January 2004: 3.

Carvin, G., Angela, B. and Zoubair, A. Help us stop school killings, begs Cronjé. *The Mercury,* 4 September 2004: 1.

Comins, L. Guard dies in 'Russian Roulette'. *The Mercury,* 5 November 2003: 3.

Dumisane, L. Killer describes rampage – but takes motive to the grave. *The Sunday Times,* 27 February 2000: 7.

Goldstone, C. Two die in shooting: City agent shot by ex-lover. *The Mercury,* 7 June 2005: 3.

Hooper-Box, C. South African road death toll bombshell. *The Sunday Tribune,* 25 May 2003: 3.

Horner, B. and Fredricks, I. Suicide rate among Blacks hits new highs. *The Sunday Times,* 12 June 2005: 13.

Hosken, G. Fourth suicide hits Pretoria schools. *Pretoria News,* 21 July 2004: 1.

Jorden, B. Golfer's family in suicide pact. *The Sunday Times*, 1 October 2000: 3.

Kalideen, N. Our son's suicide could have been prevented. *The Mercury*, 14 January 2002: 3.

———. Health body vows to get up to speed. *The Natal Mercury*, 31 March 2005: 2.

Keeton, C. Concerns over pain-killers abuse. *The Sunday Times*, 8 August 2004: 9.

Khan, F. Teen Hotline. *The Daily News*, 10 October 2003: 1.

———. Matrics swamp suicide line. *The Daily News*, 23 October 2004: 3.

Lee-Ann, N. Man kills mother and daughter. *The Mercury*, 19 December 2000: 1.

Loewe, M. and Majekula, L. 'If I die, you will die too'. *The Star*, 3 February 2004: 1.

McCarthy, M. Voting for the right to die with dignity. *The Natal Mercury*, 5 May 1991: 7.

Mkhwanazi, S. Siblings tried to disguise murder as suicide, court told. *The Mercury*, 3 March 2005: 5.

Mthembu, B. Suicide follows mercy killing. *The Daily News*, 25 February 2005: 1.

Mthembu, B. and Hosken, G. Killer's Warning: KZN suicide soldier phoned family before shooting. *The Daily News*, 24 May 2005: 1.

Naran, J. Durban's suicide anguish. *The Sunday Tribune Herald*, 27 March 2005: 1.

Ndaba, B. I would rather die in my own house. *The Natal Mercury*, 22 March 2005: 4.

Ngalwa, S. Two killers and nowhere to go: Some of South Africa's family killings this year. *The Sunday Tribune*, 5 June 2005: 15.

Nkosi, K. Three suicides rock school. *The Mercury*, 15 October 1999: 4.

Nwandiko, E. Lady luck turned a blind eye on Russian Roulette. *The Independent on Saturday*, 2 January 1999: 1.

Nyembezi, N. Teenager writes her own funeral. *The Independent on Saturday*, 7 March 1998: 3.

Nzama, W. and Leeman, P. Suicide priest faced 2 sex claims. *The Mercury*, 19 December 2003: 1.

Padayachee, N. White suicides outnumber murders. Report warns young African men that they are more likely to die a violent death than anyone else – at 9pm on a weekend. *The Sunday Times*, 13 April 2003: 9.

Premdev, D. Dying to restore human dignity. *The Sunday Tribune Herald*, 19 June 2005: 4.

Ramsamy, P. When cops kill themselves. *The Independent on Saturday*, 11 August 2001: 3.

Rondganger, L. and Hoskins, G. Train incidents kill one – and suicide bid fails. *The Daily News*, 27 May 2005: 1.

SAPA. Warning 'does not link drug to suicides'. *The Mercury*, 18 January 2002: 5.

Schoonakker, B. Portraits of the artist as a young woman. *The Sunday Times*, 10 June 2001a: 21.

———. 'Small slashed his wrists in my kitchen'. *The Sunday Times*, 24 June 2001b: 3.

Sukraj, P. Custody battle raging over prize show dog. *The Sunday Times*, 23 May 2004: 8.

Trench, A. Princess or priestess? *The Sunday Times*, 28 December 1997: 16.

Tse, J. Gran dead after allegedly killing daughter and wounding granddaughter. *The Mercury*, 21 June 2005: 4.

Van de Berg, C. Dale McDermott: Brought to his knees by Kamp Staaldraad. *The Sunday Times*, 16 January 2005: 20.

Venter, B. Distraught Brenda Fassie fan commits suicide. *The Mercury*, 12 May 2004: 2.

Vernon, M. and Nel, L.A. Teenagers survive harbour plunge. *The Mercury*, 25 July 2000: 1.

Zondi, M. A murder, failed suicide and man gone missing. *The Daily News*, 11 April 2005: 1.

Index

A list of figures and tables appears on page ix.

academic problems, school-related and 95
acetaminophen poisoning, renal failure due to 79
acetylsalicyclic acid *see* aspirin
Addington Hospital, Durban 202
adolescents, suicidal 94
Adult Respiratory Distress Syndrome (ARDS) 144
adult suicide rates 55
aetiology of suicidal behaviour, co-morbid factors in 102, 195
aetiology, underlying, and risk factors 195
Afrikaans-speaking families, family murders 99
African situation, the 37–39
AFRO region 38
    AFRO D and E 36, 39
    age-standardised death rates for 39
    see also sub-Saharan Africa
age distribution 47–48
age in non-fatal suicidal behaviour 51–52
age-standardised death rates for South Africa, the AFRO region and GBD 39
aggression 97
agony of a survivor, the 11–25
alcohol abuse in South Africa 107
alcohol-related substance-use disorder 103, 128

AN *see* analgesic nephropathy (AN)
analgesic abuse 128
    a major health problem 75
    and abnormal familial attitudes 83
    disorders stemming from 83
    functional model to understand and manage 134–43
    hazards associated with 75
    leading to chronic disease 74
    mood-altering properties 90
    pain, headaches and 86–90
    pain management and 125–31
    psychocultural aspects of 81–82
    psychological problems and 82–83
    reasons given for 75–76
    research on 83
analgesic nephropathy (AN) 75–77, 78–79
    and end-stage renal disease (ESRD) 74–75
    and long-standing psychological problems 83
    cumulative doses of analgesics leading to 77–78
    high figures reported in Durban 77
    in different geographic regions 76
    papillary necrosis (characteristic underlying pathology of) 75
    psychopathogenesis of 75

analgesics, cumulative doses
    leading to analgesic
    nephropathy 77–78
analgesics, opiate-related 85
anti-inflammatory substances, non-
    steroidal, the role of 80–81
apartheid, legacy of 107–08
ARDS *see* Adult Respiratory
    Distress Syndrome (ARDS)
arts, history and religion, suicide in
    27–34
aspirin
    history of 79
    role of 79–80
    uses, effects, toxicity 80
assisted suicide 61
attempted suicide *see* suicide
attempted suicide and parasuicide,
    difference between 6

BAC (blood alcohol content) 107
bereavement support group 19
Bible, the, five suicides mentioned
    in 31
biology psycho-, and suicidal
    behaviour 171–72
black non-fatal suicidal behaviour
    in Johannesburg, survey of 70
black South Africans 1, 42
    high suicide rate among 44
black youths 57

caffeinism, clinical manifestations
    of 86
cancer 109–12
    cervical, in adult black South
        African women 109–10
    patients and suicidal behaviour
        109
    patients, factors implicated in
        suicidal behaviour 111–12
    patients, major stressors
        amongst 112

psychological stress associated
    with 130
Catholic Church and suicide 30
cervical cancer *see* cancer
Childline 15
children and adolescents 55–58
    fatal suicidal behaviour 55–56
    non-fatal suicidal behaviour
        56–57
choice, method of, factors
    influencing 71
chronic
    disease, people with 46
    interstitial nephritis 75
    pain, MMPI scores 127
clinical depression 103
clinical management of suicidal
    persons 183
clinical psychology services 186
codeine 76
collective suicide 31
Coloured males, young, in Paarl 46
common methods in suicidal
    behaviour 72
co-morbid factors in the aetiology
    of suicidal behaviour 102
co-morbidity, somatic, suicidal
    behaviour and 108, 143–49
copycat effect (or Werther effect)
    30, 59, 66
crime, violence and, interpersonal
    and gender-based 3
cry for help 6
cultural and other influences
    37, 106
cultural and traditional role
    expectations 159–60
culture of violence 3
cumulative doses of analgesics
    leading to analgesic
    nephropathy 77–78

Daily News, The 65
DALY *see* disability adjusted life year (DALY)
data collection and storage 189
data, research-based data on fatal suicidal behaviour 42
death
 external causes of 69
 figures for and causes of 48
 leading causes of in young age group 56
 transport-related 56
Department of Behavioural Medicine, Nelson R. Mandela School of Medicine 185
Department of Medicine 123
depression 30, 93, 103, 195
 and fatal suicidal behaviour 96–97
 and other psychological disorders 101–06
 as a common psychological disorder 29
 as a contributing factor to suicide 34
 associated with suicidal behaviour 104
 clinical 103
 dysfunctional relationships and 102
 in cancer patients 110–12
 in the aetiology of suicidal behaviour 102
 of survivors 18
 prevalence of amongst adolescents 106
 stress and mood disorders 106
 throughout history 29
Dignitas (charity) 61
disability adjusted life year (DALY) 38
disease and suicidal behaviour, relationship between 108–09

divorce 94, 102, 119, 120, 166
DPS *see* Durban Parasuicide Study (DPS), The
Durban Parasuicide Study (DPS), The 42, 56, 57, 69, 95, 183, 185–93
 conceptual model for the future and a national suicide prevention programme 190–93
 database 192
 family issues, cautions 95
 found in general practice 102–06
 origins, design and aims of 186–87
 problem areas 188–90
 protocol regarding referral of suicide patients 123
 research on non-fatal suicidal behaviour 71
 research on stress and suicidal behaviour 151
 showing high prevalence of analgesics abuse 74, 75
 study of non-fatal suicidal behaviour 69, 70
 suicidal behaviour in early stages of HIV infection 115
Durkheim Emile (*Le Suicide*) 27
dysfunctional relationships and depression 102

educators, high level of HIV-positive 113
end-stage renal disease (ESRD) 74, 75
 acetaminophen, causative agent 79
 ethnic differences in local aetiology 76
 epidemiological data about non-natural deaths 42

ESRD *see* end-stage renal disease (ESRD)
ethical and legal issues in suicide prevention 183–84
ethnic distribution 48–50
euthanasia 7, 124
extended suicide/murder-suicide 62–63, 97–100

factors leading to suicidal behaviour 120
family
    dynamics in suicidal behaviour (suicide risk factors) 93, 120
    killings 44, 98
    murders in white, Afrikaans-speaking families 99
    practice, suicidal behaviour in 69
    problems 95
    violence, trends in 45
famous people in history, suicide records of 28
fatal suicidal behaviour 42–46, 67–69, 97
    common methods in 67
    in children and adolescents 55–56
    prevalence rates 53
financial implications of suicidal behaviour 3
firearm-related deaths 66, 68
functional model to understand and manage analgesic abuse 134

GBD statistics *see* Global Burden of Disease (GBD) statistics
gender distribution 46–47
Global Burden of Disease (GBD) statistics 39
global situation 35–37

global variations 37
Goethe *see* Von Goethe, J.W.
headaches, pain and analgesic abuse 86–90
Health Belief Model (HBM) 140
health-risk behaviour 139
Heaven's Gate cult 61
history, the arts and religion, suicide in 27–30
    suicidal deaths amongst the more famous 27–29
HIV/Aids 112–20
    co-morbid factor in suicide 195
    co-morbidity, somatic 142–49
    counselling, the need for 116
    factors contributing to suicidal behaviour 120
    impact on households and the private sector 113
    in educators 113
    in gay and bi-sexual men 114
    in South Africa 112
    incidence 113
    mortality statistics 114
    KwaZulu-Natal, highest patients with polytrauma 118
    neuropsychiatric complications 144, 145
    pandemic in sub-Saharan Africa 112, 195
    sexual behaviour and 8
    socio-cultural context 117
    somatic co-morbidity 143–49
    South African Health Review findings report 2003/2004 113
    stressors, unique 116–17
    suicidal behaviour and 108, 113, 115, 116
    suicide and, correlation between 113
    suicide attempts, reasons given for 119

suicide risk in patients 148
testing and suicidal ideation 114
homicide 48, 49
Hospice care 131
hospital, suicidal behaviour in 52
household poisons 70
household utility products, use of in fatal and non-fatal suicidal behaviour 72
human suffering in suicidal behaviour 4

IASP *see* International Association for Suicide Prevention (IASP)
iatrogenic suicide 63
ICU psychosis 146–47
ideation, suicidal 7, 45, 57, 94, 121
and HIV testing 113
Independent on Saturday, The 38, 45, 46, 64, 65, 100
Indian schoolchildren 57
indirect self-destructive behaviour (ISDB) and analgesic abuse 73–91, 138, 139, 142
  analgesic nephropathy 75–77
  cumulative doses of analgesics leading to analgesic nephropathy 77–78
  headaches, pain and analgesic abuse 86–91
  potential through substance abuse 135
  psychocultural aspects of analgesic abuse 81–82
  psychological problems and analgesic abuse 82–86
  role of aspirin (acetylsalicylic acid) 79–80
  role of non-steroidal anti-inflammatory substances 80–81

  role of phenacetin and paracetomol (acetaminophen) 78–79
International Association for Suicide Prevention (IASP) 125, 170–71
International Network for Suicide Prevention (WHO) 153
intervention and prevention programmes 95
ISDB *see* indirect self-destructive behaviour

'Kamp Staaldraad' 66
killings, family 44
learning disabilities 96
legal and ethical issues in suicide prevention 183

Le Suicide (E. Durkheim) 27
Letaba Hospital (Limpopo Province) 56
Letaba (Limpopo Province), studies of suicides 70
life expectancy 47
Lifeline 19, 125
life-threatening conditions, stress and, research on 1
Los Angeles County Chief Medical Examiner/Coroner (use of psychological autopsy) 160
Los Angeles Suicide Prevention Centre in California 160

male to female ratio of suicides 46–47
management and prevention 121–84
  cultural and traditional role expectations 159–60
  ethics and suicide prevention 183–84

functional model to understand
  analgesic abuse 134–43
pain management and analgesic
  abuse 125–31
prevention 170–82
prevention and the youth
  156–59
prevention of suicidal behaviour
  in South Africa 149–56, 185
somatic morbidity 143–49
stress associated with chronic
  disease 131–34
value of the psychological
  autopsy: a South African
  adaptation 160–69
managing and preventing suicidal
  behaviour, organisational
  system for 172–82
media *see* South African press,
  reports in
media responsibility on reporting
  suicidal behaviour 66
medication, overdose 69
medico-legal investigations 42
melancholia 29
  see also depression
Mercury see Natal Mercury, The
method of choice 67–72
  factors influencing 71
  fatal suicidal behaviour 67–69
  non-fatal suicidal behaviour
    69–72
Metropolitan Durban (major
  religions in) 32
migraine 87–88
MIMS 75
Mind Shift (L. Schlebusch) 74
Minnesota Multiphasic Personality
  Inventory (MMPI) 127
mood disorders 128
  diagnoses of 103

leading to suicidal behaviour
  29, 102
  see also depression
moral atrophy 3
mortuaries, data on deaths 43
Movement for the Restoration of
  the Ten Commandments 61
murderous impulses 98
murder-suicide/extended suicide
  62–63, 97–100
murder-suicides 44, 99, 100

Natal Mercury, The 44, 61, 62, 63, 64,
  65, 102, 119, 125
National Injury Mortality
  Surveillance System (NIMSS)
  42, 43, 45, 48, 49, 55, 68, 69
national suicide prevention
  programme, conceptual
  model for 190–93
  socio-political and socio-
    economic factors, changes
    associated with 190
  stress management skills,
    teaching of 190
  suicide researchers 190
Nelson R. Mandela School of
  Medicine, University of
  KwaZulu-Natal 185
nephropathy, analgesic 77–78
nephrotoxicity, clinical syndromes
  81
nicotine and caffeine 85–86
NIMSS *see* National Injury
  Mortality Surveillance System
non-fatal 189
  suicidal behaviour as crisis-
    management strategy 96
  fatal versus, South African 51
  suicidal behaviour 2, 6, 51,
    56–57, 69–72
  suicide attempts 2, 55
  suicide methods, common 70

non-natural deaths 49
  in young people 55
non-prescriptive analgesics *see*
  over-the-counter (OTC)
non-steroidal anti-inflammatory
  substances, the role of 80–81
NSAIDS *see* non-steroidal anti-
  inflammatory substances, the
  role of

occupational groups, suicide
  figures for 45
opiate-related analgesics 85
over-the-counter (OTC)
  analgesics, easy accessibility of
    127
  analgesics, prolonged ingestion
    of 82
  and substance abuse 107
  commercial exploitation of 128,
    143
  concern over role of in suicide
    attempts 72
  substance overdose 69, 70
Oxford English Dictionary 27

Paarl, young Coloured males in 46
PAC *see* pituitary-
  adrenocortical (PAC) axis
pain, headaches and analgesic
  abuse 86–90
pain management and analgesic
  abuse 125–31
pain, types of 125–26
painkillers *see* analgesic abuse and
  over-the-counter (OTC)
papillary necrosis 75
paracetamol, phenacetin and, the
  role of 78–79
parasuicide
  and attempted suicide,
    difference between 6
  in blacks 50

study *see* Durban Parasuicide
  Study, The
peak days and peak times for
  suicides 68–69
personality characteristics and
  psychopathology of
  substance abusers 136
personality, role of in pain 127
pervasive suicidal behaviour 1
pesticides, availability of 153
phenacetin, role of, and
  paracetamol 78–79
Pietermaritzburg, data study 47, 48
pituitary-adrenocortical (PAC) axis
  132
Plath, Sylvia (*The Bell Jar*) 28
political suicides 32
poor problem-solving skills 96
post-apartheid South Africa 42
post-traumatic stress disorder 101
pre-emptive suicide 115
press reports on suicidal behaviour
  in South Africa 66
Pretoria News 64
prevention 170–82
  and managing, organisational
    system for 172–82
  and the youth 156–59
    stress management and
      conflict-resolution skills 159
    suitable school prevention
      programmes 156
    teacher-counsellors in schools
      157
  basic steps in (WHO) 170
  guidelines on 153
  levels of intervention 156
  national prevention programme
    153
  of suicidal behaviour 3, 150–51
  programmes, designing of 158
  programmes, development of
    149–50

programmes, intervention and 95
programmes, psychobiological aspects of 171–72
programmes, school-based 57, 158
strategies 70
prior suicidal behaviour and substance abuse 107
problems, inter-personal 96
problem-solving skills, poor 96–97
psychiatric in-patient studies 53
psychobiology and the prevention of suicidal behaviour 171–72
psychocultural aspects of analgesic abuse 81–82
psychogenic headaches 87
psychological autopsy, assessment
    considerations 164–69, 196
    autopsy: a South African adaptation 160–69
    disorders, depression and other 101–06
    pain, unbearable 98, 123
    pre-morbid 147
psychological problems
    and analgesic abuse 82–83
    and the AN syndrome 83
psychology services, clinical 186
psychonephrology service 74
psychopathology and HIV/Aids 144
psychotherapy, follow-up 123
public health concern 42
    see also suicidal behaviour
public health responsibility 150–51
    see also suicidal behaviour

reading impairment 95–96
referral protocol 186
renal failure, acute, following acetaminophen poisoning 79

religion, history, the arts and, suicide in 27–34
religious exceptions regarding suicide 31
religious fundamentalism 32
reports in the South African press 59–66
susceptibility to suicide caused by media reports 59
risk factors and assessment 188
risk factors and causes 93–120
    aggression 97
    cancer 109–12
    extended suicide and murder-suicide 97–100
    family dynamics and related issues 93–96
    HIV/Aids 112–20
    poor problem-solving skills 96–97
    post-traumatic stress disorder 101
    prior suicidal behaviour and substance abuse 107
    South Africa's historical legacy 107–08
    stress 100–06
    suicidal behaviour and somatic morbidity 108–09
    that correlate with suicide 162
    underlying aetiology and 195
role expectations, cultural and traditional 159–60
role of
    aspirin (acetylsalicylic acid) 79–80
    non-steroidal anti-inflammatory substances (NSAIDS) 80–81
    phenacetin and paracetamol (acetaminophen) 78–79
rural China 36

SAM *see* sympathetic-adrenal medullary (SAM) system

Index

SANDF *see* South African National Defence Force (SANDF)
SAPS *see* South African Police Services (SAPS)
school-based prevention programmes 57, 158
school-related and academic problems 95
self-destructive behaviour, direct and indirect 8
self-destructive behaviour, indirect, and analgesic abuse 73–91
self-medication abuse, risks associated with 77
serotonin disturbance and suicidal behaviour 171
sexual abuse 94
sex distribution for suicides 68
simulated suicide 61
social stigma 1, 155
social taboo 1, 155
Solar Temple Cult 60
SOLOS *see* Survivors of Loved Ones' Suicide (SOLOS)
somatoform disorders 138
somatic co-morbidity: HIV/Aids 143–49
somatic diseases 120
Sorrows of Young Werther (J.W. von Goethe) 59
South Africa
   age-standardised death rates for, in 2000 39
   divergent suicidal behaviour prevalence rates reported in 41
   gravity of the situation in 42
   historical legacy 107–08
   incidence of suicidal behaviour in 41
   post-apartheid 42
   suicidal population in 41
South African
   context, differences between suicidal types in 4
   context, trends within the 41–54
   fatal suicidal behaviour rates 43
   press, reports in 32
   statistics 2
South African Depression and Anxiety Support Group 125
South African Dialysis and Transplantation Registry (SADTR)
   report on AN figures in South Africa 77
South African Health Review 2003/2004 (report on HIV/Aids) 113
South African National Defence Force (SANDF) 99
   suicide statistics 45
South African Police Services (SAPS)
   countrywide suicide rates 45
   figures for suicide 67
   post-traumatic stress disorder 101
   suicide prevention programme 151
   Western Cape, suicide rates 45
South African press, reports in 59–66
South African suicide conferences 56
South African youth, aetiological factors affecting suicidal behaviour 56
Southern African Conferences on Suicidology 186–87
Star, The 63
statistics
   for suicide in South Africa 2
   omissions in reports 2

stress
    and cancer patients 110
    and disease, link between 130, 131
    and life-threatening conditions, research on 1
    and mood disorders 106
    and suicidal behaviour 1, 100
    -diathesis models 121
    -vulnerability models 121
    sources of 133
stress associated with chronic disease 131–34
stress research 132
stressors, psychologically associated 132
stressors unique to HIV/Aids patients 116–17
studies of
    Cape Town high school students 57
    Limpopo Province, parasuicide rates amongst high school children 57
studies, South African non-hospital-based 57
sub-Saharan Africa (AFRO) region injury mortality rates 35
substance abuse 142, 195
    and suicidal behaviour, link between 74, 120, 135
    and transport-related deaths 107
    coping strategy 137
    development of, understanding 137
    prior suicidal behaviour and 107
    relapse 140, 141
substance dependence, psychological basis of 141

substances used in suicides 67–72
substance-use disorder, alcohol-related 103
suicidal
    adolescents 94
    ideation 7, 45, 57, 94, 114, 122
    population in South Africa 41
    process, development and dynamics of 121
    types within South African context, essential differences between 4
suicidal behaviour 1, 2, 6, 29, 35
    adolescent, recommendations 157
    analgesic abuse 134
    and somatic co-morbidity 108–09
    amongst black South Africans 2, 42, 44
    behaviour, fatal, South Africans affected by 50
    cancer patients and 109
    children with 158
    co-morbid factors in 107, 134
    cost in human suffering 4
    data, standardised format to record 196
    defining 5
    depression, associated with 104
    diagnosis, accurate, and appropriate treatment of risk factors 184
    disease and, relationship between 108
    divergent prevalence rates reported in South Africa 41
    effective preventative measures 196
    ethnic distribution 48–50
    factors leading to 121
    fatal and non-fatal 2, 6, 35, 42, 45, 51, 63, 67

fatal, in South Africa 6, 42–46, 55–56
financial implications 3
gravity of the situation in South Africa 42
hidden burden of 37
high incidence of, in South Africa 41
identifying 188
imitating others 59
in Africa, contemporary data on 38
in black youths, 18 years and younger 57
in children and adolescents 55
in chronic disease 53
incidence of in South Africa 41
in family practice 69
in HIV/Aids-infected people 113, 115, 116
in hospital 52–53
in South Africa 3, 195
in South Africa, prevention of 3, 149–56
in South Africa, risk factors 100–01
in South Africa, widely pervasive 155
in young people 55
major public health responsibility 9–10
management of 142
management and prevention of suicidal behaviour in South Africa 185
managing and preventing, organisational system for 172–82
methods used in 48
mood disorders leading to 29
mood indicators of 103
murderous impulses (primary motive for) 98

national imperatives 191–92
non-fatal 2, 35, 50–52, 55, 56, 69–72, 189
organisational system for managing and preventing 172–82
OTC substances, abuse of 71, 82
predisposition to 121
prevalence rates, divergent, in South Africa 41
prevention of 3, 124, 159, 179
prevention of fatal outcome 152
prevention of in South Africa 149–56
prevention of, basic issues around psychobiology and 171–72
primary motives 98
prior, and substance abuse 107
psychological pain, unbearable (primary motive) 98
public health concern, significant, in South Africa 42
ratio of fatal versus non-fatal 51, 53
related to HIV/Aids 118
research on, contextualising 185
risk factors in 100–01
romanticising of 30
serotonin disturbance and 171
somatic co-morbidity and 107–08
statistics regarding, in South Africa 2
stress associated with 1, 131
sub-intentioned 189
substance abuse as co-morbid factor in 134
terminology and definitions of 189
types and variants of 4–9
warning signs 159–60

suicide
  adult rates 55–56
  annual figures for South
    Africans 50
  assisted 7, 61–62, 124, 125
  attempted, and parasuicide 6
  attempts 2
  biological factors associated
    with 162
  choice of method 71
  collective, religious, mass 31, 32
  conferences in South Africa 56
  cost in human suffering 4
  cults/mass suicides/religious
    suicides 60–61
  emotional, rational or 124
  ethics and 183–84
  examples that gain respect
    31–32
  extended/murder- 62–63,
    97–100
  fake 8, 61, 163
  figures for occupational groups
    45
  figures for South Africa 50
  financial implications 3
  global increase 36
  global variations 37
  history of 34
  iatrogenic 63
  in Africa, religious
    understandings of 32
  inappropriate publicity 30
  in children and adolescents
    55–58
  literature on 27
  male to female ratio 57
  management and prevention
    121–84
  mass 60–61
  method of choice, factors
    influencing 71
  murder-suicide/extended
    suicide 62–63, 97–100
  notes 14, 24, 43, 61, 64, 65, 162,
    164, 174
  origins of the word 27
  pacts 60
  peak days and peak times for
    68–69
  prevention 170–82
  prevention, guidelines on 153
  prevention, national programme
    153
  prevention programmes 151
  prevention programmes, school-
    based 57
  rates, fatal, South African 42–44
  rates reported 45
  rational, or emotional 124
  religion and 30–33
  religious perspective of writers
    on 33
  religious suicides 60–61
  retrospective approach to 160
  risk factors and causes 93–120
  seasonal trends 68, 71
  sex distribution 68
  simulated 61
  South African National Defence
    Force (SANDF) 45
  South African Police Services
    (SAPS) 45, 51, 67
  statistics in South Africa 2
  survivor programmes 172
  survivors 19
  treatment, organisational system
    for 122
  trends within an international
    and South African context
    35–40
  well-known South Africans 29
suicide in history, the arts and
    religion 27–34

copycat effect, the 30
   history and the arts 27–30
   suicide and religion 30–33
suicide notes 14, 24, 43, 61, 64, 65, 162, 164, 174
suicide prevention, ethics and 183–84
suicide prevention, guidelines on 153
Suicide Prevention, International Network for (WHO) 153
suicidology 5, 27
Sunday Times, The 44, 49, 60, 62, 64, 65, 76, 77
Sunday Tribune, The 44, 45, 46
Sunday Tribune Herald, The 44
survivor programmes 172
Survivors of Loved Ones' Suicide (SOLOS) 20, 125
sympathetic-adrenal medullary (SAM) system 132

teachers *see* educators
tension headache 86, 87
The Bell Jar (S. Plath) 28
therapy, psycho-, follow-up 123
traditional expectations, cultural and 159–60
traditional herbal remedies, abuse of 76
traffic-related injuries 3
transport-related deaths 48
   and BAC (blood-alcohol concentration) 107
   in under 14 age group 56
trauma, effects of 195
treatment, organisational system for 122
trends within an international and African context 35–40
   the African situation 37–39
   the global situation 35–37
trends within the South African context 41–54
   age distribution 47–48
   ethnic distribution 48–50
   fatal suicidal behaviour 42–46
   gender distribution 46–47
   non-fatal suicidal behaviour 50–52
   suicidal behaviour in hospital 52–53
types and variants of suicidal behaviour 4–9

'ungreying' phenomenon 36, 55
United Nations peace mission 45

violence
   and crime, interpersonal and crime based 3
   and health-risk behaviours, relationship between 2
   culture of 3
   family 45
Von Goethe, J.W. (*The Sorrows of Young Werther*) 59

Werther effect (or copycat effect) 30, 59, 66
World Health Organization (WHO) 35, 36, 37, 44, 45, 46, 47, 48, 49, 55, 67, 153, 170, 193
   AFRO region of 35, 36
   International Network for Suicide Prevention 153

You Magazine 65
youth, prevention and 156–59